"If you wish to hear Mass as it should be heard, you must follow with eye, heart and lips all that happens on the altar."

St. Pius X

✠ ✠ ✠

"Place the Missal in the hands of the faithful so that they may take part more easily and more fruitfully in the Mass; and that the faithful, united with the Priest, may pray together in the very words and sentiments of the Church."

Pius XII

✠ ✠ ✠

"They are especially worthy of praise who use a small Missal suitable to their understanding and pray along with the Priest in the very words of the Church."

Decree of S.C. of Rites, Sept. 3, 1958

✠ ✠ ✠

"The most pressing duty of Christians is to live the liturgical life, and increase and cherish its supernatural spirit."

Pius XII

Saint Joseph

SUNDAY MISSAL

Confraternity Version
Word-for-Word as Read from the Pulpit

GREATER LOVE THAN THIS, NO MAN HATH

SAINT JOSEPH
SUNDAY MISSAL

A SIMPLIFIED ARRANGEMENT OF
PRAYING THE MASS ON ALL
SUNDAYS AND FEAST DAYS

with

A TREASURY OF PRAYERS

●

LARGE TYPE
Latin—English Edition

Edited by
REV. HUGO HOEVER, S.O.Cist., Ph.D.

CATHOLIC BOOK PUBLISHING CO.
NEW YORK

De Permissu Superiorum.

NIHIL OBSTAT:

JOHN A. GOODWINE, J.C.D.

Censor Librorum

IMPRIMATUR:

✠ FRANCIS CARDINAL SPELLMAN, D.D.

Archbishop of New York

Feast of Saint Joseph, March 19, 1957

(T-820)

SAINT JOSEPH

This
New Sunday Missal
is dedicated to

Saint Joseph

Patron
of the
Universal Church

— CONTENTS —

The Mass re-creates the Last Supper and
the Sacrifice of the Cross

THE HOLY SACRIFICE OF THE MASS

Love the Mass

AS a true Catholic you must love the Mass,
and that means that you must understand
it and make it *part of your life.*

You can love things only when they are in
some way yours, things into which you have
put a *part of yourself.* You can love the Mass
only insofar as you pray it in such close union
with the priest that it becomes *your* Mass.

Understanding the Mass

The Mass commemorates and re-creates two
cardinal events in the Life of Christ: the Last
Supper and the Sacrifice of the Cross.

The Mass re-enacts what took place at the Last Supper on Holy Thursday. At the Consecration the priest repeats the words and acts of Jesus our High Priest. Secondly, the Mass also recalls and sacramentally renews the Sacrifice of the Cross on Good Friday.

Jesus died shedding His Blood for us. In the Mass, this bloody aspect of the death of Jesus is not re-enacted. It is recalled, however, by the fact that on the altar, the host which becomes the Body, and the wine which becomes the Blood of Jesus Christ are separate, as His Body and Blood were separate on Calvary after His death. But on the Cross, Jesus, while shedding His Blood to the last drop, offered to His Divine Father, the suffering and death He was enduring for us. *Now in the Mass, Jesus again offers to His Father* the *suffering and death* He endured for us on Calvary.

In the Mass, there is something that was not at the Last Supper or upon Calvary. It is not only Jesus Who offers Himself to His Father on the altar, and not only is He offered by the celebrating priest, but also *by all those participating in the Mass.* Moreover, the priest and all those participating in Holy Mass *offer themselves* to God *with Jesus.* With Jesus, they offer up to God the Father, their joys, their sufferings, their whole lives. It is well to recall that, although it was by the Cross that Christ redeemed us, it is chiefly through the Mass that He brings us the benefits of that Redemption.

The Cross without the Mass would be a sealed well; the Mass without the Cross would be an idle ceremony.

The Mass and You

On the Cross, Jesus offered Himself alone. In Holy Mass, you also make an offering. You offer to God, in the first place, Jesus Himself; and *you must offer yourself to God* with Him, in a very practical way, offering your daily work, your troubles during the week, your labor, your suffering, your trials, your griefs and your joys—in a word, your whole life.

But the Mass is not merely a half-hour devoted each Sunday in sacrificing to the Father the death of His Son, and to offering yourself, with His Son, to God the Father.

The *Mass* must *come into your life,* just as *your life* must *go into your Mass.* That half-hour must exert its influence not only over your entire Sunday, but also over your entire week.

Assisting at Mass on Sunday should influence and effect a change in your life for the entire week.

Your entire week should be, so to speak, "centered" upon the Mass. Holy Mass should be like the sun, illuminating all your actions during that whole week. It should be the culmination, the climax, the biggest and most beautiful event of the week.

Your Sunday Mass should increase your value in your own eyes, obligate you, lay duties upon you, keep you from evil.

It should uplift you, elevate your life and your humanity. *It should help you to become a more devout Catholic and worthier apostle.*

Using the Missal at Mass

Endeavor, therefore, to "follow" the priest, his gestures and his motions. Instead of merely following him with your eyes, speak, in unison with him, the words which the Church bids him to say. To "participate" more fully in the Mass, place yourself where you can see the priest and the altar — *and use a missal.* A missal, the Church's own Mass prayer book, will help you to understand what is spoken and done by the priest.

Principal Parts of the Mass

I. PREPARATION — the prayers which the priest recites at the foot of the altar up to the Introit. Their object is to prepare us for the Holy Sacrifice of the Mass. The celebrant and the server, who represents the congregation, exchange words of humility and confidence by reciting Psalm 42. Then, both alternately recite the Confiteor, humbly confessing their sins.

At this moment recall your sins and examine the good you have done during the whole week. Have you followed the Christian way of life? Have you nourished your inner life with prayer and devout reading?

II. MASS OF THE CATECHUMENS — After the *Introit* (excerpts from a Psalm), the *Kyrie* and *Gloria* (a prayer of the highest praise), the priest presents to God in the *Prayer* on your behalf, all the needs of the Church in general, and yours in particular.

The *Epistle* and *Gospel* repeat to us the teachings of Jesus—to instruct us and prompt our wills to follow His teaching in our conduct.

Inspired by these lessons, you are ready to affirm your faith in the *Credo,* a profession of faith in union with the entire Catholic world. By living this profession of faith, you will spread the light which is Christ, and influence your indifferent or unbelieving friends.

III. MASS OF THE FAITHFUL — Consists of three parts: the Offertory, the Consecration and the Communion.

1. *The Offertory.* At the Last Supper, our Blessed Lord took bread and wine and offered them to His Father. In the same manner the celebrant takes bread and wine and makes the same offering. But the priest also pours a few drops of water into the wine in the chalice. In this union you recall the mystery of God becoming man and your own union with God. You may also see in it the need of making divine all the elements of your life—your daily work, your family life, your tears, your joys, your devotion, your trials, your suffering—it is

all this that is going to become divine, just as the drops of water mixed in the wine become the Blood of Christ.

During the Offertory offer to God the lives and sufferings of all those who fail to offer them, so that their labors and sufferings may be united to those of our Lord who died for all.

2. *The Consecration.* The Preface introduces the most important part of the Mass usually called the Canon, because it contains unchangeable and essential prayers. The Canon, in this narrow sense, is announced by the ringing of the bell.

During the prayers of the Canon before the Consecration, there are two important intentions. The first is for yourself. Do you know what is the most pressing thing you should ask from God? It might be the grace to resist a certain temptation, or that of having a better understanding and greater love of a truly Christian life.

The second intention concerns those who come under your influence. They may need the power of your good example, the encouragement of your words, the grace obtained through your prayers. Finally, pray for those who are not Christians so as to obtain for them the light and blessing of the true faith.

At the Consecration, the offering which a moment ago was nothing but bread is going to become Someone—your Savior. You have seen, you have willed with the priest this transformation of bread and wine into the Body and Blood of Christ. This is the moment you should transform your human life into a truly divine life—to change what is too human, too inferior and too shabby in your life. During the intervals following the Consecration fervently pray for all the faithful departed.

At the Minor Elevation realize that nothing in your life has any value if it be not done for the honor and glory of God. Do, bear, suffer all things . . . THROUGH CHRIST, WITH CHRIST, IN CHRIST. In this is true Christian life.

3. *The Communion.* In order to *live* your Mass during the coming week or day, so that it be truly lived in Christ for your own sanctification and the benefit of your neighbor, you must fulfill the conditions demanded by Christ Himself. He invites you to His Sacred Banquet. A moment ago, during the *Our Father* you asked for material bread and for this Spiritual Bread, without which the soul cannot live spiritually. Through Holy Communion Jesus wants to expand your life, making it His own life.

After Holy Communion, and even if you have not received Holy Communion, you should give thanks to Jesus for giving Himself to you at Mass. Thank Him for having offered your life to His Father at the same time as He offered His own.

At the end of Mass the priest blesses you, and together with him you should affirm through the last Gospel your faith in Jesus, His Incarnation and Redemption.

THE MASS VESTMENTS

THE Mass vestments were originally ordinary garments of the ancient Roman world. Thus, the priest, vested for Mass, is a wonderful witness to the historical continuity of the Catholic Church with the primitive Church of Rome, founded by the Prince of the Apostles.

The AMICE: A white linen cloth which covers the neck and shoulders. It symbolizes the helmet of salvation, i.e., trust in Jesus Christ.

The ALB: A long white linen garment reaching to the feet. The Alb symbolizes the innocence and purity that should adorn the soul of the priest who ascends the altar.

The CINCTURE: A white cord, with which the Alb is bound round the waist, is the emblem of purity.

The MANIPLE: Worn over the left forearm. Originally a handkerchief carried in the left hand or thrown over the left arm. It symbolizes the labor and hardship the priest must expect in his ardent apostolate.

The STOLE: Hangs round the neck and is crossed over the breast. It symbolizes the spiritual powers and dignity of the priest.

The CHASUBLE: The outer garment put on over the others. The Chasuble symbolizes the virtue of charity, and the yoke of unselfish service for the Lord, which the priest assumes at ordination.

The DALMATIC: An outer, sleeved tunic that came to Rome from Dalmatia, whence its name. It is worn in place of the Chasuble, by the deacon and subdeacon during Solemn Mass. It symbolizes the joy and happiness that are the fruit of dedication to God.

THE SACRED VESSELS NEEDED FOR MASS

The CHALICE: A cup of precious metal (the inside must be gold or gold-plated), that holds the wine consecrated at Mass.

The PATEN: A small plate of precious metal that holds the Sacred Host.

The CIBORIUM: A large cup of precious metal with a cover of the same material, that contains the hosts consecrated for distribution to the Faithful in Holy Communion.

The PALL: A small square of stiffened linen, or of cardboard covered with linen, used to cover the chalice.

The PURIFICATOR: A small linen cloth used by the priest to dry his fingers and the chalice, when he has washed and purified them after Communion. The CORPORAL: The linen cloth spread by the priest on the altar at the beginning of Mass. The chalice and host rest upon this cloth.

The CHALICE VEIL: A cloth covering of the same color as the Chasuble, that conceals the chalice and paten up to the Offertory and after the Communion. The BURSE: A flat, square container of cloth, the same color as the vestments, in which the corporal is carried to and from the altar. It is placed over the veil on top of the chalice.

THE COLORS OF THE VESTMENTS

THE ecclesiastical colors speak a language of their own; a language of faith and love, as does the whole Liturgy.

WHITE: Signifies the *joy* and *purity* of the soul. The white vestment is the peaceable garment for the feast days of Christ, of the Holy Trinity, our Lady; the Angels, Confessors and Virgins. It is also worn from Christmas to the Epiphany, and during Eastertide.

RED: Signifies the fire of *love* towards God, and is the color for Pentecost, the feast of the Holy Spirit; for the feast days on which the suffering and the Cross of Christ are recalled to the mind; for the feast days of the Apostles and the Martyrs, who shed their blood for the Faith and out of love for the Redeemer.

GREEN: The color of *hope,* worn on the Sundays between Pentecost and Advent, and from the Epiphany to Septuagesima.

VIOLET: The color of *humility* and *penance* is worn in times of repentance, during Advent and Lent, that is, between Septuagesima and Easter, on the Ember Days, Vigils and Rogation Days.

BLACK: The contrast to the cheerful and pure white, is the expression of *mourning*. Black is used on Good Friday, when the Church mourns the death of her Founder, Jesus Christ, on All Souls' Day, at funeral services and during Masses for the Dead.

SIMPLE WAY TO FOLLOW THE MASS

1. Before Mass starts, see the Liturgical Calendar, pages 474-479, for the exact *date* and *page* for Today's Mass.

2. Mark with a ribbon or picture bookmark each of the following:

    (a) The "Ordinary of the Mass," page 18.

    (b) The "Mass for Today" in the Proper of the Season.

3. Mass begins on page 18.

All references from the "Ordinary" to the "Proper" and vice versa are clearly indicated.

The arrow (↴) means *continue to read*.

THE DIALOGUE MASS—The pause marks (I) in the Latin Text of the Ordinary facilitate the recitation of the *Dialogue Mass*.

For Mass during the week, use the Mass of the preceding Sunday or the Requiem Mass, page 405.

MASS GUIDE

Our Participation in the Mass

Main Parts of the Mass	Our Participation
I. Preparation	
1. Prayers at the foot of the altar.	WE COME to Mass longing for God and with great sorrow for our sins.
II. Prayerful Worship	
1. Introit. 5. Epistle. 2. Kyrie. 6. Gospel. 3. Gloria. 7. Creed. 4. Collects.	WE LISTEN to the word of God in the Epistle and Gospel and respond with the Credo, "I believe."
III. Sacrificial Preparation	
1. Offertory Verse. 2. Offertory Prayers. 3. Washing the Fingers. 4. Orate Fratres. 5. Secret Prayers.	WE ARE PREPARED to offer to God that sacrifice which is the most pleasing to Him, self-surrender.
IV. Sacrificial Action	
1. Preface and Sanctus. 2. Memento of the Living and of the Saints. 3. Consecration. 4. Offering the Victim. 5. Commemoration of the Dead and petition for Communion with the Saints.	JESUS CHANGES our gifts into His Body and Blood. We offer Him and He offers Himself with us and for us to His heavenly Father.
V. Sacrificial Banquet	
1. Our Father. 2. Agnus Dei. 3. Communion. 4. Communion Verse. 5. Postcommunion.	THE FATHER GIVES us His Son in Holy Communion. We abide in God and God in us.
VI. Dismissal	
1. Ite Missa est. 2. Blessing. 3. Last Gospel.	WE GO AS children of God with Jesus and like Jesus to our work.

PREPARATION FOR MASS

RECEIVE, O Holy Trinity, One God, this Holy Sacrifice of the Body and Blood of our Lord Jesus Christ, which I, Your unworthy servant, desire now to offer to Your Divine Majesty by the hands of this Your minister, with all the sacrifices which have ever been or will be offered to You, in union with that most holy sacrifice offered by the same Christ our Lord at the Last Supper, and on the Altar of the Cross. I offer it to You with the utmost affection of devotion, out of pure love for Your infinite goodness, and according to the most holy intention of the same Christ our Lord, and of our Holy Mother the Church.

O GOD, almighty and merciful, grant us through this Holy Sacrifice, joy and peace, a better life, time to do penance, grace and consolation of the Holy Spirit, and perseverance in good works. Amen.

820-2

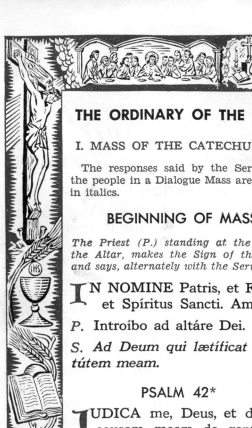

THE ORDINARY OF THE MASS

I. MASS OF THE CATECHUMENS

The responses said by the Server and the people in a Dialogue Mass are printed in italics.

BEGINNING OF MASS

KNEEL

The Priest (P.) standing at the foot of the Altar, makes the Sign of the Cross, and says, alternately with the Server (S.):

IN NOMINE Patris, et Fílii, ✠ et Spíritus Sancti. Amen.

P. Introíbo ad altáre Dei.

S. *Ad Deum qui lætíficat juventútem meam.*

PSALM 42*

JUDICA me, Deus, et discérne causam meam de gente non sancta: ab hómine iníquo et dolóso érue me.

*This Ps. 42, with the Antiphon, is omitted in Masses for the Dead, and from Passion Sunday until Holy Thursday inclusive.

THE ORDINARY OF THE MASS

I. MASS OF THE CATECHUMENS

BEGINNING OF MASS

KNEEL

The Priest (P.) standing at the foot of the Altar, makes the Sign of the Cross, and says, alternately with the Server (S.):

IN THE Name of the Father, ✠ and of the Son, and of the Holy Spirit. Amen.

P. I will go in to the altar of God.

S. The God of my gladness and joy.

PSALM 42*

OUR JOY AND CONFIDENCE IN GOD

DO me justice, O God, and fight my fight against a faithless people; from the deceitful and impious man rescue me.

---

*This Ps. 42, with the Antiphon, is omitted in Masses for the Dead, and from Passion Sunday until Holy Thursday inclusive.

S. Quia tu es, Deus, fortitúdo mea: I *quare me repulísti,* I *et quare tristis incédo,* I *dum afflígit me inimícus?*

P. Emítte lucem tuam et veritátem tuam: ipsa me deduxérunt et adduxérunt in montem sanctum tuum, et in tabernácula tua.

S. Et introíbo ad altáre Dei: I *ad Deum qui lætíficat juventútem meam.*

P. Confitébor tibi in cíthara, Deus, Deus meus: quare tristis es ánima mea, et quare contúrbas me?

S. Spera in Deo, I *quóniam adhuc confitébor illi:* I *salutáre vultus mei,* I *et Deus meus.*

P. Glória Patri, et Fílio, et Spirítui Sancto.

S. Sicut erat in princípio, et nunc, et semper: I *et in sǽcula sæculórum. Amen.*

The Antiphon is repeated:

P. Introíbo ad altáre Dei.

S. Ad Deum qui lætíficat juventútem meam.

P. Adjutórium nostrum ✠ in nómine Dómini.

S. For You, O God, are my strength. Why do You keep me so far away? Why must I go about in mourning, with the enemy oppressing me?

P. Send forth Your light and Your fidelity; they shall lead me on and bring me to Your holy mountain and to Your dwelling-place.

S. Then will I go in to the altar of God, the God of my gladness and joy.

P. Then will I give You thanks upon the harp, O God, my God! Why are you so downcast, O my soul? Why do you sigh within me?

S. Hope in God! For I shall again be thanking Him, in the presence of my Savior and my God.

P. Glory be to the Father, and to the Son, and to the Holy Spirit.

S. As it was in the beginning, is now, and ever shall be, world without end. Amen.

The Antiphon is repeated:

P. I will go in to the altar of God.

S. The God of my gladness and joy.

P. Our help ✠ is in the Name of the Lord.

S. Qui fecit cœlum et terram.

Bowing down, the Priest says the "Confiteor."

P. Confíteor Deo, etc.

S. Misereátur tui omnípotens Deus, | et dimíssis peccátis tuis, | perdúcat te ad vitam ætérnam.

P. Amen.

Then the Server, bowing, recites the "Confiteor."

CONFITEOR Deo omnipoténti, | beátæ Maríæ semper Vírgini, | beáto Michaéli Archángelo, | beáto Joánni Baptístæ, | sanctis Apóstolis Petro et Paulo, | ómnibus Sanctis, et tibi, Pater: | quia peccávi nimis cogitatióne verbo, et ópere: (strike breast three times) | mea culpa, mea culpa, mea máxima culpa. | Ideo precor beátam Maríam semper Vírginem, | beátum Michaélem Archángelum, | beátum Joánnem Baptístam, | sanctos Apóstolos Petrum et Paulum, | omnes Sanctos, et te Pater, | oráre pro me ad Dóminum Deum nostrum.

P. Misereátur vestri omnípotens Deus, et dimíssis peccátis vestris, perdúcat vos ad vitam ætérnam. *S.* Amen.

S. Who made heaven and earth.

Bowing down, the Priest says the "Confiteor."

P. I confess to Almighty God, etc.

S. May Almighty God have mercy on you, forgive you your sins, and bring you to life everlasting.

P. Amen.

OUR CONFESSION TO GOD

I CONFESS to Almighty God, to Blessed Mary, ever Virgin, to Blessed Michael the Archangel, to Blessed John the Baptist, to the Holy Apostles Peter and Paul, and to all the Saints, and to you, Father, that I have sinned exceedingly in thought, word and deed, (*strike breast three times, saying:*) through my fault, through my fault, through my most grievous fault. Therefore I beseech Blessed Mary, ever Virgin, Blessed Michael the Archangel, Blessed John the Baptist, the Holy Apostles Peter and Paul, and all the Saints, and you, Father, to pray to the Lord our God for me.

P. May Almighty God have mercy on you, forgive you your sins, and bring you to life everlasting. *S.* Amen.

INDULGENTIAM, ✠ absolutiónem, et remissiónem peccatórum nostrórum, tríbuat nobis omnípotens et miséricors Dóminus. *S. Amen.*

P. Deus, tu convérsus vivificábis nos.

S. Et plebs tua lætábitur in te.

P. Osténde nobis Dómine, misericórdiam tuam. *S. Et salutáre tuum da nobis.*

P. Dómine, exáudi oratiónem meam.

S. Et clamor meus ad te véniat.

P. Dóminus vobíscum.

S. Et cum spíritu tuo.

P. Orémus.

Going up to the Altar, he prays silently:

AUFER a nobis, quǽsumus, Dómine, iniquitátes nostras: ut ad Sancta sanctórum puris mereámur méntibus introíre. Per Christum Dóminum nostrum. Amen.

Bowing down and kissing the Altar, the Priest says:

ORAMUS te, Dómine, per mérita Sanctórum tuórum, quorum relíquiæ hic sunt, et ómnium Sanctórum: ut indulgére dignéris ómnia peccáta mea. Amen.

OUR PETITION FOR REMISSION OF SINS

MAY the Almighty and Merciful Lord grant us pardon, ✠ absolution, and remission of our sins.

S. Amen.

P. Will You not, O God, give us life?

S. And shall not Your people rejoice in You?

P. Show us, O Lord, Your kindness.

S. And grant us Your salvation.

P. O Lord, hear my prayer.

S. And let my cry come to You.

P. The Lord be with you.

S. And with your spirit.

P. Let us pray.

OUR PRAYER FOR PURITY

TAKE away from us our sins, O Lord, we beseech You, that we may enter with pure minds into the Holy of Holies. Through Christ our Lord. Amen.

OUR SORROW FOR SIN

WE BESEECH You, O Lord, by the merits of Your Saints whose relics are here, and of all the Saints: deign in Your mercy to pardon me all my sins. Amen.

Standing at the right side (Epistle side) of the Altar, the Priest reads the "Introit" which belongs to the Changeable parts of the Mass.

THE INTROIT

● Turn to —INTROIT — Today's Mass. ●

THE KYRIE

Returning to the center of the Altar, the Priest, alternately with the Server, says:

P. Kyrie eléison. S. *Kyrie eléison.* P. Kyrie eléison. S. *Christe eléison.* P. Christe eléison. S. *Christe eléison.* P. Kyrie eléison. S. *Kyrie eléison.* P. Kyrie eléison.

THE GLORIA

This chant of joy is omitted during Advent, Septuagesima, Lent and Requiem Masses.

GLORIA in excélsis Deo. Et in terra pax homínibus bonæ voluntátis. l *Laudámus te.* l *Benedícimus te.* l *Adorámus te.* l *Glorificámus te.* l *Grátias ágimus tibi* l *propter magnam glóriam tuam.* l *Dómine Deus,* l *Rex cœléstis,* l *Deus Pater omnípotens.* l

THE INTROIT

WE PRAISE GOD

● *Turn to —* **INTROIT** *— Today's Mass.* ●

THE KYRIE

WE BEG THE HOLY TRINITY FOR MERCY

P. Lord, have mercy. *S.* Lord, have mercy. *P.* Lord, have mercy. *S.* Christ, have mercy. *P.* Christ, have mercy. *S.* Christ, have mercy. *P.* Lord, have mercy. *S.* Lord, have mercy. *P.* Lord, have mercy.

THE GLORIA

OUR HYMN OF PRAISE

GLORY to God in the highest. And on earth peace to men of good will. We praise You. We bless You. We adore You. We glorify You. We give You thanks for Your great glory. O Lord God, heavenly King, God the Father Almighty. O Lord Jesus Christ, the Only-begotten Son. O Lord God, Lamb of God, Son of the Father: You Who take

Dómine Fili unigénite, | Jesu Christe. | Dómine Deus, | Agnus Dei, | Fílius Patris. | Qui tollis peccáta mundi, | miserére nobis. | Qui tollis peccáta mundi, | súscipe deprecatiónem nostram. | Qui sedes ad déxteram Patris, | miserére nobis. | Quóniam tu solus Sanctus. | Tu solus Dóminus. | Tu solus Altíssimus, | Jesu Christe. | Cum Sancto Spíritu ✠ *in glória Dei Patris. Amen.*

The Priest kisses the Altar, and, turning to the people, says:

P. Dóminus vobíscum.

S. *Et cum spíritu tuo.*

P. Orémus.

THE PRAYER

● Turn to — PRAYER — Today's Mass. ●

After having read the one or more Prayers of the day, he continues to read the "Epistle," "Gradual" and "Alleluia" or "Tract."

At the end of the Prayer:

P. Per ómnia sǽcula sæculórum. S. Amen.

At the end of the Epistle:

S. Deo grátias.

away the sins of the world, have mercy on us. You Who take away the sins of the world, receive our prayer. You Who sit at the right hand of the Father, have mercy on us. For You alone are holy. You alone are the Lord. You alone, O Jesus Christ, are most high. Together with the Holy Spirit ✠ in the glory of God the Father. Amen.

P. The Lord be with you.
S. And with your spirit.
P. Let us pray.

THE PRAYER
OUR PRAYER OF PETITION TO GOD

● *Turn to —* **PRAYER** *— Today's Mass.* ●

After having read the one or more Prayers of the day, he continues to read the "Epistle," "Gradual" and "Alleluia" or "Tract."

At the end of the Prayer:

P. World without end. *S.* Amen.

At the end of the Epistle:

S. Thanks be to God.

Bowing down at the center of the Altar, he says:

Prayer: CLEANSE MY HEART

MUNDA cor meum ac lábia mea, omnípotens Deus, qui lábia Isaíæ Prophétæ cálculo mundásti igníto: ita me tua grata miseratióne dignáre mundáre, ut sanctum Evangélium tuum digne váleam nuntiáre. Per Christum Dóminum nostrum. Amen.

The following Prayer is omitted in Requiem Masses.

Jube, Dómine benedícere. Dóminus sit in corde meo et in lábiis meis: ut digne et competénter annúntiem evangélium suum. Amen.

THE GOSPEL
STAND

P. Dóminus vobíscum.

S. Et cum spíritu tuo.

P. ✠ Sequéntia (*or* Inítium) sancti Evangélii secúndum *N.*

S. Glória tibi, Dómine.

The Priest and people make the Sign of the Cross on forehead, lips and breast.

● Turn to — GOSPEL — Today's Mass. ●

At the end of the "Gospel," the Server says: Laus tibi, Christe. *The Priest (except in Requiem Masses) kisses the book and says:* Per evangélica dicta deleántur nostra delícta.

Prayer: CLEANSE MY HEART

CLEANSE my heart and my lips, O Almighty God, Who cleansed the lips of the Prophet Isaias with a burning coal. In Your gracious mercy deign so to purify me that I may worthily proclaim Your holy Gospel. Through Christ our Lord. Amen.

The following Prayer is omitted in Requiem Masses.

Lord, grant Your blessing. The Lord be in my heart and on my lips, that I may worthily and fittingly proclaim His holy Gospel. Amen.

THE GOSPEL

OUR DIVINE INSTRUCTION

STAND

P. The Lord be with you.

S. And with your spirit.

P. ✠ The continuation (*or* The beginning) of the holy Gospel according to Saint *N.*

S. Glory be to You, O Lord.

● *Turn to —* **GOSPEL** *— Today's Mass.* ●

At the end of the "Gospel," the Server says: Praise be to You, O Christ. *The Priest (except in Requiem Masses) kisses the book and says:* By the words of the Gospel may our sins be taken away.

THE NICENE CREED   STAND

At the middle of the Altar the Priest says:

CREDO in unum Deum, Patrem omni- poténtem, I factórem cœli et terræ, I visibílium ómnium et invisibílium. I *Et in unum Dóminum Jesum Christum,* I *Fíli- um Dei unigénitum.* I *Et ex Patre na- tum* I *ante ómnia sǽcula.* I *Deum de Deo,* I *lumen de lúmine,* I *Deum verum de Deo vero.* I *Génitum, non factum,* I consub- stantiálem Patri: I per quem ómnia facta sunt. I Qui propter nos hómines, I et propter nostram salútem I descéndit de cœlis. I (Here all genuflect.) *Et incarnátus est de*

 *Spíritu Sancto* I *ex María Vírgine:* I *ET HOMO FAC- TUS EST.* I *Crucifíxus étiam pro nobis;* I *sub Póntio Pi- láto* I *passus, et sepúltus est.* I *Et resurréxit tértia die,* I *secúndum Scriptúras.* I *Et ascéndit in cœlum:* I *se- det ad déxteram Patris.* I *Et íterum ventúrus est cum glória* I *judicáre vi- vos et mórtuos:* I *cujus regni non erit finis.* I *Et in Spíritum Sanctum,* I *Dóminum et vivi- ficántem:* I *qui ex Patre Filióque procédit.*

THE NICENE CREED STAND

OUR PROFESSION OF FAITH

I BELIEVE in one God, the Father Almighty, Maker of heaven and earth, and of all things visible and invisible. And in one Lord Jesus Christ, the Only-begotten Son of God. Born of the Father before all ages. God of God; Light of Light; true God of true God. Begotten not made; of one being with the Father; by Whom all things were made. Who for us men, and for our salvation, came down from heaven. (*Here all genuflect.*) And was made Flesh by the Holy Spirit of the Virgin Mary: AND WAS MADE MAN. He was also crucified for us, suffered under Pontius Pilate and was buried. And on the third day He rose again according to the Scriptures. And ascending into heaven, He sits at the right hand of the Father. And He shall come again in glory to judge the living and the dead; and of His kingdom there shall be no end. And I believe in the Holy Spirit, Lord and Giver of life, Who proceeds from the

Qui cum Patre, et Fílio I *simul adorátur,* I *et conglorificátur:* I *qui locútus est per Prophétas.* I *Et unam, sanctam, cathólicam* I *et apostólicam Ecclésiam.* I *Confíteor unum baptísma* I *in remissiónem peccatórum.* I *Et exspécto resurrectiónem mortuórum.* I ✠ *Et vitam ventúri sǽculi. Amen.*

II. MASS OF THE FAITHFUL

The Offertory

The Priest turns to the people and says:

P. Dóminus vobíscum.

S. *Et cum spíritu tuo.*

P. Orémus.

SIT

He then reads the "Offertory Verse."

● Turn to — OFFERTORY — Today's Mass. ●

OFFERTORY PRAYERS

The Priest now uncovers the chalice, places the host on the paten and offering it up, says:

SUSCIPE, sancte Pater, omnípotens ætérne Deus, hanc immaculátam hóstiam, quam ego indígnus fámulus tuus óffero tibi, Deo meo vivo et vero, pro innumera-

Father and the Son. Who together with the Father and the Son is no less adored, and glorified: Who spoke by the Prophets. And I believe in One, Holy, Catholic and Apostolic Church. I confess one Baptism for the remission of sins. And I look for the resurrection of the dead. ✠ And the life of the world to come. Amen.

II. MASS OF THE FAITHFUL

The Offertory

P. The Lord be with you.
S. And with your spirit.
P. Let us pray.

SIT

OUR OFFERING OF PETITION

● *Turn to —* **OFFERTORY** *— Today's Mass.* ●

OFFERTORY PRAYERS

WE OFFER OURSELVES TO GOD

ACCEPT, O Holy Father, Almighty and Eternal God, this spotless host, which I, Your unworthy servant, offer to You, my living and true God,

bílibus peccátis, et offensiónibus, et negligéntiis meis, et pro ómnibus circumstántibus, sed et pro ómnibus fidélibus Christiánis vivis atque defúnctis: ut mihi, et illis profíciat ad salútem in vitam ætérnam. Amen.

He pours wine and water into the chalice, blessing the water before it is poured, except in Requiem Masses.

DEUS, qui humánæ substántiæ dignitátem mirabíliter condidísti, et mirabílius reformásti: da nobis per hujus aquæ et vini mystérium, ejus divinitátis esse consórtes, qui humanitátis nostræ fíeri dignátus est párticeps, Jesus Christus Fílius tuus Dóminus noster: Qui tecum vivit et regnat in unitáte Spíritus Sancti Deus: per ómnia sæcula sæculórum. Amen.

Offering up the chalice, the Priest says:

OFFERIMUS tibi, Dómine, cálicem salutáris tuam deprecántes cleméntiam: ut in conspéctu divínæ majestátis tuæ, pro nostra et totíus mundi salúte cum odóre suavitátis ascéndat. Amen.

to atone for my numberless sins, offenses, and negligences; on behalf of all here present and likewise for all faithful Christians living and dead, that it may profit me and them as a means of salvation to life everlasting. Amen.

OUR UNION WITH CHRIST

O GOD, Who established the nature of man in wondrous dignity, and still more admirably restored it, grant that through the mystery of this water and wine, we may be made partakers of His Divinity, Who has condescended to become partaker of our humanity, Jesus Christ, Your Son, our Lord. Who with You lives and reigns in the unity of the Holy Spirit, God, world without end. Amen.

OUR PRAYER FOR THE WORLD

WE OFFER You, O Lord, the chalice of salvation, humbly begging of Your mercy that it may arise before Your divine Majesty, with a pleasing fragrance, for our salvation and for that of the whole world. Amen.

Bowing down, the Priest says:

IN spíritu humilitátis, et in ánimo contríto suscipiámur a te, Dómine: et sic fiat sacrifícium nostrum in conspéctu tuo hódie, ut pláceat tibi, Dómine Deus.

Raising his eyes and blessing the offering, he says:

VENI, Sanctificátor omnípotens ætérne Deus: et béne ✠ dic hoc sacrifícium tuo sancto nómini præparátum.

WASHING THE FINGERS

The Priest washes his fingers and recites Psalm 25:

LAVABO inter innocéntes manus meas: et circúmdabo altáre tuum, Dómine. Ut áudiam vocem laudis: et enárrem univérsa mirabília tua. Dómine, diléxi decórem domus tuæ: et locum habitatiónis glóriæ tuæ. Ne perdas cum ímpiis, Deus ánimam meam: et cum viris sánguinum vitam meam: In quorum mánibus iniquitátes sunt: déxtera eórum repléta est munéribus. Ego autem in innocéntia mea ingréssus sum: rédime me, et miserére mei.

IN A humble spirit and with a contrite heart, may we be accepted by You, O Lord, and may our sacrifice so be offered in Your sight this day as to please You, O Lord God.

OUR INVOCATION TO THE HOLY SPIRIT

COME, O Sanctifier, Almighty and Eternal God, and bless ✠ this sacrifice prepared for the glory of Your holy Name.

WASHING THE FINGERS

I WASH my hands in innocence, and I go around Your altar, O Lord, giving voice to my thanks, and recounting all Your wondrous deeds. O Lord, I love the house in which You dwell, the tenting-place of Your glory. Gather not my soul with those of sinners, nor my life with men of blood. On their hands are crimes, and their right hands are full of bribes. But I walk in integrity; redeem me, and have pity on me. My foot stands on level

Pes meus stetit in dirécto: in ecclésiis be-
nedícam te, Dómine.

*The following "Glory be" is omitted in Requiem
Masses and in Masses during Passion Time.*

Glória Patri, et Fílio, et Spirítui Sancto.
Sicut erat in princípio, et nunc, et semper:
et in sǽcula sæculórum. Amen.

*Bowing before the middle of the Altar, with hands
joined, the Priest says:*

SUSCIPE, sancta Trí-
nitas, hanc oblatió-
nem, quam tibi offérimus
ob memóriam passiónis,
resurrectiónis, et ascen-
siónis Jesu Christi Dó-
mini nostri: et in honó-
rem beátæ Maríæ sem-
per Vírginis, et beáti Joánnis Baptístæ, et
sanctórum Apostolórum Petri et Pauli, et
istórum, et ómnium Sanctórum: ut illis profíciat ad honorem, nobis autem ad salútem:
et illi pro nobis intercédere dignéntur in
cœlis, quorum memóriam ágimus in terris.
Per eúmdem Christum Dóminum nostrum.
Amen.

The Priest turns toward the people and says:

ORATE fratres, ut meum ac véstrum
sacrifícium acceptábile fiat apud Deum
Patrem omnipoténtem.

ground; in the assemblies I will bless You,
O Lord.

*The following "Glory be" is omitted in Requiem
Masses and in Masses during Passion Time.*

Glory be to the Father, and to the Son,
and to the Holy Spirit.

As it was in the beginning, is now, and
ever shall be, world without end. Amen.

OUR OFFERING TO THE BLESSED TRINITY

ACCEPT, Most Holy Trinity, this
offering which we are making to
You in remembrance of the Passion,
Resurrection, and Ascension of Jesus
Christ, our Lord; and in honor of Blessed
Mary, ever Virgin, Blessed John the
Baptist, the Holy Apostles, Peter and
Paul, and of these (*Saints whose relics
are on the Altar*) and of all the Saints;
that it may add to their honor and aid
our salvation; and may they deign to
intercede in heaven for us who honor
their memory here on earth. Through
the same Christ our Lord. Amen.

THE PRIEST REMINDS US THAT WE OFFER WITH HIM

PRAY, brethren, that my sacrifice
and yours may become acceptable
to God the Father Almighty.

S. Suscípiat Dóminus sacrifícium de mánibus tuis ⎮ *ad laudem et glóriam nóminis sui,* ⎮ *ad utilitátem quoque nostram,* ⎮ *totiúsque Ecclésiæ suæ sanctæ.*

P. Amen.

THE SECRET

● Turn to — SECRET — Today's Mass. ●

At the end of the "Secret" the Priest says audibly:

P. Per ómnia sǽcula sæculórum.

S. Amen.

PREFACE—CANON

P. Dóminus vobíscum.

S. Et cum spíritu tuo.

P. Sursum corda.

S. Habémus ad Dóminum.

P. Grátias agámus Dómino Deo nostro.

S. Dignum et justum est.

The "Preface" for Sundays

VERE dignum et justum est, æquum et salutáre, nos tibi semper, et ubíque grátias ágere: Dómine sancte, Pater omnípotens, ætérne Deus: Qui cum unigénito Fílio tuo, et Spíritu Sancto, unus es Deus,

S. May the Lord accept this sacrifice from your hands to the praise and glory of His Name, for our advantage, and that of all His holy Church.

P. Amen.

THE SECRET

OUR OFFERING PRAYER

● *Turn to — * **SECRET** *— Today's Mass.* ●

P. World without end.

S. Amen.

PREFACE—CANON

P. The Lord be with you.

S. And with your spirit.

P. Lift up your hearts.

S. We have lifted them up to the Lord.

P. Let us give thanks to the Lord, our God.

S. It is fitting and just.

The following Preface of the Most Holy Trinity is said on all Sundays except on Feasts that have a proper Preface, and during Lent and Paschaltime.

The "Preface" for Sundays

OUR PRAYER OF THANKSGIVING

IT IS fitting indeed and just, right and helpful to salvation, for us always

unus es Dóminus: non in uníus singularitáte persónæ, sed in uníus Trinitáte substántiæ. Quod enim de tua glória, revelánte te, crédimus, hoc de Fílio tuo, hoc de Spíritu Sancto, sine differéntia discretiónis sentímus. Ut in confessióne veræ sempiternǽque Deitátis, et in persónis propríetas, et in esséntia únitas, et in majestáte adorétur æquálitas. Quam laudant Angeli atque Archángeli, Chérubim quoque ac Séraphim: qui non cessant clamáre quotídie, una voce dicéntes:

The Sanctus   KNEEL

Here the bell is rung three times, announcing the beginning of the Canon.

SANCTUS, Sanctus, Sanctus, | Dóminus Deus Sábaoth. | Pleni sunt cœli et terra | glória tua. | Hosánna in excélsis. | ✠ Benedíctus qui venit in nómine Dómini. | Hosánna in excélsis.

and everywhere to give thanks to You,
O Holy Lord, Father Almighty, Everlasting God, Who with Your Only-begotten
Son and the Holy Spirit are one God, one
Lord; not in the unity of a single person,
but in the trinity of a single nature. For
that which we believe on Your revelation
concerning Your glory, that same we believe of Your Son, that same of the Holy
Spirit, without difference or discrimination. So that in confessing the true and
everlasting Godhead, we shall adore distinction in Persons, oneness in being, and
equality in Majesty. This the Angels and
Archangels, the Cherubim, too, and the
Seraphim do praise; day by day they cease
not to cry out as with one voice, saying:

KNEEL

OUR HYMN OF PRAISE

HOLY, HOLY, HOLY, Lord God of
Hosts. Heaven and earth are filled
with Your glory. Hosanna in the highest.
✠ Blessed is He Who comes in the Name
of the Lord. Hosanna in the highest.

THE CANON OF THE MASS

𝕿E IGITUR, clementíssime Pater, per Jesum Christum Fílium tuum, Dóminum nostrum, súpplices rogámus ac pétimus *(he kisses the altar)* uti accépta hábeas, et benedícas hæc ✠ dona, hæc ✠ múnera, hæc ✠ sancta sacrifícia illibáta; in primis, quæ tibi offérimus pro Ecclésia tua sancta cathólica; quam pacificáre, custodíre, adunáre, et régere dignéris toto orbe terrárum: una cum fámulo tuo Papa nostro *N.*, et Antístite nostro *N.*, et ómnibus orthodóxis, atque cathólicæ et apostólicæ fídei cultóribus.

COMMEMORATION OF THE LIVING

𝕸EMENTO, Dómine, famulórum, famularúmque tuárum *N.* et *N.*,

Pray for those you wish to remember:

et ómnium circumstántium, quorum tibi fides cógnita est, et nota devótio, pro qui-

WE PRAY FOR THE CHURCH

HEREFORE, most gracious Father, we humbly beg of You and entreat You through Jesus Christ Your Son, our Lord, (*he kisses the altar*) to deem acceptable and bless these ✠ gifts, these ✠ offerings, these ✠ holy and un-spotted oblations which, in the first place, we offer You for Your Holy Catholic Church, that You would deign to give her peace and protection, to unite and guard her throughout the world, together with Your servant *N.*, our Pope, and *N.*, our Bishop; and all true believers who cherish the Catholic and Apostolic Faith.

COMMEMORATION OF THE LIVING

WE PRAY FOR THE LIVING

REMEMBER, O Lord, Your servants and handmaids, *N.* and *N.*,

Pray for those you wish to remember:

and all here present, whose faith and de-votion are known to You, on whose be-half we offer to You, or who themselves

bus tibi offérimus: vel qui tibi ófferunt hoc sacrifícium laudis pro se, suísque ómnibus: pro redemptióne animárum suárum, pro spe salútis, et incolumitátis suæ: tibíque reddunt vota sua ætérno Deo, vivo et vero.

COMMEMORATION OF THE SAINTS

COMMUNICANTES, et memóriam venerántes in primis gloriósæ semper Vírginis Maríæ, Genitrícis Dei et Dómini nostri Jesu Christi: sed et beatórum Apostolórum ac Mártyrum tuórum, Petri et Pauli, Andréæ, Jacóbi, Joánnis, Thomæ, Jacóbi, Philíppi, Bartholomǽi, Matthǽi, Simónis, et Thaddǽi: Lini, Cleti, Cleméntis, Xysti, Cornélii, Cypriáni, Lauréntii, Chrysógoni, Joánnis et Pauli, Cosmæ et Damiáni: et ómnium Sanctórum tuórum; quorum méritis precibúsque concédas, ut in ómnibus protectiónis tuæ muniámur auxílio. Per eúmdem Christum Dóminum nostrum. Amen.

Spreading his hands over the oblation, he says:

HANC IGITUR oblatiónem servitútis nostræ, sed et cunctæ famíliæ tuæ

offer to You, this sacrifice of praise for themselves, families and friends, for the good of their souls, for their hope of salvation and deliverance from all harm, and who offer their homage to You, Eternal, Living and True God.

COMMEMORATION OF THE SAINTS

WE ASK THE INTERCESSION OF THE SAINTS

IN THE unity of holy fellowship we observe the memory, first of all, of the glorious and ever Virgin Mary, Mother of our Lord and God Jesus Christ; next, that of Your Blessed Apostles and Martyrs, Peter and Paul, Andrew, James, John, Thomas, James, Philip, Bartholomew, Matthew, Simon and Thaddeus; of Linus, Cletus, Clement, Sixtus, Cornelius, Cyprian, Lawrence, Chrysogonus, John and Paul, Cosmas and Damian, and of all Your Saints, by whose merits and prayers grant that we may be always fortified by the help of Your protection. Through the same Christ our Lord. Amen.

WE RENEW OUR OFFERING

GRACIOUSLY accept, then, we beseech You, O Lord, this service of

820-3

quǽsumus, Dómine, ut placátus accípias: diésque nostros in tua pace dispónas, atque ab ætérna damnatióne nos éripi, et in electórum tuórum júbeas grege numerári. Per Christum Dóminum nostrum. Amen.

QUAM oblatiónem tu, Deus, in ómnibus, quǽsumus, bene ✠ díctam, adscríp ✠ tam, ra ✠ tam, rationábilem, acceptabilémque fácere dignéris: ut nobis Cor ✠ pus, et San ✠ guis fiat dilectíssimi Fílii tui Dómini nostri Jesu Christi.

The Consecration
CONSECRATION OF THE HOST

QUI prídie quam paterétur, accépit panem in sanctas ac venerábiles manus suas, et elevátis óculis in cœlum ad te Deum Patrem suum omnipoténtem tibi grátias agens, bene ✠ díxit, fregit, dedítque discípulis suis, dicens: Accípite, et manducáte ex hoc omnes:

Hoc est enim Corpus meum.

When he elevates the Sacred Host, look at It and say: My Lord and my God!

our worship and that of all Your household. Provide that our days be spent in Your peace, save us from everlasting damnation, and cause us to be numbered in the flock You have chosen. Through Christ our Lord. Amen.

WE ASK GOD TO BLESS OUR OFFERING

O GOD, deign to bless ✠ what we offer, and make it approved, ✠ effective, ✠ right, and wholly pleasing in every way, that it may become for our good, the Body ✠ and Blood ✠ of Your dearly beloved Son, Jesus Christ our Lord.

The Consecration

CONSECRATION OF THE HOST

WHO, the day before He suffered, took bread into His holy and venerable hands, and having raised His eyes to heaven, to You, O God, His Almighty Father, giving thanks to You, He blessed it, ✠ broke it, and gave it to His disciples, saying: All of you take and eat of this:

For this is My Body.

When he elevates the Sacred Host, look at It and say: My Lord and my God!

CONSECRATION OF THE WINE

SIMILI modo postquam cœnátum est, accípiens et hunc præclárum Cálicem in sanctas ac venerábiles manus suas: item tibi grátias agens, bene ✠ díxit, dedítque discípulis suis, dicens: Accípite, et bíbite ex eo omnes:

Hic est enim Calix Sánguinis mei, novi et ætérni testaménti: mystérium fidei: qui pro vobis et pro multis effundétur in remissiónem peccatórum.

After replacing the chalice on the corporal, he says:
Hæc quotiescúmque fecéritis, in mei memóriam faciétis.

The Priest adores the Precious Blood: you do likewise. The bell rings 3 times.

OFFERING OF THE VICTIM

UNDE et mémores, Dómine, nos servi tui, sed et plebs tua sancta, ejúsdem Christi Fílii tui Dómini nostri tam beátæ Passiónis,

CONSECRATION OF THE WINE

IN LIKE manner, when the supper was done, taking also this goodly chalice into His holy and venerable hands, again giving thanks to You, He blessed ✠ it, and gave it to His disciples, saying: All of you take and drink of this:

For this is the Chalice of My Blood of the new and eternal covenant: the mystery of faith: which shall be shed for you and for many unto the forgiveness of sins.

After replacing the chalice on the corporal, he says:

As often as you shall do these things, in memory of Me shall you do them.

The Priest adores the Precious Blood: you do likewise. The bell rings 3 times.

OFFERING OF THE VICTIM
WE OFFER THE VICTIM TO GOD

MINDFUL, therefore, O Lord, not only of the blessed Passion of the same Christ, Your Son, our Lord, but also

nec non et ab ínferis Resurrectiónis, sed et in cœlos gloriósæ Ascensiónis: offérimus præcláræ majestáti tuæ de tuis donis ac datis hóstiam ✠ puram, hóstiam ✠ sanctam, hóstiam ✠ immaculátam, Panem ✠ sanctum vitæ ætérnæ, et cálicem ✠ salútis perpétuæ.

SUPRA quæ propítio ac seréno vultu respícere dignéris; et accépta habére, sícuti accépta habére dignátus es múnera púeri tui justi Abel, et sacrifícium patriárchæ nostri Abrahæ, et quod tibi óbtulit summus sacérdos tuus Melchísedech, sanctum sacrifícium, immaculátam hóstiam.

SUPPLICES te rogámus, omnípotens Deus: jube hæc perférri per manus sancti Angeli tui in sublíme altáre tuum, in conspéctu divínæ majestátis tuæ: ut quotquot ex hac altáris participatióne, sacrosánctum Fílii tui Cor ✠ pus, et Sán ✠ guinem sumpsérimus, omni benedictióne

of His Resurrection from the dead, and finally His glorious Ascension into heaven, we, Your ministers, as also Your holy people, offer to Your supreme Majesty, of the gifts bestowed upon us, the pure ✠ Victim, the holy ✠ Victim, the all-perfect ✠ Victim: the holy ✠ Bread of life eternal and the Chalice ✠ of unending salvation.

WE ASK GOD TO ACCEPT OUR GIFT

AND this deign to regard with gracious and kindly attention and hold acceptable, as You deigned to accept the offerings of Abel, Your just servant, and the sacrifice of Abraham our patriarch, and that which Your chief priest Melchisedec offered to You, a holy sacrifice and a spotless victim.

WE PRAY FOR BLESSINGS

MOST humbly we implore You, Almighty God, bid these offerings to be brought by the hands of Your holy angel to Your altar above; before the face of Your Divine Majesty; that those of us who, by sharing in the Sacrifice of this altar, shall receive the most sacred

cœlésti et grátia repleámur. Per eúmdem
Christum Dóminum nostrum. Amen.

COMMEMORATION OF THE DEAD

MEMENTO étiam,
Dómine, famuló-
rum famularúmque tuá-
rum *N.* et *N.*, qui nos
præcessérunt cum signo
fídei, et dórmiunt in
somno pacis.

*Here pray for such of the
Dead as you wish.*

Ipsis, Dómine, et ómni-
bus in Christo quiescéntibus, locum refri-
gérii, lucis et pacis, ut indúlgeas, deprecámur.
Per eúmdem Christum Dóminum nostrum.
Amen.

*Striking his breast and slightly raising his voice
for the first three words, he says:*

NOBIS quoque peccatóribus fámulis tuis,
de multitúdine miseratiónum tuárum
sperántibus, partem aliquam, et societátem
donáre dignéris, cum tuis sanctis Apóstolis
et Martýribus: cum Joánne, Stéphano,
Matthía, Bárnaba, Ignátio, Alexándro, Mar-

✠ Body and ✠ Blood of Your Son, may be filled with every grace and heavenly blessing. Through the same Christ our Lord. Amen.

COMMEMORATION OF THE DEAD

WE PRAY FOR THE DEAD

REMEMBER also, O Lord, Your servants and handmaids, *N.* and *N.,* who have gone before us with the sign of faith, and rest in the sleep of peace.

Here pray for such of the Dead as you wish.

To these, O Lord, and to all who rest in Christ, we beseech You to grant of Your goodness, a place of comfort, light and peace. Through the same Christ our Lord. Amen.

WE PRAY FOR ETERNAL HAPPINESS

TO US sinners also, Your servants, trusting in the greatness of Your mercy, deign to grant some part and fellowship with Your holy Apostles and Martyrs: with John, Stephen, Matthias, Barnabas, Ignatius, Alexander, Marcellinus, Peter, Felicitas, Perpetua, Agatha,

cellíno, Petro, Felicitáte, Perpétua, Agatha, Lúcia, Agnéte, Cæcília, Anastásia, et ómnibus Sanctis tuis: intra quorum nos consórtium, non æstimátor mériti, sed véniæ, quæsumus, largítor admítte. Per Christum Dóminum nostrum.

PER quem hæc ómnia, Dómine, semper bona creas, sanctí ✠ ficas, viví ✠ ficas, bene ✠ dícis, et præstas nobis.

He uncovers the chalice and genuflects. Taking the Host in his right hand, and the chalice in his left, he makes the Sign of the Cross with the Host five times, saying:

THE MINOR ELEVATION

Per ip ✠ sum, et cum ip ✠ so, et in ip ✠ so, est tibi Deo Patri ✠ omnipoténti, in unitáte Spíritus ✠ Sancti, omnis honor et glória.

He elevates the chalice and the Sacred Host and then replaces them upon the corporal, covers the chalice, and genuflects. Rising again he says aloud:

P. Per ómnia sǽcula sæculórum.

S. Amen.

Lucy, Agnes, Cecilia, Anastasia, and all Your Saints; into whose company, we implore You to admit us, not weighing our merits, but freely granting us pardon. Through Christ our Lord.

WE PRAY FOR EUCHARISTIC BLESSINGS

THROUGH Whom, O Lord, You always create, ✠ sanctify, ✠ fill with life, ✠ bless, and bestow upon us all good things.

THE MINOR ELEVATION

WE PRAISE GOD IN UNION WITH CHRIST

Through ✠ Him, and with ✠ Him, and in ✠ Him, is to You, God the Father ✠ Almighty, in the unity of the Holy ✠ Spirit, all honor and glory.

He elevates the chalice and the Sacred Host and then replaces them upon the corporal, covers the chalice, and genuflects. Rising again he says aloud:

P. World without end.
S. Amen.

The Communion and Thanksgiving

The complete "Our Father" (from Pater to Amen) may be recited aloud by the people with the Priest—but only in Latin.

Orémus.

Præcéptis salutáribus móniti, et divína institutióne formáti, audémus dícere:

P̶ATER noster, qui es in cœlis: I *sanctificétur nomen tuum:* I *advéniat regnum tuum:* I *fiat volúntas tua, sicut in cœlo, et in terra.* I *Panem nostrum quotidiánum da nobis hódie,* I *et dimítte nobis débita nostra,* I *sicut et nos dimíttimus debitóribus nostris.* I *Et ne nos indúcas in tentatiónem:*

S. *Sed líbera nos a malo.*

P. Amen.

He takes the paten between his first and second fingers, and says:

L̶IBERA nos, quǽsumus, Dómine, ab ómnibus malis, prætéritis, præséntibus, et futúris: et intercedénte beáta et gloriósa semper Vírgine Dei Genitríce María, cum beátis Apóstolis tuis Petro et Paulo, atque

The Communion and Thanksgiving

The preparation for intimate union with Christ in Holy Communion fittingly begins with "The Lord's Prayer." The Priest joins his hands, and says:

Let us pray.

Prompted by saving precepts, and taught by Your divine teaching, we dare to say:

OUR FATHER, Who art in heaven, hallowed be Thy name: Thy kingdom come: Thy will be done on earth as it is in heaven. Give us this day our daily bread; and forgive us our trespasses, as we forgive those who trespass against us. And lead us not into temptation:

S. But deliver us from evil.

P. Amen.

WE PRAY FOR GOD'S PROTECTION

DELIVER us, we beseech You, O Lord, from all evils, past, present, and to come; and by the intercession of the Blessed and glorious Mary, ever Virgin, Mother of God, together with Your Blessed Apostles Peter and Paul, and

Andréa, et ómnibus Sanctis, da propítius pacem in diébus nostris: ut ope misericórdiæ tuæ adjúti, et a peccáto simus semper líberi, et ab omni perturbatióne secúri.

The Priest genuflects and breaks the Sacred Host in two over the chalice. He places the portion in his right hand on the paten and breaks off a particle from the portion in his left hand, saying:

Per eúmdem Dóminum nostrum Jesum Christum Fílium tuum. Qui tecum vivit et regnat in unitáte Spíritus Sancti Deus.

P. Per ómnia sǽcula sæculórum. *S. Amen.*

P. Pax ✠ Dómini sit ✠ semper vo ✠ bíscum. *S. Et cum spíritu tuo.*

He puts a small particle into the chalice, saying:

Hæc commíxtio et consecrátio Córporis et Sánguinis Dómini nostri Jesu Christi, fiat accipiéntibus nobis in vitam ætérnam. Amen.

*A*GNUS Dei, ᛁ *qui tollis peccáta mundi,* ᛁ *miserére nobis.*

Agnus Dei, ᛁ *qui tollis peccáta mundi,* ᛁ *miserére nobis.*

Agnus Dei, ᛁ *qui tollis peccáta mundi,* ᛁ *dona nobis pacem.*

Andrew, and all the Saints, grant of Your goodness, peace in our days, that aided by the riches of Your mercy, we may be always free from sin and safe from all disturbance.

Through the same our Lord, Jesus Christ, Your Son, Who lives and reigns with You in the unity of the Holy Spirit, God.

P. World without end. *S.* Amen.

P. May the peace ✠ of the Lord be ✠ always with ✠ you.

S. And with your spirit.

May this mingling and consecration of the Body and Blood of our Lord Jesus Christ help us who receive it to life everlasting. Amen.

WE PRAY FOR FORGIVENESS AND PEACE

LAMB of God, You Who take away the sins of the world, have mercy on us.

Lamb of God, You Who take away the sins of the world, have mercy on us.

Lamb of God, You Who take away the sins of the world, grant us peace.

In Requiem Masses he says twice, Dona eis réquiem; *and lastly,* Dona eis réquiem sempitérnam. *Then inclining toward the Altar, with hands joined upon it, the Priest says the following:*

PRAYERS BEFORE HOLY COMMUNION

The following prayer is omitted in Requiem Masses.

DOMINE Jesu Christe, qui dixísti Apóstolis tuis: Pacem relínquo vobis, pacem meam do vobis: ne respícias peccáta mea, sed fidem Ecclésiæ tuæ: eámque secúndum voluntátem tuam pacificáre et coadunáre dignéris: qui vivis et regnas Deus, per ómnia sǽcula sæculórum. Amen.

DOMINE Jesu Christe, Fili Dei vivi, qui ex voluntáte Patris, cooperánte Spíritu Sancto, per mortem tuam mundum vivificásti: líbera me per hoc sacrosánctum Corpus et Sánguinem tuum ab ómnibus iniquitátibus meis, et univérsis malis: et fac me tuis semper inhærére mandátis, et a te numquam separári permíttas. Qui cum eódem Deo Patre et Spíritu Sancto vivis et regnas Deus in sǽcula sæculórum. Amen.

In Requiem Masses he says twice, Grant them rest; *and lastly,* Grant them eternal rest. *Then inclining toward the Altar, with hands joined upon it, the Priest says the following:*

PRAYERS BEFORE HOLY COMMUNION

OUR PRAYER FOR UNITY AND PEACE

The following prayer is omitted in Requiem Masses.

O LORD Jesus Christ, Who said to Your Apostles: "Peace I leave with you, My peace I give to you," regard not my sins but the faith of Your Church, and deign to give her peace and unity according to Your Will: Who live and reign, God, world without end. Amen.

OUR PRAYER FOR HOLINESS

O LORD Jesus Christ, Son of the living God, Who, by the will of the Father, with the co-operation of the Holy Spirit, have by Your death given life to the world, deliver me by this Your Most Sacred Body and Blood from all my sins and from every evil. Make me always cling to Your commandments, and never permit me to be separated from You. Who with the same God the Father and the Holy Spirit, live and reign, God, world without end. Amen.

PERCEPTIO Córporis tui, Dómine Jesu Christe, quod ego indígnus súmere præsúmo, non mihi provéniat in judícium et condemnatiónem; sed pro tua pietáte prosit mihi ad tutaméntum mentis et córporis, et ad medélam percipiéndam. Qui vivis et regnas cum Deo Patre in unitáte Spíritus Sancti Deus, per ómnia sæcula sæculórum. Amen.

COMMUNION OF THE PRIEST

Panem cœléstem accípiam, et nomen Dómini invocábo.

Slightly inclining, he takes both parts of the Sacred Host and paten in his left hand; then, striking his breast with his right hand, he says three times:

DOMINE, non sum dignus, ‖ ut intres sub tectum meum: ‖ sed tantum dic verbo, ‖ et sanábitur ánima mea.

Making the Sign of the Cross with the Sacred Host, he says:

CORPUS Dómini nostri Jesu Christi custódiat ánimam meam in vitam ætérnam. Amen.

OUR PRAYER FOR A WORTHY COMMUNION

LET not the partaking of Your Body, O Lord Jesus Christ, which I, though unworthy, presume to receive, turn to my judgment and condemnation; but through Your goodness, may it become a safeguard and an effective remedy, both of soul and body. Who live and reign with God the Father, in the unity of the Holy Spirit, God, world without end. Amen.

COMMUNION OF THE PRIEST

I will take the Bread of heaven, and call upon the Name of the Lord.

HUMILITY AND FAITH

LORD, I am not worthy that You should come under my roof; but only say the word, and my soul will be healed. (3 *times.*)

THE LIVING BREAD OF HEAVEN

MAY the Body of our Lord Jesus Christ preserve my soul to life everlasting. Amen.

After consuming the Sacred Host, he uncovers the chalice, makes a genuflection, collects whatever particles may remain and puts them in the chalice, and gives thanks, saying:

QUID retríbuam Dómino pro ómnibus quæ retríbuit mihi? Cálicem salutáris accípiam, et nomen Dómini invocábo. Laudans invocábo Dóminum, et ab inimícis meis salvus ero.

Making the Sign of the Cross with the chalice, he says:

SANGUIS Dómini nostri Jesu Christi custódiat ánimam meam in vitam ætérnam. Amen.

The Priest reverently consumes the Precious Blood.

(If Communion is not distributed omit part with red line.)

COMMUNION OF THE FAITHFUL

The Priest removes the ciborium from the Tabernacle and places it upon the corporal. He opens it, places the lid on the corporal and makes a genuflection. Then he takes a Sacred Host with his right hand and the ciborium with his left, and, turning to the people, says:

ECCE Agnus Dei, ecce qui tollit peccáta mundi.

ACT OF HOPE

WHAT return shall I make to the Lord for all He has given me? I will take the Chalice of salvation, and I will call upon the Name of the Lord. Praising will I call upon the Lord and I shall be saved from my enemies.

SHORT ACT OF FAITH

MAY the Blood of our Lord Jesus Christ preserve my soul to life everlasting. Amen.

(If Communion is not distributed omit part with red line.)

COMMUNION OF THE FAITHFUL

To be free from mortal sin, to be fasting from solids (and alcohol) for three hours and from liquids for one hour, and to have a right intention, are the conditions for worthy reception of Holy Communion.

WE HUMBLY CONFESS OUR UNWORTHINESS

BEHOLD the Lamb of God, behold Him Who takes away the sins of the world.

DOMINE, non sum dignus | ut intres sub tectum meum; | sed tantum dic verbo, | et sanábitur ánima mea. (3 times.)

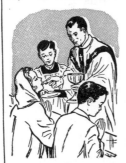

Descending the steps, the Priest goes to the Altar rail and administers Holy Communion. Each time, he makes the sign of the Cross with the Sacred Host and says to each person:

CORPUS Dómini nostri Jesu Christi custódiat ánimam tuam in vitam ætérnam. Amen.

Having finished distributing Communion, the Priest returns to the Altar in silence. He places the ciborium on the corporal and genuflects. After covering the ciborium with the lid and the veil, the Priest places it in the Tabernacle, genuflects and closes the Tabernacle. (If no Hosts remain in the ciborium, he does not place it in the Tabernacle, but purifies it at the the same time as the chalice.)

SIT

THE ABLUTIONS

He then purifies the chalice with a little wine, saying:

QUOD ore súmpsimus, Dómine, pura mente capiámus: et de múnere temporáli fiat nobis remédium sempitérnum.

L ORD, I am not worthy that You should come under my roof; but only say the word, and my soul will be healed. (3 *times.*)

When the Priest holds the Sacred Host before you, look at It and say: My Lord and my God!

M AY the Body of our Lord Jesus Christ preserve your soul to life everlasting. Amen.

The faithful who do not receive sacramentally should at least say the following act of Spiritual Communion:

My Jesus, I believe that You are in the Blessed Sacrament. I love You above all things, and I long for You in my soul. Since I cannot now receive You sacramentally, come at least spiritually into my heart. As though You have already come, I embrace You and unite myself entirely to You; never permit me to be separated from You.

SIT

THE ABLUTIONS

WE ADORE GOD WITH FAITH, HOPE AND CHARITY

W HAT has passed our lips as food, O Lord, may we possess in purity of heart, that what is given to us in time, be our healing for eternity.

He purifies his fingers with wine and water, saying:

CORPUS tuum, Dómine, quod sumpsi, et Sánguis quem potávi, adhǽreat viscéribus meis: et præsta, ut in me non remáneat scélerum mácula, quem pura et sancta refecérunt sacraménta. Qui vivis et regnas in sǽcula sæculórum. Amen.

He consumes the ablution and wipes his lips and then the chalice, which he covers, and places in the center of the Altar.

COMMUNION AND POSTCOMMUNION

● *Turn to —*
COMMUNION AND POSTCOMMUNION
— *Today's Mass.* ●

Having said the Communion verse, the Priest kisses the Altar, and turning to the people, says: Dóminus vobíscum. *S.* Et cum spíritu tuo. *P.* Orémus. *At the end of the Postcommunion the response is: S.* Amen.

FINAL PRAYERS

After the Postcommunion, the Priest turns again toward the people, and says:

P. Dóminus vobíscum.

S. Et cum spíritu tuo.

P. Ite, Missa est.

S. Deo grátias.

WE PRAY FOR THE GRACE OF HOLY COMMUNION

MAY Your Body, O Lord, which I have eaten, and Your Blood which I have drunk, cleave to my very soul, and grant that no trace of sin be found in me, whom these pure and holy mysteries have renewed. Who live and reign, world without end. Amen.

COMMUNION AND POSTCOMMUNION

PRAYERS OF GRATITUDE AND PETITION

* *Turn to —*

COMMUNION AND POSTCOMMUNION
— Today's Mass. ●

Having said the Communion verse, the Priest kisses the Altar, and turning to the people, says: The Lord be with you. S. And with your spirit. P. Let us Pray. *At the end of the Postcommunion the response is:* S. Amen.

FINAL PRAYERS

After the Postcommunion, the Priest turns again toward the people, and says:

P. The Lord be with you.

S. And with your spirit.

P. Go, you are dismissed.

S. Thanks be to God.

In Masses followed by a procession, the Priest turns to the Altar and says: Let us bless the Lord. *S.* Thanks be to God. *In Requiem Masses he says:* May they rest in peace. *S.* Amen. *(In both cases the Last Blessing is omitted.)*

KNEEL

PLACEAT tibi, sancta Trínitas, obséquium servitútis meæ: et præsta, ut sacrifícium quod óculis tuæ majestátis indígnus óbtuli, tibi sit acceptábile, mihíque, et ómnibus pro quibus illud óbtuli, sit te miseránte propitiábile. Per Christum Dóminum nostrum. Amen.

THE LAST BLESSING

He kisses the Altar, and facing the people, gives the blessing. (Omitted in Requiem Masses and in Masses followed by a procession.)

BENEDICAT vos omnípotens Deus Pater, ✠ et Fílius, et Spíritus Sanctus.

S. Amen.

THE LAST GOSPEL

Going to the Gospel side of the Altar, he says:

P. Dóminus vobíscum.

S. *Et cum spíritu tuo.*

In Masses followed by a procession, the Priest turns to the Altar and says: Let us bless the Lord. S. Thanks be to God. *In Requiem Masses he says:* May they rest in peace. S. Amen. *(In both cases the Last Blessing is omitted.)*

WE OFFER OUR WORSHIP TO GOD

KNEEL

MAY the tribute of my worship be pleasing to You, most holy Trinity, and grant that the sacrifice which I, all unworthy, have offered in the presence of Your Majesty, may be acceptable to You, and through Your mercy obtain forgiveness for me and all for whom I have offered it. Through Christ our Lord. Amen.

THE LAST BLESSING

THE PRIEST BLESSES US IN THE NAME OF THE BLESSED TRINITY

MAY Almighty God bless you: ✠ the Father, and the Son, and the Holy Spirit.

S. Amen.

THE LAST GOSPEL

P. The Lord be with you.

S. And with your spirit.

The Priest and people make the Sign of the Cross on forehead, lips and breast.

STAND

P. ✠ **Inítium** sancti Evangélii secúndum **Joánnem.**

S. *Glória tibi, Dómine.*

IN princípio erat Verbum et Verbum erat apud Deum, et Deus erat Verbum. Hoc erat in princípio apud Deum. Omnia per ipsum facta sunt, et sine ipso factum est nihil quod factum est; in ipso vita erat, et vita erat lux hóminum; et lux in ténebris lucet, et ténebræ eam non comprehendérunt. Fuit homo missus a Deo cui nomen erat Joánnes. Hic venit in testimónium, ut testimónium perhibéret de lúmine, ut omnes créderent per illum. Non erat ille lux; sed ut testimónium perhibéret de lúmine. Erat lux vera quæ illúminat omnem hóminem veniéntem in hunc mundum. In mundo erat, et mundus per ipsum factus est et mundus eum non cognóvit. In própria venit, et sui eum non recepérunt. Quotquot

The Priest and people make the Sign of the Cross on forehead, lips and breast.

STAND

P. ✠ The beginning of the holy Gospel according to St. John.

S. Glory be to You, O Lord.

CHRIST THE SON OF GOD IS THE LIGHT AND LIFE OF MANKIND

IN THE beginning was the Word, and the Word was with God; and the Word was God. He was in the beginning with God. All things were made through Him, and without Him was made nothing that has been made. In Him was life, and the life was the light of men. And the light shines in the darkness; and the darkness grasped it not. There was a man, one sent from God, whose name was John. This man came as a witness, to bear witness concerning the Light, that all might believe through Him. He was not himself the Light, but was to bear witness to the Light. It was the true Light that enlightens every man who comes into the world. He was in the world, and the world was made by Him, and the world knew Him not. He

autem recepérunt eum, dedit eis potestátem fílios Dei fíeri; his qui credunt in nómine ejus, qui non ex sanquínibus, neque ex voluntáte carnis, neque ex voluntáte viri, sed ex Deo nati sunt. **ET VERBUM CARO FACTUM EST** (*Here all genuflect*) et habitávit in nobis; et vídimus glóriam ejus, glóriam quasi Unigéniti a Patre, plenum grátiæ et veritátis.

S. Deo grátias.

came unto His own, and His own received Him not. But to as many as received Him He gave the power of becoming sons of God; to those who believe in His Name: who were born not of blood, nor of the will of the flesh, nor of the will of man, but of God. AND THE WORD WAS MADE FLESH (*Here all genuflect*), and dwelt among us. And we saw His glory, the glory as of the Only-begotten of the Father, full of grace and of truth.

S. Thanks be to God.

PRAYERS AFTER LOW MASS

Prescribed by Leo XIII; by Pius XI for the Church in Russia. An indulgence of 17 years. (No. 675.)

Hail Mary (*three times*)

HAIL, Holy Queen, Mother of Mercy, our life, our sweetness, and our hope! To you do we cry, poor banished children of Eve; to you do we send up our sighs, mourning and weeping in this valley of tears. Turn then, most gracious advocate, your eyes of mercy toward us; and after this our exile, show unto us the blessed fruit of your womb, Jesus. O clement, O loving, O sweet Virgin Mary.

P. Pray for us, O holy Mother of God.

S. That we may be made worthy of the promises of Christ.

Let us pray.

O GOD, our refuge, and our strength, look down in mercy on Your people who cry to You; and by the intercession of the glorious and Immaculate Virgin Mary, Mother of God, of Saint Joseph her spouse, of Your blessed Apostles Peter and Paul, and of all the Saints, in mercy and goodness hear our prayers for the conversion of sinners, and for the liberty and exaltation of our holy mother the Church. Through the same Christ our Lord. Amen.

HOLY Michael, the Archangel, defend us in battle; be our safeguard against the wickedness and snares of the devil. May God rebuke him we humbly pray; and do you, Prince of the heavenly host, by the power of God cast into hell Satan and all the evil spirits, who wander through the world seeking the ruin of souls. Amen.

P. Most Sacred Heart of Jesus.

S. Have mercy on us. (*Three times.*)

THANKSGIVING AFTER MASS

Act of Thanksgiving

O GOD, Whose mercies are without number and Whose goodness is an infinite treasure, we render thanks to Your most gracious Majesty, for the gifts You have bestowed upon us, always imploring Your mercy, that as You grant the prayers of those who ask You, You will never forsake them, but will prepare them for the future reward. Through Christ our Lord. Amen.

Petitions of St. Augustine

An indulgence of 500 days. A plenary indulgence if these petitions are repeated daily for a month. (No. 88.)

LORD Jesus, let me know myself; let me know You,
And desire nothing else but You.
Let me hate myself and love You,
And do all things for Your sake.
Let me humble myself and exalt You,
And think of nothing else but You.
Let me die to myself and live in You,
And take whatever happens as coming from
    You.

820-4

Let me forsake myself and walk after You,
And ever desire to follow You.
Let me flee from myself and turn to You,
That so I may merit to be defended by You.
Let me fear for myself, let me fear You,
And be among those that are chosen by You.
Let me distrust myself and trust in You,
And ever obey for the love of You.
Let me cleave to nothing but You,
And ever be poor for the sake of You.
Look upon me that I may love You,
Call me, that I may see You,
And forever possess You, for all eternity.
  Amen.

A Prayer for the Holy Souls in Purgatory

An indulgence of 500 days. (No. 594.)

O LORD God Almighty, I beseech You, by the Precious Blood which Your Divine Son Jesus shed in the garden, deliver the souls in purgatory, and especially that soul among them all which is most destitute of spiritual aid; and vouchsafe to bring it to Your glory, there to praise and bless You forever. Amen.

Our Father, Hail Mary, Eternal rest, etc.

————◆————

PRAYER CONCLUSIONS

The conclusions of the Prayers, Secrets and Post-communions in the Proper of the Season vary according as they are addressed to either of the three Persons of the Blessed Trinity. Throughout the Missal the first few words of the Prayer conclusions, are indicated. The complete conclusions which should be memorized are as follows:

For Prayers addressed to God the Father:

Through our Lord Jesus Christ, Your Son, Who lives and reigns with You in the unity of the Holy Spirit, God, world without end. *S.* Amen.

When our Lord is mentioned at the beginning or in the body of the Prayer:

Through the same our Lord Jesus Christ, Your Son, Who lives and reigns with You in the unity of the Holy Spirit, God, world without end. *S.* Amen.

For Prayers mentioning the Holy Spirit:

Through . . . in the unity of the same. Through our Lord Jesus Christ, Your Son, Who lives and reigns with You in the unity of the same Holy Spirit, God, world without end. *S.* Amen.

For Prayers whose final clause mentions our Blessed Lord:

Who with You lives and reigns in the unity of the Holy Spirit, God, world without end. *S.* Amen.

When the Prayer is addressed to God the Son:

Who live and reign with God the Father, in the unity of the Holy Spirit, God, world without end. *S.* Amen.

"It is now the hour for us to rise from sleep."

PROPER OF THE SEASON

ADVENT is the season of longing for the Redeemer. Knowing our weakness and sinfulness we turn to the Divine Savior for help and grace. Now we prepare ourselves for the coming of the forgiving Christ that we may receive Him without fear when He comes as our Judge.

FIRST SUNDAY OF ADVENT
PURPLE VESTMENTS

THOUGHT FOR TODAY: It is now the hour for us to rise from the sleep of sin and of religious indifference. Let us start our preparation for the blessing of Christmas with great confidence in Jesus, for "no one who waits for (Him) shall be put to shame."

● *Beginning of Mass, page 19.*

Introit. *Ps. 24, 1-3.* To You I lift up my soul: in You, O my God, I trust; let me not be put to shame: let not my enemies exult over me: no one who waits for You shall be put to shame. *Ps. 24, 4.* Your ways, O Lord, make known to me; teach me Your paths. ℣. Glory be to the Father, and to the Son, and to the Holy Spirit. As it was in the beginning, is now, and ever shall be, world without end. Amen. — To You...

The Introit *is repeated up to the Psalm-verse (Ps.) in all Masses throughout the year. The* Gloria *is omitted during Advent, except on Feast days when the color of the vestments is not Purple.*

● Kyrie, page 27. Omit Gloria.

Prayer. O Lord, we beseech You, stir up Your power, and come; that by Your protection we may deserve to be rescued from the threatening dangers of our sins, and to be saved by Your deliverance. Who live, * etc. S. Amen. ↻

Epistle. *Rom. 13, 11-14.* Brethren: Understand, for it is now the hour for us to rise from sleep, because now our salvation is nearer than when we came to believe. The night is far advanced; the day is at hand. Let us therefore lay aside the works of darkness, and put on the armor of light. Let us walk becomingly as in the day, not in revelry and drunkenness, not in debauchery and wantonness, not in strife and jeal-

---

*The different endings of the Prayers, Secrets, and Postcommunions are found on page 83.

ousy. But put on the Lord Jesus Christ. S. Thanks be to God. ⌐

Gradual. *Ps. 24, 3. 4.* No one who waits for You shall be put to shame. ℣. Your ways, O Lord, make known to me; teach me Your paths.

Alleluia, alleluia. ℣. *Ps. 84, 8.* Show us, O Lord, Your kindness, and grant us Your salvation. Alleluia.

● *Prayer: Cleanse My Heart, page* 31.

Gospel. *Luke 21, 25-33.* At that time, Jesus said to His disciples: "There will be signs in the sun and moon and stars, and upon the earth distress of nations bewildered by the roaring of sea and waves; men fainting for fear and for expectation of the things that are coming on the world; for the powers of heaven will be shaken. And then they will see the Son of Man coming upon a cloud with great power and majesty. But when these things begin to come to pass, look up, and lift up your heads, because your redemption is at hand." And He spoke to them a parable. "Behold the fig tree, and all the trees. When they now put forth their buds, you know that summer is near. Even so, when you see these things coming to pass, know that the kingdom of God is near. Amen I say to you, this generation will not pass away till all things have been accomplished. Heaven and earth will pass away, but My words will not pass away." S. Praise be to You, O Christ.

● Creed, page 33.

Offertory. *Ps. 24, 1-3.* To You I lift up my soul; in You, O my God, I trust; let me not be put to shame: let not my enemies exult over me: no one who waits for You shall be put to shame.

● Offertory Prayers, page 35.

Secret. Grant, O Lord, that these sacred mysteries may cleanse us by their powerful virtue, and bring us with more purity to Him, Who was the author of them. Through our Lord, etc.

● Preface, page 43.

Communion. *Ps. 84, 13.* The Lord will give His benefits: and our earth shall yield its increase.

P. The Lord be with you. *S.* And with your spirit. ↱

Postcommunion. May we receive Your mercy in the midst of Your temple, O Lord; that we may anticipate with due honor the coming solemnities of our renewal. Through our Lord, etc. *S.* Amen.

● Final Prayers, page 73.

———◆———

John sent two of his disciples to Christ.

SECOND SUNDAY OF ADVENT
PURPLE VESTMENTS

THOUGHT FOR TODAY: We need not wait for another Savior. We are certain that Jesus is the Son of God become man, the Anointed Priest-Victim, Redeemer of all mankind. We want to show our love for Him by purifying our hearts.

● *Beginning of Mass, page 19.*

Introit. *Isa. 30, 30.* People of Sion, behold the Lord shall come to save the nations; and the Lord shall make the glory of His voice to be heard, in the joy of your heart. *Ps. 79.* O Shepherd of Israel, hearken, O Guide of the flock of Joseph! ℣. Glory be.

● *Kyrie, page 27. Omit Gloria.*

Prayer. Stir up our hearts, O Lord, to prepare the ways of Your Only-begotten Son, that we may attain to serve You with purified minds, through His advent. Who with You, etc. S. Amen. ↰

– 88 –

Epistle. *Rom. 15, 4-13.* Brethren: Whatever things have been written have been written for our instruction, that through the patience and the consolation afforded by the Scriptures we may have hope. May then the God of patience and of comfort grant you to be of one mind towards one another according to Jesus Christ; that, one in spirit, you may with one mouth glorify the God and Father of our Lord Jesus Christ. Wherefore receive one another, even as Christ has received you to the honor of God. For I say that Christ Jesus has been a minister of the circumcision in order to show God's fidelity in confirming the promises made to our fathers, but that the Gentiles glorify God because of His mercy, as it is written, "Therefore will I praise You among the Gentiles, and will sing to Your name." And again He says, "Rejoice, you Gentiles, with His people." And again, "Praise the Lord, all you Gentiles; and sing His praises, all you peoples." And again Isaias says, "There shall be the root of Jesse, and He Who shall arise to rule the Gentiles . . . in Him the Gentiles shall hope." Now may the God of hope fill you with all joy and peace in believing, that you may abound in hope and in the power of the Holy Spirit. *S.* Thanks be to God. ꜗ

Gradual. *Ps. 49, 2-3. 5.* From Sion, perfect in beauty, God shines forth. ℣. Gather His faithful ones before Him, those who have made a covenant with Him by sacrifice.

Alleluia, alleluia. ℣. *Ps. 121, 1.* I rejoiced because they said to me: "We will go up to the house of the Lord." Alleluia.

● *Prayer: Cleanse My Heart, page* 31.

Gospel. *Matt. 11, 2-10.* At that time, when John had heard in prison of the works of Christ, he sent two of his disciples to say to Him, "Are You He Who is to come, or shall we look for another?" And Jesus answering said to them, "Go and report to John what you have heard and seen: the blind see, the lame walk, the lepers are cleansed, the deaf hear, the dead rise, the poor have the gospel preached to them. And blessed is he who is not scandalized in Me." Then, as they went away, Jesus began to say to the crowds concerning John, "What did you go out to the desert to see? A reed shaken by the wind? But what did you go out to see? A man clothed in soft garments? Behold, those who wear soft garments are in the houses of kings. But what did you go out to see? A prophet? Yes, I tell you, and more than a prophet. This is he of whom it is written, 'Behold, I send My messenger before Your face, who shall make ready Your way before You.'" S. Praise be to You, O Christ.

● Creed, page 33.

Offertory. *Ps. 84, 7-8.* Will You not, O God, give us life; and shall not Your people rejoice in You? Show us, O Lord, Your kindness, and grant us Your salvation.

● Offertory Prayers, page 35.

Secret. Be appeased, we beseech You, O Lord, by the prayers and offerings of our humility; and where no merit can avail, You Yourself help us with Your aid. Through our Lord, etc.

● Preface, page 43.

Communion. *Bar. 5, 5; 4, 36.* Arise, O Jerusalem, and stand on high; and behold the joy that comes to you from your God.

P. The Lord be with you. *S.* And with your spirit. ➜

Postcommunion. Filled with the food of this spiritual nourishment, we suppliantly entreat You, O Lord, that by participation in this mystery You would teach us to despise earthly things, and to love those of heaven. Through our Lord, etc. S. Amen.

● Final Prayers, page 73.

———◆———

"I am the voice of one crying in the desert."

THIRD SUNDAY OF ADVENT
PURPLE VESTMENTS

THOUGHT FOR TODAY: While we are rejoicing "for the Lord is near," there are millions who do not know the One who should stand in the midst of them. The unbelievers must find a guiding beacon in the shining light of our Christian life.

● *Beginning of Mass, page 19.*

Introit. *Phil. 4, 4-6.* Rejoice in the Lord always: again I say, rejoice. Let your moderation be known to all men: for the Lord is near. Have no anxiety, but in everything by prayer let your petitions be made known to God. *Ps. 84, 2.* You have favored, O Lord, Your land; You have restored the well-being of Jacob. ℣. Glory be.

● *Kyrie, page 27. Omit Gloria.*

Prayer. Incline Your ear to our prayers, we beseech You, O Lord, and brighten the

– 92 –

darkness of our minds by the grace of Your visitation. Who live, etc. S. Amen. ⤵

Epistle. *Phil. 4, 4-7.* Brethren: Rejoice in the Lord always; again I say, rejoice. Let your moderation be known to all men. The Lord is near. Have no anxiety, but in every prayer and supplication with thanksgiving let your petitions be made known to God. And may the peace of God which surpasses all understanding guard your hearts and your minds in Christ Jesus, our Lord. S. Thanks be to God. ⤵

Gradual. *Ps. 79, 2.3.2.* From Your throne, O Lord, upon the Cherubim, rouse Your power, and come. ℣. O Shepherd of Israel, hearken, O Guide of the flock of Joseph.

Alleluia, alleluia. ℣ Rouse, O Lord, Your power, and come to save us. Alleluia.

● *Prayer: Cleanse My Heart, page* 31.

Gospel. *John 1, 19-28.* At that time, the Jews sent to John from Jerusalem priests and Levites to ask him, "Who are you?" And he acknowledged and did not deny; and he acknowledged, "I am not the Christ." And they asked him, "What then? Are you Elias?" And he said, "I am not." "Are you the Prophet?" And he answered, "No." They therefore said to him, "Who are you? that we may give an answer to those who sent us. What have you to say of yourself?" He said, "I am the voice of one crying in the desert, 'Make straight the way of the Lord,' as said Isaias the prophet." And they who had been sent were from among the Pharisees. And they asked him, and said to him, "Why, then, do you baptize, if you are not the Christ, nor Elias, nor the Prophet?" John said to them in answer, "I baptize with water; but in the midst of you there has stood One Whom you do not know. He it is Who is to come after me, Who has been set above me, the strap of Whose sandal I am not worthy to loose." These things took place at Bethany, beyond the Jordan, where John was baptizing. S. Praise be to You, O Christ.

● Creed, page 33.

Offertory. *Ps. 84, 2.* You have favored, O Lord, Your land; You have restored the well-being of Jacob; You have forgiven the guilt of Your people.

● Offertory Prayers, page 35.

Secret. May the sacrifice of our devotion ever be offered up to You, O Lord, and both carry out the institution of this sacred mystery, and in us, wonderfully work Your salvation. Through our Lord, etc.

● *Preface, page 43.*

Communion. *Isa. 35, 4.* Say to the faint-hearted, take courage, and fear not; behold, our God will come and will save us.

P. The Lord be with you. *S.* And with your spirit. ↰

Postcommunion. We entreat Your mercy, O Lord, that these divine aids, having cleansed us from our vices, may prepare us for the coming festivities. Through our Lord, etc. *S.* Amen.

● *Final Prayers, page 73.*

"And he went ... about the Jordan preaching a baptism of repentance."

FOURTH SUNDAY OF ADVENT

PURPLE VESTMENTS

THOUGHT FOR TODAY: As Mary is about to give her Divine Son to the world and to us, we cleanse our hearts in sincere confession to prepare the way of the Lord. The most precious Christmas gift is Christ Himself, Whom we receive in Holy Communion.

● *Beginning of Mass, page* 19.

Introit. *Isa. 45, 8.* Drop down dew, you heavens, from above, and let the clouds rain the just: let the earth be opened and bud forth a Savior. *Ps. 18, 2.* The heavens declare the glory of God, and the firmament proclaims His handiwork. ℣. Glory be.

● *Kyrie, page* 27. *Omit Gloria.*

Prayer. Stir up, we beseech You, O Lord, Your power, and come, and succor us with great might; that, by the help of Your grace, what is hindered by our sins, may be hastened by the bounty of Your mercy. Who live, etc. S. Amen. ⇒

Epistle. *1 Cor. 4, 1-5.* Brethren: Let a man so account us, as servants of Christ and stewards of the mysteries of God. Now here it is required in stewards that a man be found trustworthy. But with me it is a very small matter to be judged by you or by man's tribunal. Nay, I do not even judge my own self. For I have nothing on my conscience, yet I am not thereby justified; but he who judges me is the Lord. Therefore, pass no judgment before the time, until the Lord comes, Who will both bring to light the things hidden in darkness and make manifest the counsels of hearts; and then everyone will have his praise from God. S. Thanks be to God. ⇒

Gradual. *Ps. 144, 18. 21.* The Lord is near to all who call upon Him, to all who call upon Him in truth. ℣. May my mouth speak the praise of the Lord, and may all flesh bless His holy Name.

Alleluia, alleluia. ℣. Come, O Lord, and delay not; forgive the sins of Your people Israel. Alleluia.

● *Prayer: Cleanse My Heart, page* **31.**

Gospel. *Luke 3, 1-6.* Now in the fifteenth year of the reign of Tiberius Cæsar, when Pontius Pilate was procurator of Judea, and Herod tetrarch of Galilee, and Philip his brother tetrarch of the district of Iturea and Trachonitis, and Lysanias tetrarch of Abilene, during the high priesthood of Annas and Caiphas, the word of God came to John, the son of Zachary, in the desert. And he went into all the region about the Jordan, preaching a baptism of repentance for the forgiveness of sins, as it is written in the book of the words of Isaias the prophet, "The voice of one crying in the desert, 'Make ready the way of the Lord, make straight His paths. Every valley shall be filled, and every mountain and hill shall be brought low, and the crooked ways shall be made straight, and the rough ways smooth; and all mankind shall see the salvation of God.' " *S.* Praise be to You, O Christ.

- Creed, page 33.

Offertory. *Luke 1, 28.* Hail, Mary full of grace, the Lord is with you, blessed are you among women, and blessed is the fruit of your womb.

- Offertory Prayers, page 35.

Secret. Look favorably on these sacrifices, we beseech You, O Lord, that they may profit us both for our devotion and salvation. Through our Lord, etc.

● *Preface, page 43.*

Communion. *Isa. 7, 14.* Behold, a virgin shall conceive, and bring forth a Son, and His Name shall be called Emmanuel.

P. The Lord be with you. *S.* And with your spirit. ↰

Postcommunion. Having received Your sacred gifts, we beseech You, O Lord, that our assistance at these mysteries may result in an increase of our salvation. Through our Lord, etc. *S.* Amen.

● *Final Prayers, page 73.*

THIS DAY IS BORN TO YOU A SAVIOR

CHRISTMAS DAY

CHRISTMASTIDE: The Church at this period of the year deals with the mysteries of the Infancy of Christ. She reminds us of the great mystery of the Incarnation, which consists of the union of the Divine with the human nature in Jesus. This mystery is made complete by the union of our souls with Christ.

———————

FIRST MASS AT MIDNIGHT

WHITE VESTMENTS

THOUGHT FOR TODAY: May our hearts express our love and gratitude and our resolve to belong entirely to Jesus, as we contemplate this manifestation that God is Love, and that He so loved the world as to give us His Only-begotten Son.

● *Beginning of Mass, page 19.*

Introit. *Ps. 2, 7.* The Lord said to Me, "You are My Son; this day I have begotten You." *Ps. 2, 1.* Why do the nations rage and the peoples utter folly? ℣. Glory be.

● *Kyrie and Gloria, page 27.*

Prayer. O God, You have illumined this most holy night with the brightness of the True Light; grant, we beseech You, that we, who have known the mystery of His light on earth, may also attain to the full enjoyment of His joys in heaven. Who with You, etc. S. Amen. ↄ

Epistle. *Titus 2, 11-15.* Beloved: The grace of God our Savior has appeared to all men, instructing us, in order that, rejecting ungodliness and worldly lusts, we may live temperately and justly and piously in this world; looking for the blessed hope and glorious coming of our great God and Savior, Jesus Christ, Who gave Himself for us that He might redeem us from all iniquity and cleanse for Himself an acceptable people, pursuing good works. Thus speak, and exhort, in Christ Jesus our Lord. S. Thanks be to God. ↄ

Gradual. *Ps. 109, 3. 1.* Yours is princely power in the day of Your birth, in holy splendor; before the daystar I have begotten You. ℣. The Lord said to my Lord: "Sit at My right hand, till I make Your enemies Your footstool."

Alleluia, alleluia. ℣. *Ps. 2, 7.* The Lord said to Me, "You are My Son; this day I have begotten You." Alleluia.

● *Prayer: Cleanse My Heart, page* **31.**

Gospel. *Luke 2, 1-14.* At that time, there went forth a decree from Cæsar Augustus that a census of the whole world should be taken. This first census took place while Cyrinus was governor of Syria. And all were going, each to his own town, to register. And Joseph also went from Galilee out of the town of Nazareth into Judea to the town of David, which is called Bethlehem —because he was of the house and family of David—to register, together with Mary his espoused wife, who was with child. And it came to pass while they were there, that the days for her to be delivered were fulfilled. And she brought forth her firstborn Son, and wrapped Him in swaddling clothes, and laid Him in a manger, because there was no room for them in the inn. And there were shepherds in the same district living in the fields and keeping watch over their flock by night. And behold, an angel of the Lord stood by them and the glory of God shone round about them, and they feared exceedingly. And the angel said to them, "Do not be afraid, for behold, I bring you good news of great joy which shall be to all the people; for today in the town of David a Savior has been born to you, Who is Christ the Lord. And this shall be a sign to you: you will find an infant wrapped in

swaddling clothes and lying in a manger."
And suddenly there was with the angel a
multitude of the heavenly host praising God
and saying, "Glory to God in the highest,
and on earth peace among men of good
will." *S.* Praise be to You, O Christ.

● *Creed, page* 33.

Offertory. *Ps. 95, 11. 13.* Let the heavens be glad and the earth rejoice before the
Lord, for He comes.

● *Offertory Prayers, page* 35.

Secret. May the offering of this day's
festival be pleasing to You, O Lord, that
by Your bountiful grace, we may, through
this sacred intercourse, be found conformed
to Him, in Whom our substance is united
to You. Who with You, etc. ➤

Preface for Christmas

P. World without end. *S.* Amen. *P.* The Lord
be with you. *S.* And with your spirit. *P.* Lift up
your hearts. *S.* We have lifted them up to the
Lord. *P.* Let us give thanks to the Lord, our
God. *S.* It is fitting and just.

It is fitting indeed and just, right and
helpful to salvation, for us always and everywhere to give thanks to You, O Holy Lord,
Father Almighty, Everlasting God. Because

by the mystery of the Word made flesh the new light of Your glory has shone upon the eyes of our mind: that while we acknowledge Him to be God seen by men, we may be drawn by Him to the love of things unseen. And therefore with Angels and Archangels, with Thrones and Dominations, and with the whole host of the heavenly army, we sing a hymn to Your glory, saying again and again: Holy, Holy, Holy, Lord God of hosts. Heaven and earth are filled with Your glory. Hosanna in the highest. Blessed is He Who comes in the name of the Lord. Hosanna in the highest.

● *Canon, page 47.*

Communion. *Ps. 109, 3.* In holy splendor before the daystar I have begotten You.

P. The Lord be with you. *S.* And with your spirit. ↱

Postcommunion. Grant, we beseech You, O Lord our God, that we, who rejoice in celebrating these mysteries of the Nativity of our Lord Jesus Christ, may by a fitting life become worthy to attain to His fellowship. Who with You, etc. *S.* Amen.

● *Final Prayers, page 73.*

———◆———

Simeon said, "Behold, this Child is destined for the fall and for the rise of many in Israel."

SUNDAY WITHIN OCTAVE OF CHRISTMAS

WHITE VESTMENTS

THOUGHT FOR TODAY: Mary and Joseph were wondering at the things which were spoken about Jesus. They realized better that their hearts would be pierced with the sword of sorrow because they were so closely associated with the "Man of Sorrows."

● *Beginning of Mass, page 19.*

Introit. *Wis. 18, 14. 15.* When a profound stillness compassed everything and the night in its swift course was half spent, Your all-powerful Word, O Lord, bounded from heaven's royal throne. *Ps. 92, 1.* The Lord is King, in splendor robed; robed is the Lord, and girt about with strength. ℣. Glory be.

● *Kyrie and Gloria, page 27.*

Prayer. Almighty and everlasting God, direct our actions according to Your good pleasure; that we may deserve to abound in good works, in the Name of Your beloved Son. Who with You, etc. *S.* Amen. ➘

Epistle. *Gal. 4, 1-7.* Brethren: As long as the heir is a child, he differs in no way from a slave, though he is the master of all; but he is under guardians and stewards until the time set by his father. So we too, when we were children, were enslaved under the elements of the world. But when the fullness of time came, God sent His Son, born of a woman, born under the Law, that He might redeem those who were under the Law, that we might receive the adoption of sons. And because you are sons, God has sent the Spirit of His Son into our hearts, crying, "Abba, Father." So that He is no longer a slave, but a son; and if a son, an heir also through God. *S.* Thanks be to God. ➘

Gradual. *Ps. 44, 3. 2.* Fairer in beauty are You than the sons of men; grace is poured out upon Your lips. ℣. My heart overflows with a goodly theme; as I sing my ode to the King, my tongue is nimble as the pen of a skillful scribe.

Alleluia, alleluia. ℣. *Ps. 92, 1.* The Lord is King, in splendor robed; robed is the Lord and girt about with strength. Alleluia.

● Prayer: *Cleanse My Heart, page* 31.

Gospel. *Luke 2, 33-40.* At that time, Joseph and Mary, the Mother of Jesus, were marvelling at the things spoken concerning Him. And Simeon blessed them, and said to Mary His Mother, "Behold, this Child is destined for the fall and for the rise of many in Israel, and for a sign that shall be contradicted. And your own soul a sword shall pierce, that the thoughts of many hearts may be revealed." There was also Anna, a prophetess, daughter of Phanuel, of the tribe of Aser. She was of a great age, having lived with her husband seven years from her maidenhood, and by herself as a widow to eighty-four years. She never left the temple, with fastings and prayers worshipping night and day. And coming up at that very hour, she began to give praise to the Lord, and spoke of Him to all who were awaiting the redemption of Jerusalem. And when they had fulfilled all things as prescribed in the Law of the Lord, they returned to Galilee, into their own town of Nazareth. And the Child grew and became strong. He was full of wisdom and the grace of God was upon Him. *S.* Praise be to You, O Christ.

● *Creed, page 33.*

Offertory. *Ps. 92, 1. 2.* God has made the world firm, not to be moved; Your throne, O God, stands firm from of old; from everlasting You are.

● *Offertory Prayers, page 35.*

Secret. Grant, we beseech You, almighty God, that the offering made in the sight of Your Majesty may obtain for us the grace of a holy devotion, and the reward of a blessed eternity. Through our Lord, etc.

● *Preface for Christmas, page 104.*

Communion. *Matt. 2, 20.* Take the Child and His Mother, and go into the land of Israel, for those who sought the Child's life are dead.

P. The Lord be with you. *S.* And with your spirit. ⇥

Postcommunion. O Lord, by the working of this mystery, may our vices be purged away and our just desires fulfilled. Through our Lord, etc. *S.* Amen.

● *Final Prayers, page 73.*

———◆———

"His Name was called Jesus."

OCTAVE DAY OF CHRISTMAS
WHITE VESTMENTS

THOUGHT FOR TODAY: At the beginning of the new civil year we firmly resolve to live "temperately and justly, and piously" in the New Year, looking for the "glorious coming of our great God."

● *Beginning of Mass, page 19.*

Introit. *Isa. 9, 6.* A Child is born to us, and a Son is given to us; Whose government is upon His shoulder; and His Name shall be called the Angel of great counsel. *Ps. 97, 1.* Sing to the Lord a new song; for He has done wondrous deeds. ℣. Glory be.

● *Kyrie and Gloria, page 27.*

Prayer. O God, by the fruitful virginity of Blessed Mary, You bestowed upon the human race the rewards of eternal salvation; grant, we beseech You, that we may feel the power of her intercession, through whom we have been made worthy to receive the Author of Life, Jesus Christ Your Son, our Lord. Who with You, etc. S. Amen. ⤸

Epistle. *Titus 2, 11-15.* Beloved: The grace of God our Savior has appeared to all men, instructing us, in order that, rejecting ungodliness and worldly lusts, we may live temperately and justly and piously in this world; looking for the blessed hope and glorious coming of our great God and Savior, Jesus Christ, Who gave Himself for us that He might redeem us from all iniquity and cleanse for Himself an acceptable people, pursuing good works. Thus speak, and exhort, in Christ Jesus our Lord. S. Thanks be to God. ⤸

Gradual. *Ps. 97, 3. 4. 2.* All the ends of the earth have seen the salvation by our God; sing joyfully to God, all you lands. ℣. The Lord has made His salvation known; in the sight of the nations He has revealed His justice.

Alleluia, alleluia. ℣. *Heb. 1, 1. 2.* God, Who in diverse ways spoke in times past to the fathers by the prophets, last of all, in these days, has spoken to us by His Son. Alleluia.

● *Prayer: Cleanse My Heart, page* 31.

Gospel. *Luke 2, 21.* At that time, when eight days were fulfilled for the circumcision of the Child, His Name was called Jesus, the Name given Him by the angel before He was conceived in the womb. S. Praise be to You, O Christ.

• Creed, page 33.

Offertory. *Ps. 88, 12. 15.* Yours are the heavens, and Yours is the earth; the world and its fullness You have founded; justice and judgment are the foundation of Your throne.

• Offertory Prayers, page 35.

Secret. Receive, we beseech You, O Lord, our offerings and prayers; and through these heavenly mysteries cleanse us, and grant what we ask. Through our Lord, etc.

• Preface for Christmas, page 104.

Communion. *Ps. 97, 3.* All the ends of the earth have seen the salvation by our God.

P. The Lord be with you. *S.* And with your spirit. ↰

Postcommunion. May this Communion, O Lord, cleanse us from guilt; and by the intercession of Blessed Mary the Virgin-Mother of God, make us share in the heavenly remedy. Through, etc. S. Amen.

• Final Prayers, page 73.

———◆———

"At the Name of Jesus every knee should bend."

HOLY NAME OF JESUS

WHITE VESTMENTS

THOUGHT FOR TODAY: The Son of God made Man, was called Jesus, that is, Savior. This name recalls God's ineffable mercy "for there is no other name under heaven given to men, by which we must be saved." Let us always use it with gratitude and respect.

If no Sunday occurs between the Octave Day of Christmas and Epiphany, this Feast is celebrated on January 2.

● *Beginning of Mass, page 19.*

Introit. *Phil. 2, 10-11.* At the Name of Jesus every knee should bend of those in heaven, on earth, and under the earth, and every tongue should confess that the Lord Jesus Christ is in the glory of God the Father. *Ps. 8, 2.* O Lord, our Lord, how glorious is Your Name over all the earth! ℣. Glory be.

– 113 –

● *Kyrie and Gloria, page* 27.

Prayer. O God, You have established Your Only-begotten Son as the Savior of mankind and commanded that He should be called Jesus; mercifully grant that we who venerate His holy Name on earth, may also be filled with the enjoyment of the vision of Him in heaven. Through the same, etc. S. Amen. ⮑

Epistle. *Acts 4, 8-12.* In those days, Peter, filled with the Holy Spirit, said, "Rulers of the people and elders, if we are on trial today about a good work done to a cripple, as to how this man has been cured, be it known to all of you and to all the people of Israel that in the Name of Jesus Christ of Nazareth, Whom you crucified, Whom God has raised from the dead, even in this Name does he stand here before you, sound. This is 'The stone that was rejected by you, the builders, which has become the cornerstone.' Neither is there salvation in any other. For there is no other name under heaven given to men by which we must be saved." S. Thanks be to God. ⮑

Gradual. *Ps. 105, 47.* Save us, O Lord, our God, and gather us from among the nations, that we may give thanks to Your holy Name and glory in praising You. ℣. *Isa. 63, 16.* You, O Lord, are our Father and our Redeemer; from everlasting is Your Name.

Alleluia, alleluia. ℣ *Ps. 144, 21* May my mouth speak the praise of the Lord, and may all flesh bless His holy Name. Alleluia.

● Prayer: Cleanse My Heart, page 31.

Gospel. *Luke 2, 21.* At that time, when eight days were fulfilled for the circumcision of the Child, His Name was called Jesus, the Name given Him by the angel before He was conceived in the womb. *S.* Praise be to You, O Christ.

● Creed, page 33.

Offertory. *Ps. 85, 12. 5.* I will give thanks to You, O Lord my God, with all my heart, and I will glorify Your Name forever; for You, O Lord, are good and forgiving, abounding in kindness to all who call upon You. Alleluia.

● Offertory Prayers, page 35.

Secret. May Your blessing, most merciful God, by which every creature lives, sanctify, we beseech You, this our sacrifice, which we offer to You, to the glory of the Name of Your Son our Lord Jesus Christ, that it may please Your Majesty as an act of praise, and profit us to salvation. Through the same, etc.

● *Preface for Christmas, page 104.*

Communion. *Ps. 85, 9-10.* All the nations You have made shall come and worship You, O Lord, and glorify Your Name; for You are great, and You do wondrous deeds; You alone are God. Alleluia.

P. The Lord be with you. *S.* And with your spirit. ➷

Postcommunion. Almighty and eternal God, You have created and redeemed us; graciously regard our prayers, and vouchsafe to accept with a benign and favorable countenance the sacrifice of the Saving Victim which we have offered to Your Majesty, in honor of the Name of Your Son, our Lord Jesus Christ: that, through the infusion of Your grace into us, we may rejoice over our names having been written under the glorious Name of Jesus, as a pledge of eternal predestination. Through the same, etc. *S.* Amen.

● *Final Prayers, page 73.*

———◇———

"Entering the house, they found the Child with Mary His Mother, and falling down they worshipped Him."

THE EPIPHANY OF OUR LORD

WHITE VESTMENTS

THOUGHT FOR TODAY: Following the example of the Wise Men we adore the newborn King, and offer Him the gold of a loving heart, the frankincense of persevering prayers, and the myrrh of our readiness to labor and suffer for Him.

● *Beginning of Mass, page 19.*

Introit. *Mal. 3, 1; 1 Par. 29, 12.* Behold the Lord the Ruler is come; and the kingdom is in His hand, and power, and dominion. *Ps. 71, 1.* O God, with Your judgment endow the king, and with Your justice, the king's son. ℣. Glory be.

● *Kyrie and Gloria, page 27.*

Prayer. O God, on this day, by the guiding star, You revealed Your Only-begotten Son to the Gentiles; mercifully grant, that we who now know You by faith, may be led on even to look upon the beauty of Your Majesty. Through the same, etc. *S.* Amen. ↵

Epistle. *Isa. 60, 1-6.* Arise, be enlightened, O Jerusalem; for your light is come, and the glory of the Lord is risen upon you. For behold, darkness shall cover the earth, and a mist the people; but the Lord shall arise upon you, and His glory shall be seen upon you. And the Gentiles shall walk in your light, and kings in the brightness of your rising. Lift up your eyes round about, and see; all these are gathered together: they are come to you; your sons shall come from afar, and your daughters shall rise up at your side. Then shall you see, and abound; and your heart shall wonder and be enlarged, when the multitude of the sea shall be converted to you, the strength of the Gentiles shall come to you. The multitude of camels shall cover you, the dromedaries of Madian and Epha; all they from Saba shall come, bringing gold and frankincense, and showing forth praise to the Lord. *S.* Thanks be to God. ↵

Gradual. *Isa. 60, 6. 1.* All they from Saba shall come, bringing gold and frankincense, and showing forth praise to the

THE EPIPHANY OF OUR LORD 119

Lord. ℣. Arise, and be enlightened, O Jerusalem, for the glory of the Lord is risen
upon you.

Alleluia, alleluia. ℣. *Matt. 2, 2.* We have
seen His star in the East: and have come
with gifts to worship the Lord. Alleluia.

● *Prayer: Cleanse My Heart, page 31.*

Gospel. *Matt. 2, 1-12.* When Jesus was
born in Bethlehem of Judea, in the days
of King Herod, behold, Magi came from the
East to Jerusalem, saying, "Where is He
that is born King of the Jews? For we have
seen His star in the East and have come to
worship Him." But when King Herod heard
this, he was troubled, and so was all Jerusalem with him. And gathering together all
the chief priests and Scribes of the people,
he inquired of them where the Christ was
to be born. And they said to him, "In Bethlehem of Judea; for thus it is written by
the prophet, 'And you, Bethlehem, of the
land of Juda, are by no means least among
the princes of Juda; for from you shall
come forth a leader who shall rule My
people Israel.'" Then Herod summoned the
Magi secretly, and carefully ascertained
from them the time when the star had appeared to them. And sending them to Bethlehem, he said, "Go and make careful in-

quiry concerning the Child, and when you have found Him, bring me word, that I too may go and worship Him." Now they, having heard the king, went their way. And behold, the star that they had seen in the East went before them, until it came and stood over the place where the Child was. And when they saw the star they rejoiced exceedingly. And entering the house, they found the Child with Mary His Mother, and falling down they worshipped Him. (*Here genuflect.*) And opening their treasures they offered Him gifts of gold, frankincense and myrrh. And being warned in a dream not to return to Herod, they went back to their own country by another way. *S.* Praise be to You, O Christ.

● Creed, page 33.

Offertory. *Ps. 71, 10-11.* The kings of Tharsis and the Isles shall offer gifts; the kings of Arabia and Saba shall bring tribute; all kings shall pay homage; all nations shall serve Him.

● Offertory Prayers, page 35.

Secret. Graciously regard, we beseech You, O Lord, the offerings of Your Church, in which gold, frankincense, and myrrh are no longer laid before You, but He is sacrificed and received, Who by those gifts was signified, Jesus Christ, Your Son our Lord. Who with You, etc. ➤

Preface of the Epiphany

P. World without end. *S.* Amen. *P.* The Lord be with you. *S.* And with your spirit. *P.* Lift up your hearts. *S.* We have lifted them up to the Lord. *P.* Let us give thanks to the Lord, our God. *S.* It is fitting and just.

It is fitting indeed and just, right and helpful to salvation, for us always and everywhere to give thanks to You, O Holy Lord, Father Almighty, Everlasting God; for when Your Only-begotten Son showed Himself in the substance of our mortal nature, He restored us by the new light of His own immortality. And therefore with Angels and Archangels, with Thrones and Dominations and with the whole host of the heavenly army we sing a hymn to Your glory, saying again and again: Holy, Holy, Holy, Lord God of hosts. Heaven and earth are filled with Your glory. Hosanna in the highest. Blessed is He Who comes in the Name of the Lord. Hosanna in the highest.

● *Canon, page 47.*

Communion. *Matt. 2, 2.* We have seen His star in the East; and have come with gifts to worship the Lord.

P. The Lord be with you. *S.* And with your spirit. ↱

Postcommunion. Grant, we beseech You, almighty God, that we may attain by the understanding of a purified mind what we have celebrated in a solemn office. Through our Lord, etc. *S.* Amen.

● *Final Prayers, page 73.*

"He went down with them and came to Nazareth, and was subject to them."

FEAST OF THE HOLY FAMILY

WHITE VESTMENTS

THOUGHT FOR TODAY: The family is the smaller unit from which society develops. As long as the love of God binds the members of the family together, and the Christian virtues rule in our homes, society will be prosperous and at peace. Ask in your Mass and Holy Communion that your conduct in family life may be guided by the example of the Holy Family at Nazareth.

● *Beginning of Mass, page 19.*

Introit. *Prov. 23, 24. 25.* The father of the Just will exult with glee; let Your father and mother have joy; let her who bore You exult. *Ps. 83, 2. 3.* How lovely is Your dwelling place, O Lord of hosts; my soul yearns and pines for the courts of the Lord. ℣. Glory be.

● *Kyrie and Gloria, page 27.*

Prayer. O Lord Jesus Christ, by subjecting Yourself to Mary and Joseph, You consecrated family life with wonderful virtues: grant that, by their joint assistance, we may fashion our lives after the example of Your Holy Family, and obtain everlasting fellowship with it. Who live, etc S. Amen. ⇁

Epistle. *Col. 3, 12-17.* Brethren: Put on, as God's chosen ones, holy and beloved, a heart of mercy, kindness, humility, meekness, patience. Bear with one another and forgive one another, if anyone has a grievance against any other; even as the Lord has forgiven you, so also do you forgive. But above all these things have charity, which is the bond of perfection. And may the peace of Christ reign in your hearts; unto that peace, indeed, you were called in one body. Show yourselves thankful. Let the word of Christ dwell in you abundantly: in all wisdom teach and admonish one another by psalms, hymns and spiritual songs, singing in your hearts to God by His grace. Whatever you do in word or in work, do all in the Name of the Lord Jesus Christ, giving thanks to God the Father through Him. S. Thanks be to God. ⇁

Gradual. *Ps. 26, 4.* One thing I ask of the Lord; this I seek: to dwell in the house of the Lord all the days of my life. ℣ *Ps. 83, 5.* Happy they who dwell in Your house, O Lord; continually they praise You.

Alleluia, alleluia. ℣. *Isa. 45, 15.* Truly, You are a hidden God, the God of Israel, the Savior. Alleluia.

● *Prayer: Cleanse My Heart, page* 31.

Gospel. *Luke 2, 42-52.* When Jesus was twelve years old, they went up to Jerusalem according to the custom of the feast. And after they had fulfilled the days, when they were returning, the Boy Jesus remained in Jerusalem, and His parents did not know it. But thinking that He was in the caravan, they had come a day's journey before it occurred to them to look for Him among their relatives and acquaintances. And not finding Him, they returned to Jerusalem in search of Him. And it came to pass after three days, that they found Him in the temple, sitting in the midst of the teachers, listening to them and asking them questions. And all who were listening to Him were amazed at His understanding and His answers. And when they saw Him, they were astonished. And His mother said to Him, "Son, why have You done so to us? Behold, in sorrow Your father and I have been seeking You." And He said to them, "How is it that you sought Me? Did you not know that I must be about My Father's business?" And they did not understand the word that He spoke to them. And He went down with them and came to Nazareth, and was subject to them; and His Mother kept all these things carefully in her heart. And Jesus advanced in wisdom and age and grace before God and men. S. Praise be to You, O Christ.

● Creed, page 33.

Offertory. *Luke 2, 22.* The parents of Jesus took Him up to Jerusalem, to present Him to the Lord.

● Offertory Prayers, page 35.

Secret. We offer You, O Lord, the sacrifice of reconciliation, humbly entreating that, by the intercession of the Virgin-Mother of God and Saint Joseph, You may firmly establish our families in Your peace and grace. Through the same, etc.

● Preface of the Epiphany, page 121.

Communion. *Luke 2, 51.* Jesus went down with them and came to Nazareth, and was subject to them.

P. The Lord be with you. *S.* And with your spirit. ⮑

Postcommunion. O Lord Jesus, cause those whom You refresh with the heavenly sacrament, to imitate continually the example of Your Holy Family, that being welcomed at the hour of death by Your glorious Virgin-Mother and Saint Joseph, we may be found worthy to be received by You into Your everlasting dwellings. Who live, etc. S. Amen.

● *Final Prayers, page 73.*

Jesus said to them, "Fill the jars with water."

SECOND SUNDAY AFTER EPIPHANY
GREEN VESTMENTS

TIME AFTER EPIPHANY: This third part of the Christmas Cycle begins with January 14 and ends with Septuagesima Sunday. Its theme is the public life of our Lord, His miracles and teaching. The "Sundays after Epiphany" may be six or less, according as Easter is early or late in the year. The Sundays omitted after Epiphany are used to make up the number required after Pentecost.

THOUGHT FOR TODAY: Imitating Mary's life of charity and relying on her powerful intercession, we may find a sure way out of our daily troubles, as the bridegroom did at the wedding at Cana.

When this Mass or those of the following Sundays before Septuagesima are said on weekdays, the Gloria and Creed are omitted.

● *Beginning of Mass, page 19.*

Introit. *Ps. 65, 4.* Let all on earth worship You, O God, and sing praise to You, sing praise to Your Name, Most High. *Ps.*

65, 1-2. Shout joyfully to God, all you on earth, sing praise to the glory of His Name; proclaim His glorious praise. ℣. Glory be.

● *Kyrie and Gloria, page 27.*

Prayer. Almighty and eternal God, You govern all things in heaven and on earth, in Your mercy hear the supplication of Your people, and grant Your peace in our times. Through our Lord, etc. *S.* Amen.

Epistle. *Rom. 12, 6-16.* Brethren: We have gifts differing according to the grace that has been given us, such as prophecy to be used according to the proportion of faith; or ministry, in ministering; or he who teaches, in teaching; he who exhorts, in exhorting; he who gives, in simplicity; he who presides, with carefulness; he who shows mercy, with cheerfulness. Let love be without pretense. Hate what is evil, hold to what is good. Love one another with fraternal charity, anticipating one another with honor. Be not slothful in zeal; be fervent in spirit, serving the Lord, rejoicing in hope. Be patient in tribulation, persevering in prayer. Share the needs of the saints, practising hospitality. Bless those who persecute you; bless and do not curse. Rejoice with those who rejoice; weep with those who weep. Be of one mind towards one another.

Do not set your mind on high things but condescend to the lowly. S. Thanks be to God. ⟍

Gradual. *Ps. 106, 20-21.* The Lord sent forth His Word to heal them and to snatch them from destruction. ℣. Let them give thanks to the Lord for His kindness, and His wondrous deeds to the children of men.

Alleluia, alleluia. ℣. *Ps. 148, 2.* Praise the Lord, all you His angels; praise Him, all You His hosts. Alleluia.

● *Prayer: Cleanse My Heart, page 31.*

Gospel. *John 2, 1-11.* At that time, a marriage took place at Cana of Galilee, and the Mother of Jesus was there. Now Jesus too was invited to the marriage, and also His disciples. And the wine having run short, the Mother of Jesus said to Him, "They have no wine." And Jesus said to her, "What would you have Me do, woman? My hour has not yet come." His Mother said to the attendants, "Do whatever He tells you." Now six stone water-jars were placed there, after the Jewish manner of purification, each holding two or three measures. Jesus said to them, "Fill the jars with water." And they filled them to the brim. And Jesus said to them, "Draw out now, and take to the chief

steward." And they took it to him. Now
when the chief steward had tasted the water
after it had become wine, not knowing
whence it was (though the attendants who
had drawn the water knew), the chief
steward called the bridegroom, and said to
him, "Every man at first sets forth the good
wine, and when they have drunk freely,
then that which is poorer. But you have
kept the good wine until now." This first of
His signs Jesus worked at Cana of Galilee;
and He manifested His glory, and His disciples believed in Him. *S.* Praise be to You,
O Christ.

● *Creed, page* 33.

Offertory. *Ps.* 65, *1-2. 16.* Shout joyfully
to God, all you on earth, sing praise to the
glory of His Name; hear now, all you who
fear God, while I declare what the Lord
has done for me, alleluia.

● *Offertory Prayers, page* 35.

Secret. Sanctify, O Lord, the gifts we
offer, and purify us from the stains of our
sins. Through our Lord, etc.

● *Preface, page* 43.

Communion. *John* 2, 7. 8. 9. *10-11.* The
Lord said, "Fill the jars with water and take
to the chief steward." When the chief stew-

ard had tasted the water after it had become wine, he said to the bridegroom, "You have kept the good wine until now." This first miracle Jesus worked in the presence of His disciples.

P. The Lord be with you. *S.* And with your spirit. ⮑

Postcommunion. May the working of Your power, we beg of You, O Lord, be increased in us, that, being nourished by divine sacraments, we may by Your grace be prepared to obtain that which they promise. Through our Lord, etc. *S.* Amen.

● *Final Prayers, page 73.*

"Lord, I am not worthy . . . but only say the word, and my servant will be healed."

THIRD SUNDAY AFTER EPIPHANY
GREEN VESTMENTS

THOUGHT FOR TODAY: "Lord, I am not worthy that You should come under my roof." Receiving Christ in frequent Holy Communion with deep humility and living faith in His Divinity is the best assurance that we shall never be cast into hell.

● *Beginning of Mass, page 19.*

Introit. *Ps. 96, 7. 8.* Adore God, all you His angels; Sion hears and is glad; and the cities of Juda rejoice. *Ps. 96, 1.* The Lord is King; let the earth rejoice; let the many isles be glad. ℣. Glory be.

● *Kyrie and Gloria, page 27.*

Prayer. Almighty and everlasting God, graciously look upon our infirmity, and, for our protection, stretch forth the right hand of Your Majesty. Through our Lord, etc. S. Amen. ↝

Epistle. *Rom. 12, 16-21.* Brethren: Be not wise in your own conceits. To no man render evil for evil, but provide good things not only in the sight of God, but also in the sight of all men. If it be possible, as far as in you lies, be at peace with all men. Do not avenge yourselves, beloved, but give place to the wrath, for it is written, "Vengeance is Mine: I will repay, says the Lord." But, "If your enemy is hungry, give him food; if he is thirsty, give him drink; for by so doing you will heap coals of fire upon his head." Be not overcome by evil, but overcome evil with good. S. Thanks be to God. ⮐

Gradual. *Ps. 101, 16. 17.* The nations shall revere Your Name, O Lord, and all the kings of the earth Your glory. ℣. For the Lord has rebuilt Sion, and He shall appear in His glory.

Alleluia, alleluia. ℣. *Ps. 96, 1.* The Lord is King; let the earth rejoice; let the many isles be glad. Alleluia.

● *Prayer: Cleanse My Heart, page* 31.

Gospel. *Matt. 8, 1-13.* At that time, when Jesus had come down from the mountain, great crowds followed Him. And behold, a leper came up and worshipped Him, saying, "Lord, if You will, You can make me clean." And stretching forth His hand Jesus touched him, saying, "I will; be made clean." And immediately his leprosy was cleansed. And Jesus said to him, "See that you tell no one; but go, show yourself to the priest, and offer the gift that Moses commanded, for a witness to them." Now when He entered Capharnaum, there came to Him a centurion who entreated Him, saying, "Lord, my servant is lying sick in the house, paralyzed, and is grievously afflicted." Jesus said to him, "I will come and cure him." But in answer the centurion said, "Lord, I am not worthy that You should come under my roof; but only say the word, and my servant will be healed. For I too am a man subject to authority, and have soldiers subject to me; and I say to one, 'Go,' and he goes; and to another, 'Come,' and he comes; and to my servant, "Do this,' and he does it." And when Jesus heard this, He marvelled, and said to those who were following Him, "Amen I say to you, I have not found such great faith in Israel. And I tell you that many will come from the east and from the west, and will feast with Abraham and Isaac and Jacob in the kingdom of heaven, but the children of the kingdom will be put forth into the darkness outside;

there will be the weeping, and the gnashing of teeth." Then Jesus said to the centurion, "Go your way; as you have believed, so be it done to you." And the servant was healed in that hour. S. Praise be to You, O Christ.

● Creed, page 33.

Offertory. *Ps. 117, 16. 17.* The right hand of the Lord has struck with power: the right hand of the Lord has exalted me; I shall not die, but live, and declare the works of the Lord.

● Offertory Prayers, page 35.

Secret. May this offering, we beseech You, O Lord, cleanse away our sins, and sanctify the bodies and minds of Your servants for the celebration of this sacrifice. Through our Lord, etc.

● Preface, page 43.

Communion. *Luke 4, 22.* All marvelled at the words that came from the mouth of God.

P. The Lord be with you. *S.* And with your spirit. ↱

Postcommunion. We, O Lord, to whom You grant the use of mysteries so great, beseech You to render us truly fitted to obtain their effect. Through, etc. S. Amen.

● Final Prayers, page 73.

———◈———

"Why are you fearful, O you of little faith?"

FOURTH SUNDAY AFTER EPIPHANY

GREEN VESTMENTS

THOUGHT FOR TODAY: Our life with its temptations and struggles is often similar to a voyage on a stormy sea. If we do what is in our power and persevere in prayer, the Master of Nature will do the rest, and there will come a great calm and peace.

● *Beginning of Mass, page 19.*

Introit. *Ps. 96, 7. 8.* Adore God, all you His angels: Sion hears and is glad; and the cities of Juda rejoice. *Ps. 96, 1.* The Lord is King, let the earth rejoice; let the many isles be glad. ℣. Glory be.

● *Kyrie and Gloria, page 27.*

Prayer. O God, You know that, placed as we are amid such great dangers, we cannot by reason of our human frailty stand; grant us health of mind and of body, that, by Your help, we may overcome the things which we suffer for our sins. Through our Lord, etc. S. Amen. ⤵

Epistle. *Rom. 13, 8-10.* Brethren: Owe no man anything except to love one another; for he who loves his neighbor has fulfilled the Law. For "You shall not commit adultery. You shall not kill. You shall not steal. You shall not bear false witness. You shall not covet"; and if there is any other commandment, it is summed up in this saying, "You shall love your neighbor as yourself." Love does no evil to a neighbor. Love therefore is the fulfillment of the Law. S. Thanks be to God. ⤵

Gradual. *Ps. 101, 16-17.* The nations shall revere Your Name, O Lord, and all the kings of the earth Your glory. ℣. For the Lord has rebuilt Sion, and He shall appear in His glory. Alleluia, alleluia. ℣. *Ps. 96, 1.* The Lord is King; let the earth rejoice; let the many isles be glad. Alleluia.

● *Prayer: Cleanse My Heart, page 31.*

Gospel. *Matt. 8, 23-27.* At that time, Jesus got into a boat, and His disciples followed Him. And behold, there arose a great storm on the sea, so that the boat was covered by the waves; but He was asleep. So they came and woke Him, saying, "Lord save us! we are perishing!" But He said to them, "Why are you fearful, O you of little faith?" Then He arose and rebuked the wind and the sea, and there came a great calm. And the men marvelled, saying, "What manner of Man is this, that even the wind and the sea obey Him?" S. Praise be to You, O Christ.

● Creed, page 33.

Offertory. *Ps. 117, 16. 17.* The right hand of the Lord has struck with power: the right hand of the Lord has exalted me; I shall not die, but live, and declare the works of the Lord.

● Offertory Prayers, page 35.

Secret. Grant, we beseech You, almighty God, that the gift of this sacrifice, may ever purify and protect our frailty from all evil. Through our Lord, etc.

● Preface, page 43.

Communion. *Luke 4, 22.* All marvelled at the words that came from the mouth of God.

P. The Lord be with you. S. And with your spirit. ⤶

Postcommunion. May Your gifts, O God, detach us from earthly pleasures, and ever fill us with heavenly refreshment. Through our Lord, etc. S. Amen.

● Final Prayers, page 73.

————◇————

"His enemy came and sowed weeds among the wheat."

FIFTH SUNDAY AFTER EPIPHANY
GREEN VESTMENTS

THOUGHT FOR TODAY: God is the Creator of the world, and what He has made is good. How then do we account for the evil in the world? Because man has free will, he can misuse God's gifts and transgress His Commandments and do evil. He can become an enemy of his greatest Benefactor. It would be foolish to delay our conversion until God will separate the weeds from the wheat.

● *Beginning of Mass, page 19.*

Introit. *Ps. 96, 7. 8.* Adore God, all you His angels: Sion hears and is glad; and the cities of Juda rejoice. *Ps. 96, 1.* The Lord is King; let the earth rejoice; let the many isles be glad. ℣. Glory be.

● *Kyrie and Gloria, page 27.*

Prayer. We beseech You, O Lord, in Your unceasing goodness, guard Your family; that we who lean only upon the hope of Your heavenly grace, may always be defended by Your protection. Through our Lord, etc. *S.* Amen. ⤴

Epistle. *Col. 3, 12-17.* Brethren: Put on, as God's chosen ones, holy and beloved, a heart of mercy, kindness, humility, meekness, patience. Bear with one another and forgive one another, if anyone has a grievance against any other; even as the Lord has forgiven you, so also do you forgive. But above all these things have charity, which is the bond of perfection. And may the peace of Christ reign in your hearts; unto that peace, indeed, you were called in one body. Show yourselves thankful. Let the word of Christ dwell in you abundantly: in all wisdom teach and admonish one another by psalms, hymns and spiritual songs, singing in your hearts to God by His grace. Whatever you do in word or in work, do all in the Name of the Lord Jesus Christ, giving thanks to God the Father through Jesus Christ our Lord. *S.* Thanks be to God. ⤴

Gradual. *Ps. 101, 16-17.* The nations shall revere Your Name, O Lord, and all the kings of the earth Your glory. ℣. For the Lord has rebuilt Sion, and He shall appear in His glory.

Alleluia, alleluia. ℣. *Ps. 96, 1.* The Lord is King; let the earth rejoice; let the many isles be glad. Alleluia.

● *Prayer: Cleanse My Heart, page* 31.

Gospel. *Matt. 13, 24-30.* At that time, Jesus spoke this parable to the crowds: "The kingdom of heaven is like a man who sowed good seed in his field; but while men were asleep, his enemy came and sowed weeds among the wheat, and went away. And when the blade sprang up and brought forth fruit, then the weeds appeared as well. And the servants of the householder came and said to him, 'Sir, did you not sow good seed in your field? How then does it have weeds?' He said to them, 'An enemy has done this.' And the servants said to him, 'Will you have us go and gather them up?' 'No,' he said, 'lest in gathering the weeds you root up the wheat along with them. Let both grow together until the harvest; and at harvest time I will say to the reapers: Gather up the weeds first, and bind them in bundles to burn; but gather the wheat into my barn.' " S. Praise be to You, O Christ.

● *Creed, page* 33.

Offertory. *Ps. 117, 16. 17.* The right hand of the Lord has struck with power:

the right hand of the Lord has exalted me; I shall not die, but live, and declare the works of the Lord.

● *Offertory Prayers, page 35.*

Secret. We offer You, O Lord, sacrifices of propitiation; that, taking compassion on us, You may both absolve us from our sins, and guide our inconstant hearts. Through our Lord, etc.

● *Preface, page 43.*

Communion. *Luke 4, 22.* All marvelled at the words that came from the mouth of God.

P. The Lord be with you. *S.* And with your spirit. ⌐

Postcommunion. We beseech You, almighty God, that we may receive the effect of that salvation, whose pledge we have received in these mysteries. Through our Lord, etc. *S.* Amen.

● *Final Prayers, page 73.*

"Jesus spoke to the crowds in parables."

SIXTH SUNDAY AFTER EPIPHANY
GREEN VESTMENTS

THOUGHT FOR TODAY: We thank God for the shelter given us under the tree of Christ's Church. But it would not profit us if the teaching of Christ would not "leaven" our thoughts, words and deeds, and stimulate us to true Catholic Action.

● *Beginning of Mass, page* 19.

Introit. *Ps. 96, 7. 8.* Adore God, all you His angels: Sion hears and is glad; and the cities of Juda rejoice. *Ps. 96, 1.* The Lord is King; let the earth rejoice; let the many isles be glad. ℣. Glory be.

● *Kyrie and Gloria, page* 27.

Prayer. Grant, we beseech You, almighty God, that, ever fixing our thoughts on such things that are reasonable, we may, both in word and in work, do that which is pleasing to You. Through our Lord, etc. S. Amen. ➔

Epistle. *1 Thess. 1, 2-10.* Brethren: We give thanks to God always for you all, continually making a remembrance of you in our prayers; being mindful before God our Father of your work of faith, and labor, and charity, and your enduring hope in our Lord Jesus Christ. We know, brethren, beloved of God, how you were chosen. For our gospel was not delivered to you in word only, but in power also, and in the Holy Spirit, and in much fullness, as indeed you know what manner of men we have been among you for your sakes. And you became imitators of us and of the Lord, receiving the word in great tribulation, with joy of the Holy Spirit, so that you became a pattern to all the believers in Macedonia and in Achaia. For from you the word of the Lord has been spread abroad, not only in Macedonia and Achaia, but in every place your faith in God has gone forth, so that we need say nothing further. For they themselves report concerning us how we entered among you, and how you turned to God from idols, to serve the living and true God, and to await from heaven Jesus, His Son, Whom He raised from the dead, Who has delivered us from the wrath to come. *S.* Thanks be to God. ⟶

Gradual. *Ps. 101, 16-17.* The nations shall revere Your Name, O Lord, and all the kings of the earth Your glory. ℣. For the Lord has rebuilt Sion, and He shall appear in His glory.

Alleluia, alleluia. ℣. *Ps. 96, 1.* The Lord is King; let the earth rejoice; let the many isles be glad. Alleluia.

● *Prayer: Cleanse My Heart, page* 31.

Gospel. *Matt. 13, 31-35.* At that time, Jesus spoke this parable to the crowds: "The kingdom of heaven is like a grain of mustard seed, which a man took and sowed in his field. This indeed is the smallest of all the seeds; but when it grows up it is larger than any herb and becomes a tree, so that the birds of the air come and dwell in its branches." He told them another parable: "The kingdom of heaven is like leaven, which a woman took and buried in three measures of flour, until all of it was leavened." All these things Jesus spoke to the crowds in parables, and without parables He did not speak to them; that what was spoken by the prophet might be fulfilled, "I will open My mouth in parables, I will utter things hidden since the foundation of the world." S. Praise be to You, O Christ.

● *Creed, page* 33.

Offertory. *Ps. 117, 16. 17.* The right hand of the Lord has struck with power: the right hand of the Lord has exalted me; I shall not die, but live, and declare the works of the Lord.

● *Offertory Prayers, page* 35.

Secret. May this offering, O God, we beseech You, cleanse and renew, govern and protect us. Through our Lord, etc.

● *Preface, page* 43.

Communion. *Luke 4, 22.* All marvelled at the words that came from the mouth of God.

P. The Lord be with you. *S.* And with your spirit. ↱

Postcommunion. Being fed, O Lord, with heavenly delights, we beseech You, that we may ever seek after those things by which we truly live. Through our Lord, etc. *S.* Amen.

● *Final Prayers, page* 73.

"The last shall be first, and the first last."

SEPTUAGESIMA SUNDAY
PURPLE VESTMENTS

PRE-LENTENTIDE: The first part of the ecclesiastical year has made known to us the Divinity of Christ. The following part shows us what Jesus has done to merit our salvation and to impart it to us. The Season of Septuagesima contains three Sundays. It leads us from the joys of Christmas to the penitential time of Lent. Although fasting is not yet compulsory, the Gloria and Alleluia are omitted, and the color of the vestments is Purple.

THOUGHT FOR TODAY: God holds out a great reward to us, but we must work to receive it. Unfortunately, we are by nature more inclined to endure hardships for the perishable goods of this life than we are for our eternal happiness in the Kingdom of God.

● *Beginning of Mass, page 19.*

Introit. *Ps. 17, 5. 6. 7.* The terrors of death surged round about me, the cords of the nether world enmeshed me; in my distress I called upon the Lord; from His holy temple He heard my voice. *Ps. 17, 2. 3.* I love You, O Lord, my strength: O Lord, my rock, my fortress, my deliverer. ℣. Glory be.

● *Kyrie, page 27. Omit Gloria.*

Prayer. Graciously hear the prayers of Your people, we beseech You, O Lord, that we, who are justly punished for our sins, may be mercifully delivered for the glory of Your Name. Through our Lord, etc. S. Amen. ➘

Epistle. *1 Cor. 9, 24 — 10, 5.* Brethren: Do you not know that those who run in a race, all indeed run, but one receives the prize? So run as to obtain it. And everyone in a contest abstains from all things — and they indeed to receive a perishable crown, but we an imperishable. I, therefore, so run as not without a purpose; I so fight as not beating the air; but I chastise my body and bring it into subjection, lest perhaps after preaching to others I myself should be rejected. For I would not have you ignorant, brethren, that our fathers were all under the cloud, and all passed through the sea, and all were baptized in Moses, in the cloud and in the sea. And all ate the same spiritual food, and all drank the same spiritual drink (for they drank from the spiritual rock which followed them, and the rock was Christ). Yet with most of them God was not well pleased. S. Thanks be to God. ⸖

Gradual. *Ps. 9, 10. 11. 19. 20.* A stronghold in times of distress; they trust in You who cherish You; for You forsake not those who seek You, O Lord. ℣. For the needy shall not always be forgotten; nor shall the hope of the afflicted forever perish; rise, O Lord, let not man prevail. ⸖

Tract. *Ps. 129, 1-4.* Out of the depths I cry to You, O Lord; Lord, hear my voice. ℣. Let Your ears be attentive to the prayer of Your servant. ℣. If You, O Lord, mark iniquities: Lord, who can stand? ℣. But with You is forgiveness, and by reason of Your law I have waited for You, O Lord.

● *Prayer: Cleanse My Heart, page 31.*

Gospel. *Matt. 20, 1-16.* At that time, Jesus spoke to His disciples this parable: "The kingdom of heaven is like a householder who went out early in the morning to hire laborers for his vineyard. And having agreed with the laborers for a denarius a day, he sent them into his vineyard. And about the third hour, he went out and saw others standing in the market place idle;

and he said to them, 'Go you also into the vineyard, and I will give you whatever is just.' So they went. And again he went out about the sixth, and about the ninth hour, and did as before. But about the eleventh hour he went out and found others standing about and he said to them, 'Why do you stand here all day idle?' They said to him, 'Because no man has hired us.' He said to them, 'Go you also into the vineyard.' But when evening had come, the owner of the vineyard said to his steward, 'Call the laborers, and pay them their wages, beginning from the last even to the first.' Now when they of the eleventh hour came, they received each a denarius. And when the first in their turn came, they thought that they would receive more; but they also received each his denarius. And on receiving it, they began to murmur against the householder, saying, 'These last have worked a single hour, and you have put them on a level with us, who have borne the burden of the day's heat.' But answering one of them, he said, 'Friend, I do you no injustice; did you not agree with me for a denarius? Take what is yours and go; I choose to give to this last even as to you. Have I not a right to do what I choose? Or are you envious because I am generous?' Even so the last shall be first, and the first last; for many are called, but few are chosen." *S.* Praise be to You, O Christ.

● Creed, page 33.

Offertory. *Ps. 91, 2.* It is good to give thanks to the Lord, and to sing praise to Your Name, Most High.

● Offertory Prayers, page 35.

Secret. Receive, we beseech You, O Lord, our offerings and prayers; and, through these heavenly mysteries, both cleanse us, and also mercifully grant what we ask. Through our Lord, etc.

● Preface, page 43.

Communion. *Ps. 30, 17. 18.* Let Your face shine upon Your servant; save me in Your kindness; O Lord, let me not be put to shame, for I call upon You.

P. The Lord be with you. *S.* And with your spirit. ↱

Postcommunion. May Your faithful people, O God, be strengthened by Your gifts; that, by receiving them, they may the more desire them, and by desiring them they may receive them forever. Through our Lord, etc. *S.* Amen.

● Final Prayers, page 73.

————◇————

"The sower went out to sow his seed."

SEXAGESIMA SUNDAY
PURPLE VESTMENTS

THOUGHT FOR TODAY: Jesus is the Divine Sower. His word and example would yield fruit a hundredfold in our hearts as it did in the life of St. Paul, if we would not busy ourselves with thousands of unnecessary things which divert us from the one necessary thing, namely, the salvation of our souls.

● *Beginning of Mass, page 19.*

Introit. *Ps. 43, 23-26.* Awake! Why are You asleep, O Lord? Arise! Cast us not off forever! Why do You hide Your face, forgetting our oppression? Our bodies are pressed to the earth; arise, O Lord, help us, and deliver us. *Ps. 43, 2.* O God, our ears have heard; our fathers have declared to us. ℣. Glory be.

● *Kyrie, page 27. Omit Gloria.*

Prayer. O God, You see that we do not trust in anything which we ourselves can do; mercifully grant, that by the protection of the teacher of the Gentiles, we may be defended against all adversities. Through our Lord, etc. S. Amen. ⌐

Epistle. *2 Cor. 11, 19 — 12, 9.* Brethren: You gladly put up with fools, because you are wise yourselves! For you suffer it if a man enslaves you, if a man devours you, if a man takes from you, if a man is arrogant, if a man slaps your face! I speak to my own shame, as though we had been weak. But wherein any man is bold — I am speaking foolishly — I also am bold. Are they Hebrews? So am I! Are they Israelites? So am I! Are they offspring of Abraham? So am I! Are they ministers of Christ? I — to speak as a fool — am more: in many more labors, in prisons more frequently, in lashes above measure, often exposed to death. From the Jews five times I received forty lashes less one. Thrice I was scourged, once I was stoned, thrice I suffered shipwreck, a night and a day I was adrift on the sea; in journeyings often, in perils from floods, in perils from robbers, in perils from my own nation, in perils from the Gentiles, in perils in the city, in perils in the wilderness, in perils in the sea, in perils from false brethren; in labor and hardships, in many sleepless nights, in hunger and thirst, in fastings often, in cold and nakedness. Besides those outer things, there is my daily pressing anxiety, the care of all the churches! Who is weak, and I am not weak? Who is made to stumble, and I am not inflamed? If I must boast, I will boast of the things that concern my weakness. The God and Father of the Lord Jesus, Who is blessed forevermore, knows that I do not lie. In Damascus the governor under King Aretas was guarding the city of the Damascenes in order to arrest me, but I was lowered in a basket through a window in the wall, and escaped his hands. If I must boast — it is not indeed expedient to do so — but I will come to visions and revelations of the Lord. I know a man in Christ who fourteen years ago — whether in the body I do not know, or out of the body I do not know, God knows— such a one was caught up to the third heaven. And I know such a man — whether in the body or out of the body I do not know, God knows — that he was caught up into paradise and heard secret words that man may not repeat. Of such a man I will boast; but of myself I will glory in nothing save in my infirmities. For if I do wish to boast, I shall not be foolish; for I shall be speaking the truth. But I forbear, lest any man should reckon me beyond what he sees in me or hears from me. And lest the greatness of the revelations should puff me up, there was given me a thorn for the flesh, a messenger of Satan, to buffet me. Concerning this I thrice besought the Lord that it might leave me. And He has said to me, "My grace is sufficient for you, for strength is made perfect in weakness." Gladly therefore I will glory in my infirmities, that the strength of Christ may dwell in me. S. Thanks be to God. ⤳

Gradual. *Ps. 82, 19. 14.* Let the nations know that God is Your name; You alone are the Most High over all the earth. ℣. O my God, make them like leaves in a whirlwind, like chaff before the wind. ⤳

Tract. *Ps. 59, 4. 6.* You have rocked the country, O Lord, and split it open. ℣. Repair the cracks in it, for it is tottering. ℣. That they may flee out of bowshot; that Your loved ones may escape.

● *Prayer: Cleanse My Heart, page* 31.

Gospel. *Luke 8, 4-15.* At that time, when a very great crowd was gathering together and men from every town were resorting to Jesus, He said in a parable: "The sower went out to sow his seed. And as he sowed, some seed fell by the wayside and was trodden under foot, and the birds of the air ate it up. And other seed fell upon the rock, and as soon as it had sprung up it withered away, because it had no moisture. And other seed fell among thorns, and the thorns sprang up with it and choked it. And other seed fell upon good ground, and sprang up and yielded fruit a hundredfold." As He said these things He cried out, "He who has ears to hear, let him hear!" But His disciples then began to ask Him what this parable meant. He said to them, "To you it is given to know the mystery of the kingdom of God, but to the rest in parables, that 'Seeing they may not see, and hearing they may not understand.' Now the parable is this: the seed is the word of God. And those by the wayside are they who have heard; then the devil comes and takes away the word from their heart, that they may not believe and be saved. Now those upon the rock are they who, when they have heard, receive the word with joy; and these have no root, but believe for a while, and in time of temptation fall away. And that which fell among the thorns, these are they who have heard, and as they go their way are choked by the cares and riches and pleasures of life, and their fruit does not ripen. But that upon good ground, these are they who, with a right and good heart, having heard the word, hold it fast, and bear fruit in patience." *S.* Praise be to You, O Christ.

● *Creed, page* 33.

Offertory. *Ps. 16, 5. 6. 7.* Make my steps steadfast in Your paths, that my feet may not falter; incline Your ear to me; hear my word; show Your wondrous kindness, O Lord, Savior of those who trust in You.

● *Offertory Prayers, page* 35.

Secret. May the sacrifice offered to You, O Lord, give us life always and defend us. Through our Lord, etc.

● *Preface, page* 43.

Communion. *Ps. 42, 4.* I will go in to the altar of God, the God of my gladness and joy.

P. The Lord be with you. *S.* And with your spirit. ↲

Postcommunion. We humbly beseech You, almighty God, to grant that those whom You refresh with Your sacraments, may serve You worthily by a life well pleasing to You. Through our Lord, etc. *S.* Amen.

● *Final Prayers, page* 73.

"Jesus, Son of David, have mercy on me!"

QUINQUAGESIMA SUNDAY

PURPLE VESTMENTS

THOUGHT FOR TODAY: As the blind man asked sight of Jesus, so we ought to implore Christ to cure our spiritual blindness. We are spiritually blind if we do not see that our busy life on earth is worthless unless it be rooted in the love of God and of our neighbor.

● *Beginning of Mass, page 19.*

Introit. *Ps. 30, 3. 4.* Be my rock of refuge, O God, a stronghold to give me safety; You are my strength and my fortress; for Your Name's sake You will lead and guide me. *Ps. 30, 2.* In You, O Lord, I take refuge; let me never be put to shame; in Your justice rescue me, and deliver me. ℣. Glory be.

● *Kyrie, page 27. Omit Gloria.*

Prayer. We beseech You, O Lord, graciously hear our prayers; and having freed us from the bonds of our sins, guard us from all adversity. Through our Lord, etc. S. Amen. ❧

Epistle. *1 Cor. 13, 1-13.* Brethren: If I should speak with the tongues of men and of angels, but do not have charity, I have become as sounding brass or a tinkling cymbal. And if I have prophecy and know all mysteries and all knowledge, and if I have all faith so as to remove mountains, yet do not have charity, I am nothing. And if I distribute all my goods to feed the poor, and if I deliver my body to be burned, yet do not have charity, it profits me nothing. Charity is patient, is kind; charity does not envy, is not pretentious, is not puffed up, is not ambitious, is not self-seeking, is not provoked; thinks no evil, does not rejoice over wickedness, but rejoices with the truth; bears with all things, believes all things, hopes all things, endures all things. Charity never fails, whereas prophecies will disappear, and tongues will cease, and knowledge will be destroyed. For we know in part and we prophesy in part; but when that which is perfect has come, that which is imperfect will be done away with. When I was a child, I spoke as a child, I felt as a child, I thought as a child. Now that I have become a man,

I have put away the things of a child. We see now through a mirror in an obscure manner, but then face to face. Now I know in part, but then I shall know even as I have been known. So there abide faith, hope and charity, these three; but the greatest of these is charity. S. Thanks be to God. ↴

Gradual. *Ps. 76, 15. 16.* You are the God Who alone works wonders; among the peoples You have made known Your power. ℣. With Your strong arm You delivered Your people, the sons of Israel and Joseph. ↴

Tract. *Ps. 99, 1-2.* Sing joyfully to the Lord, all you lands; serve the Lord with gladness. ℣. Come before Him with joyful song; know that the Lord is God. ℣. He made us, His we are; His people, the flock He tends.

● *Prayer: Cleanse My Heart, page 31.*

Gospel. *Luke 18, 31-43.* At that time, Jesus taking to Himself the Twelve said to them, "Behold, we are going up to Jerusalem, and all things that have been written by the prophets concerning the Son of Man will be accomplished. For He will be delivered to the Gentiles, and will be mocked and scourged and spit upon; and after they have scourged Him, they will put Him to death; and on the third day He will rise again." And they understood none of these things, and this saying was hidden from them, neither did they get to know the things that were being said. Now it came to pass as He drew near to Jericho, that a certain blind man was sitting by the way-side, begging; but hearing a crowd passing by, he inquired what this might be. And they told him that Jesus of Nazareth was passing by. And he cried out, saying, "Jesus, Son of David, have mercy on me!" And they who went in front angrily tried to silence him. But he cried out all the louder, "Son of David, have mercy on me!" Then Jesus stopped and commanded that he should be brought to Him. And when he drew near, He asked him, saying, "What would you have Me do for you?" And he said, "Lord, that I may see." And Jesus said to him, "Receive your sight, your faith has saved you." And at once he received his sight, and followed Him, glorifying God. And all the people upon seeing it gave praise to God. S. Praise be to You, O Christ.

● Creed, page 33.

Offertory. *Ps. 118, 12-13.* Blessed are You, O Lord; teach me Your statutes;

with my lips I declare all the ordinances of Your mouth.

● *Offertory Prayers, page 35.*

Secret. May this offering, we beseech You, O Lord, cleanse away our sins, and sanctify the bodies and minds of Your servants for the celebration of this sacrifice. Through our Lord, etc.

● *Preface, page 43.*

Communion. *Ps. 77, 29-30.* They ate and were wholly surfeited; the Lord had brought them what they craved; they were not defrauded of that which they craved.

P. The Lord be with you. *S.* And with your spirit. ↱

Postcommunion. We beseech You, almighty God, that we who have received celestial food, may be defended by it against all adversities. Through our Lord, etc. *S.* Amen.

● *Final Prayers, page 73.*

"Begone, Satan, for it is written, 'The Lord your God shall you worship and Him only shall you serve.'"

FIRST SUNDAY IN LENT
PURPLE VESTMENTS

LENT: *This Sunday is the real opening of Lent which leads us to Christ Crucified. To abstain from sin, to pray, to avoid worldly amusements, to be generous in almsgiving, and to attend Mass daily are practices acceptable to God.*

THOUGHT FOR TODAY: Christ permitted Himself to be tempted by Satan. Why, then, should we be surprised if we have to struggle against the malice and snares of the devil! Our strength to resist lies in fasting, in guarding and controlling our senses, in almsgiving, in prayers, and in uniting ourselves with Christ in Holy Mass and Communion.

● *Beginning of Mass, page 19.*

Introit. *Ps. 90, 15. 16.* He shall call upon Me, and I will answer him; I will deliver him and glorify him; with length of days I will gratify him. *Ps. 90, 1.* You who dwell in the shelter of the Most High, shall abide in the shadow of the Almighty. ℣. Glory be.

● *Kyrie, page 27. Omit Gloria.*

Prayer. O God, You purify Your Church by the yearly observance of Lent; grant to Your family that what we try to obtain from You by abstinence, we may secure by good works. Through, etc. S. Amen. ⟶

Epistle. *2 Cor. 6, 1-10.* Brethren: We entreat you not to receive the grace of God in vain. For He says, "In an acceptable time I have heard you, and in the day of salvation I have helped you." Behold, now is the acceptable time; behold, now is the day of salvation! We give no offense to anyone, that our ministry may not be blamed. On the contrary, let us conduct ourselves in all circumstances as God's ministers, in much patience; in tribulations, in hardships, in distresses; in stripes, in imprisonments, in tumults; in labors, in sleepless nights, in fastings; in innocence, in knowledge, in long-sufferings; in kindness, in the Holy Spirit, in unaffected love; in the word of truth, in the power of God; with the armor of justice on the right hand and on the left; in honor and dishonor, in evil report and good report; as deceivers and yet truthful, as unknown and yet well known, as dying, and behold, we live, as chastised but not killed, as sorrowful yet always rejoicing, as poor

yet enriching many, as having nothing yet
possessing all things. S. Thanks be to God. ↴

Gradual. *Ps. 90, 11-12.* To His angels
God has given command about you, that
they guard you in all your ways. ℣. Upon
their hands they shall bear you up, lest you
dash your foot against a stone. ↴

Tract. *Ps. 90, 1-7. 11-16.* You who dwell
in the shelter of the Most High, shall abide
in the shadow of the Almighty. ℣. Say to
the Lord, "My refuge and my fortress, my
God, in Whom I trust." ℣. For He will
rescue you from the snare of the fowler,
from the destroying pestilence. ℣. With His
pinions He will cover you, and under His
wings you shall take refuge. ℣. His faithfulness is a buckler and a shield; you shall
not fear the terror of the night. ℣. Nor the
arrow that flies by day; nor the pestilence
that roams in darkness; nor the devastating
plague at noon. ℣. Though a thousand fall
at your side, ten thousand at your right
side, near you it shall not come. ℣. For to
His angels He has given command about
you, that they may guard you in all your
ways. ℣. Upon their hands they shall bear
you up, lest you dash your foot against a
stone. ℣. You shall tread upon the asp and
the viper; you shall trample down the lion

and the dragon. ℣. Because he clings to
Me, I will deliver him; I will set him on
high because he acknowledges My Name.
℣. He shall call upon Me, and I will answer
him; I will be with him in distress. ℣. I will
deliver him and glorify him; with length of
days I will gratify him and will show him
My salvation.

● *Prayer: Cleanse My Heart, page* 31.

Gospel. *Matt. 4, 1-11.* At that time,
Jesus was led into the desert by the Spirit,
to be tempted by the devil. And after fasting forty days and forty nights, He was
hungry. And the tempter came and said to
Him, "If You are the Son of God, command that these stones become loaves of
bread." But He answered and said, "It is
written, 'Not by bread alone does man live,
but by every word that comes forth from
the mouth of God.'" Then the devil took
Him into the holy city and set Him on the
pinnacle of the temple, and said to Him, "If
You are the Son of God, throw Yourself
down; for it is written, 'He has given His
angels charge concerning You; and upon
their hands they shall bear You up, lest
You dash Your foot against a stone.'" Jesus
said to him, "It is written further, 'You
shall not tempt the Lord your God.'" Again,

the devil took Him to a very high mountain, and showed Him all the kingdoms of the world and the glory of them. And he said to Him, "All these things will I give You, if You will fall down and worship me." Then Jesus said to him, "Begone, Satan, for it is written, 'The Lord your God shall you worship and Him only shall you serve.'" Then the devil left Him; and behold, angels came and ministered to Him. S. Praise be to You, O Christ.

● Creed, page 33.

Offertory. *Ps. 90, 4. 5.* With His pinions the Lord will cover you, and under His wings you shall take refuge; His faithfulness is a buckler and a shield.

● Offertory Prayers, page 35.

Secret. We solemnly offer up this sacrifice at the beginning of Lent, and beseech You, O Lord, that with the restriction of bodily food, we may also refrain from harmful pleasures. Through our Lord, etc. ↴

Preface for Lent

P. World without end. *S.* Amen. *P.* The Lord be with you. *S.* And with your spirit. *P.* Lift up your hearts. *S.* We have lifted them up to the Lord. *P.* Let us give thanks to the Lord, our God. *S.* It is fitting and just.

It is fitting indeed and just, right and helpful to salvation, for us always and everywhere to give thanks to You, O Holy Lord, Father Almighty, Everlasting God, Who by this bodily fast extinguish our vices, elevate our understanding, bestow on us virtue and its reward, through Christ our Lord. Through Whom the Angels praise Your Majesty, the Dominations adore it, the Powers are in awe. The heavens and the heavenly hosts, and the blessed Seraphim join together in celebrating their joy. With these, we pray You, join our own voices also, while we say with lowly praise: Holy, Holy, Holy, Lord God of hosts. Heaven and earth are filled with Your glory. Hosanna in the highest. Blessed is He Who comes in the Name of the Lord. Hosanna in the highest.

● *Canon, page 47.*

Communion. *Ps. 90, 4. 5.* With His pinions the Lord will cover you, and under His wings you shall take refuge; His faithfulness is a buckler and a shield.

P. The Lord be with you. *S.* And with your spirit. ⤴

Postcommunion. May the holy reception of Your sacrament, O Lord, revive us, and, cleansing us from our former life, enable us to enjoy a closer union with that saving mystery. Through our Lord, etc. *S.* Amen.

● *Final Prayers, page 73.*

"And behold, there appeared to them Moses and Elias talking together with Him."

SECOND SUNDAY IN LENT
PURPLE VESTMENTS

THOUGHT FOR TODAY: The Transfiguration of Our Lord gives us an idea of the beauty of a soul in the state of sanctifying grace. "This is the will of God, your sanctification."

● *Beginning of Mass, page 19.*

Introit. *Ps. 24, 6. 3. 22.* Remember that Your compassion, O Lord, and Your kindness are from of old; let not our enemies exult over us; deliver us, O God of Israel, from all our tribulations. *Ps. 24, 1. 2.* To You I lift my soul, O Lord; in You, O my God, I trust; let me not be put to shame. ℣. Glory be.

● *Kyrie, page 27. Omit Gloria.*

Prayer. O God, You see that we are destitute of all strength; protect us both inwardly and outwardly; that in body we may be defended from all adversities, and in mind cleansed from evil thoughts. Through our Lord, etc. S. Amen. ↴

Epistle. *1 Thess. 4, 1-7.* Brethren: Even as you have learned from us how you ought to walk to please God — as indeed you are walking — we beseech and exhort you in the Lord Jesus to make even greater progress. For you know what precepts I have given to you by the Lord Jesus. For this is the will of God, your sanctification; that you abstain from immorality; that every one of you learn how to possess his vessel in holiness and honor, not in the passion of lust like the Gentiles who do not know God; that no one transgress and overreach his brother in the matter, because the Lord is the avenger of all these things, as we have told you before and have testified. For God has not called us unto uncleanness, but unto holiness, in Christ Jesus our Lord. S. Thanks be to God. ↴

Gradual. *Ps. 24, 17. 18.* Relieve the troubles of my heart and bring me out of my distress, O Lord. ℣. Put an end to my affliction and my suffering, and take away all my sins. ↴

Tract. *Ps. 105, 1-4.* Give thanks to the Lord, for He is good, for His kindness endures forever. ℣. Who can tell the mighty deeds of the Lord, or proclaim all His praises? ℣. Happy are they who observe what is right, who do always what is just. ℣. Remember us, O Lord, as You favor Your people; visit us with Your saving help.

● Prayer: Cleanse My Heart, page 31.

Gospel. *Matt. 17, 1-9.* At that time, Jesus took Peter, James and his brother John, and led them up a high mountain by themselves, and was transfigured before them. And His face shone as the sun, and His garments became white as snow. And behold, there appeared to them Moses and Elias talking together with Him. Then Peter addressed Jesus, saying, "Lord, it is good for us to be here. If You will, let us set up three tents here, one for You, one for Moses, and one for Elias." As he was still speaking, behold, a bright cloud overshadowed them, and behold, a voice out of the cloud said, "This is My beloved Son, in Whom I am well pleased; hear Him." And on hearing it the disciples fell on their faces and were exceedingly afraid. And Jesus came near and touched them, and said to them, "Arise, and do not be afraid." But lifting up their eyes, they saw no one but Jesus only. And as they were coming down from the mountain, Jesus cautioned them, saying, "Tell the vision to no one, till the Son of Man has risen from the dead." *S.* Praise be to You, O Christ.

● Creed, page 33.

Offertory. *Ps. 118, 47. 48.* I will delight in Your commands, which I love exceedingly; and I will lift up my hands to Your commands, which I love.

● Offertory Prayers, page 35.

Secret. O Lord, we beseech You, look favorably on these present sacrifices, that they may profit us both for our devotion and our salvation. Through our Lord, etc.

● Preface for Lent, page 168.

Communion. *Ps. 5, 2-4.* Attend to my sighing; heed my call for help, my King and my God! To You I pray, O Lord.

P. The Lord be with you. *S.* And with your spirit. ⟍

Postcommunion. We humbly beseech You, almighty God, to grant that those whom You refresh with Your sacraments, may also serve You worthily by a life well pleasing to You. Through our Lord, etc. *S.* Amen.

● Final Prayers, page 73.

*"If I cast out devils by Beelzebub, by whom
do your children cast them out?"*

THIRD SUNDAY IN LENT
PURPLE VESTMENTS

THOUGHT FOR TODAY: We cannot be neutral in
our relationship with God. If we do not serve
Him, pride and selfishness will enslave us.
"Blessed are they who hear the word of God,
and keep it."

● *Beginning of Mass, page* 19.

Introit. *Ps. 24, 15-16.* My eyes are ever
toward the Lord, for He will free my feet
from the snare; look toward me, and have
pity on me, for I am alone and afflicted.
Ps. 24, 1. 2. To You I lift up my soul, O
Lord; in You, O my God, I trust; let me not
be put to shame. ℣. Glory be.

● *Kyrie, page* 27. *Omit Gloria.*

Prayer. We beseech You, almighty God,
to regard the desires of those who humble

themselves, and, for our defense, stretch forth the right hand of Your Majesty. Through our Lord, etc. S. Amen. ↴

Epistle. *Eph. 5, 1-9.* Brethren: Be imitators of God, as very dear children and walk in love, as Christ also loved us and delivered Himself up for us an offering and a sacrifice to God to ascend in fragrant odor. But immorality and every uncleanness or covetousness, let it not even be named among you, as becomes saints; or obscenity or foolish talk or scurrility, which are out of place; but rather thanksgiving. For know this and understand, that no fornicator, or unclean person, or covetous one (for that is idolatry) has any inheritance in the kingdom of Christ and God. Let no one lead you astray with empty words; for because of these things the wrath of God comes upon the children of disobedience. Do not, then, become partakers with them. For you were once darkness, but now you are light in the Lord. Walk, then, as children of light, for the fruit of the light is in all goodness and justice and truth. S. Thanks be to God. ↴

Gradual. *Ps. 9, 20. 4.* Rise, O Lord, let not man prevail; let the nations be judged in Your presence. ℣. Because my enemies are turned back, overthrown and destroyed before You. ↴

Tract. *Ps. 122, 1-3.* To You I lift up my eyes, Who are enthroned in heaven. ℣. Behold, as the eyes of servants are on the hands of their masters. ℣. As the eyes of a maid are on the hands of her mistress, so are our eyes on the Lord our God, till He have pity on us. ℣. Have pity on us, O Lord, have pity on us.

● *Prayer: Cleanse My Heart, page* 31.

Gospel. *Luke 11, 14-28.* At that time, Jesus was casting out a devil, and the same was dumb; and when He had cast out the devil, the dumb man spoke. And the crowds marvelled. But some of them said, "By Beelzebub, the prince of devils, He casts out devils." And others, to test Him, demanded from Him a sign from heaven. But He, seeing their thoughts, said to them: "Every kingdom divided against itself is brought to desolation, and house will fall upon house. If, then, Satan also is divided against himself, how shall his kingdom stand? because you say that I cast out devils by Beelzebub. Now, if I cast out devils by Beelzebub, by whom do your children cast them out? Therefore they shall be your judges. But if I cast out devils by the finger

THE INSTITUTION OF THE HOLY EUCHARIST

JESUS CALMS THE STORM

of God, then the kingdom of God has come upon you. When the strong man, fully armed, guards his courtyard, his property is undisturbed. But if a stronger than he attacks and overcomes him, he will take away all his weapons that he relied upon, and will divide his spoils. He who is not with Me is against Me; and he who does not gather with Me scatters. When the unclean spirit has gone out of a man, he roams through waterless places in search of rest; and finding none, he says, 'I will return to my house which I left.' And when he has come to it, he finds the place swept. Then he goes and takes seven other spirits more evil than himself, and they enter in and dwell there; and the last state of that man becomes worse than the first." Now it came to pass as He was saying these things, that a certain woman from the crowd lifted up her voice and said to Him, "Blessed is the womb that bore You, and the breasts that nursed You." But He said, "Rather, blessed are they who hear the word of God and keep it." *S.* Praise be to You, O Christ.

● *Creed, page* 33.

Offertory. *Ps. 18, 9-12.* The precepts of the Lord are right, rejoicing the heart, and His ordinances are sweeter than syrup or

honey from the comb; therefore Your servant is careful of them.

● *Offertory Prayers, page 35.*

Secret. May this offering, we beseech
You, O Lord, cleanse away our sins, and
sanctify the bodies and minds of Your servants for the celebration of this sacrifice.
Through our Lord, etc.

● *Preface for Lent, page 168.*

Communion. *Ps. 83, 4. 5.* The sparrow
finds a home, and the swallow a nest in
which she puts her young—Your altars, O
Lord of hosts, my King and my God! Happy
they who dwell in Your house! Continually
they praise You.

P. The Lord be with you. *S.* And with
your spirit. ⮑

Postcommunion. Mercifully absolve us,
we beseech You, O Lord, from all guilt
and danger, whom You grant to be
partakers of so great a mystery. Through
our Lord, etc. *S.* Amen.

● *Final Prayers, page 73.*

"Jesus then took the loaves, and when He had given thanks, distributed them . . ."

FOURTH SUNDAY IN LENT

PURPLE VESTMENTS

THOUGHT FOR TODAY: A true Christian life requires self-denial and penance. Nevertheless, there is enough joy in it, because self-control leads to the freedom of the children of God. The wonderful Bread which we receive in Holy Communion is another reason for joy because it unites us with God Almighty, the source of all happiness.

● *Beginning of Mass, page 19.*

Introit. *Isa. 66, 10. 11.* Rejoice, O Jerusalem, and come together all you who love her: rejoice with joy, you who have been in sorrow: that you may exult, and be filled from the breasts of your consolation. *Ps. 121, 1.* I rejoiced because they said to me: "We will go up to the house of the Lord." ℣. Glory be.

● *Kyrie, page 27. Omit Gloria.*

Prayer. Grant, we beseech You, almighty God, that we who justly suffer for our deeds, may be relieved by the comfort of Your grace. Through our Lord, etc. S. Amen. ⸱

Epistle. *Gal. 4, 22-31.* Brethren: It is written that Abraham had two sons, the one by a slave-girl and the other by a free woman. And the son of the slave-girl was born according to the flesh, but the son of the free woman in virtue of the promise. This is said by way of allegory. For these are the two covenants: one indeed from Mount Sinai bringing forth children unto bondage, which is Agar. For Sinai is a mountain in Arabia, which corresponds to the present Jerusalem, and is in slavery with her children. But that Jerusalem which is above is free, which is our mother. For it is written, "Rejoice, O barren one, that do not bear; break forth and cry, you that do not travail; for many are the children of the desolate, more than of her that has a husband." Now we, brethren, are the children of promise, as Isaac was. But as then he who was born according to the flesh, persecuted him who was born according to the spirit, so also it is now. But what does the Scripture say? "Cast out the slave-girl and

her son, for the son of the slave-girl shall
not be heir with the son of the free woman."
Therefore, brethren, we are not children of
a slave-girl, but of the free woman — in virtue of the freedom wherewith Christ has
made us free. S. Thanks be to God. ⤴

Gradual. *Ps. 121, 1. 7.* I rejoiced because
they said to me: "We will go up to the house
of the Lord." ℣. May peace be within your
walls, prosperity in your buildings. ⤴

Tract. *Ps. 124, 1. 2.* They who trust in
the Lord are like Mount Sion, which is im-
movable; which forever stands. ℣. Mountains are round about Jerusalem; so the
Lord is round about His people, both now
and forever.

● Prayer: Cleanse My Heart, page 31.

Gospel. *John 6, 1-15.* At that time, Jesus
went away to the other side of the sea of
Galilee, which is that of Tiberias. And there
followed Him a great crowd, because they
witnessed the signs He worked on those
who were sick. Jesus therefore went up the
mountain, and sat there with His disciples.
Now the Passover, the feast of the Jews,
was near. When, therefore, Jesus had lifted
up His eyes and seen that a very great
crowd had come to Him, He said to Philip,
"Whence shall we buy bread that these may

eat?" But He said this to try him, for He Himself knew what He would do. Philip answered Him, "Two hundred denarii worth of bread is not enough for them, that each one may receive a little." One of His disciples, Andrew, the brother of Simon Peter, said to Him, "There is a young boy here who has five barley loaves and two fishes; but what are these among so many?" Jesus then said, "Make the people recline." Now there was much grass in the place. The men therefore reclined, in number about five thousand. Jesus then took the loaves, and when He had given thanks, distributed them to those reclining; and likewise the fishes, as much as they wished. But when they were filled, He said to His disciples, "Gather the fragments that are left over, lest they be wasted." They therefore gathered them up; and they filled twelve baskets with the fragments of the five barley loaves left over by those who had eaten. When the people, therefore, had seen the sign which Jesus had worked, they said, "This is indeed the Prophet Who is to come into the world." So when Jesus perceived that they would come to take Him by force and make Him king, He fled again to the mountain, Himself alone. S. Praise be to You, O Christ.

- *Creed, page 33.*

Offertory. *Ps. 134, 3. 6.* Praise the Lord, for He is good; sing praise to His Name, for He is sweet; all that He wills He does in heaven and on earth.

- *Offertory Prayers, page 35.*

Secret. Look favorably on these sacrifices, we beseech You, O Lord, that they may profit us both for our devotion and our salvation. Through our Lord, etc.

- *Preface for Lent, page 168.*

Communion. *Ps. 121, 3. 4.* Jerusalem, built as a city with compact unity: to it the tribes go up, the tribes of the Lord, to give thanks to Your Name, O Lord.

P. The Lord be with you. *S.* And with your spirit. ↴

Postcommunion. Grant, we beseech You, O merciful God, that we may use with sincere veneration, and always receive with faithful minds, Your holy mysteries with which we are continually fed. Through our Lord, etc. *S.* Amen.

- *Final Prayers, page 73.*

"Before Abraham came to be, I am."

PASSION SUNDAY

PURPLE VESTMENTS

THOUGHT FOR TODAY: The misled Jewish
people tried to stone Christ after He had pro-
claimed His Divinity. But this was not yet the
hour in which Jesus was going to die for us. He
proved Himself to be the Master of time and
of His life when He "hid Himself, and went out
from the temple."

*Psalm "Do me justice" is omitted at the foot of the
altar, and the "Glory be to the Father" at the Introit,
and after the Psalm, "I wash" is not said.*

● *Beginning of Mass, page 19.*

Introit. *Ps. 42, 1. 2.* Do me justice, O God,
and fight my fight against a faithless people;
from the deceitful and impious man rescue
me; for You are my God and my strength.
Ps. 42, 3. Send forth Your light and Your
fidelity; they shall lead me on and bring

me to Your holy mountain, to Your dwelling-place. — Do me justice. . .

● *Kyrie, page 27. Omit Gloria.*

Prayer. We beseech You, almighty God, mercifully look upon Your family, that by Your bounty it may be governed in body, and by Your protection, guarded in spirit. Through our Lord, etc. S. Amen. ⤵

Epistle. *Heb. 9, 11-15.* Brethren: When Christ appeared as High Priest of the good things to come, He entered once for all through the greater and more perfect tabernacle, not made by hands (that is, not of this creation), nor again by virtue of blood of goats and calves, but by virtue of His own blood, into the Holies, having obtained eternal redemption. For if the blood of goats and bulls and the sprinkled ashes of a heifer sanctify the unclean unto the cleansing of the flesh, how much more will the blood of Christ, Who through the Holy Spirit offered Himself unblemished unto God, cleanse your conscience from dead works to serve the living God? And this is why He is mediator of a new covenant, that whereas a death has taken place for redemption from the transgressions committed under the former covenant, they who have been called may receive eternal inheritance according to the promise, in Christ Jesus our Lord. S. Thanks be to God. ⮑

Gradual. *Ps. 142, 9. 10.* Rescue me from my enemies, O Lord; teach me to do Your will. ℣. *Ps. 17, 48. 49.* O Lord, my deliverer from the angry nations: truly above my adversaries You exalt me and from the violent man You have rescued me. ⮑

Tract. *Ps. 128, 1-4.* Much have they oppressed me from my youth. ℣. Let Israel say: Much have they oppressed me from my youth. ℣. Yet they have not prevailed against me; upon my back the plowers plowed. ℣. Long did they make their furrows; but the just Lord has severed the cords of the wicked.

● *Prayer: Cleanse My Heart, page* 31.

Gospel. *John 8, 46-59.* At that time, Jesus said to the crowds of the Jews: "Which of you can convict Me of sin? If I speak the truth, why do you not believe Me? He who is of God hears the words of God. The reason why you do not hear is that you are not of God." The Jews therefore in answer said to Him, "Are we not right in saying that You are a Samaritan, and have a devil?" Jesus answered, "I have not a devil,

but I honor My Father, and you dishonor
Me. Yet, I do not seek My own glory; there
is One Who seeks and Who judges. Amen,
amen, I say to you, if anyone keep My
word, he will never see death." The Jews
therefore said, "Now we know that You
have a devil. Abraham is dead, and the
prophets, and You say, 'If anyone keep
My word he will never taste death.' Are
You greater than our father Abraham, who
is dead? And the prophets are dead. Whom
do You make Yourself?" Jesus answered,
"If I glorify Myself, My glory is nothing.
It is My Father Who glorifies Me, of Whom
you say that He is your God. And you do
not know Him, but I know Him. And if I
say that I do not know Him, I shall be like
you, a liar. But I know Him, and I keep
His word. Abraham your father rejoiced
that he was to see My day. He saw it and
was glad." The Jews therefore said to Him,
"You are not yet fifty years old, and have
You seen Abraham?" Jesus said to them,
"Amen, amen, I say to you, before Abraham came to be, I am." They therefore took
up stones to cast at Him; but Jesus hid
Himself, and went out from the temple. *S.*
Praise be to You, O Christ.

● *Creed, page* 33.

Offertory. *Ps. 118, 17. 107.* I praise You, O Lord, with all my heart; be good to Your servant, that I may live and keep Your words. O Lord, give me life according to Your word.

● *Offertory Prayers, page* 35.

Secret. May these gifts, we beseech You, O Lord, both loosen the bonds of our wickedness, and obtain for us the gifts of Your mercy. Through our Lord, etc. ➘

Preface of the Holy Cross

P. World without end. *S.* Amen. *P.* The Lord be with you. *S.* And with your spirit. *P.* Lift up your hearts. *S.* We have lifted them up to the Lord. *P.* Let us give thanks to the Lord, our God. *S.* It is fitting and just.

It is fitting indeed and just, right and helpful to salvation, for us always and everywhere to give thanks to You, O Holy Lord, Father Almighty, Everlasting God; Who set the salvation of mankind upon the tree of the Cross, so that whence came death, thence also life might rise again, and He that overcame by the tree, by the tree also might be overcome: through Christ our Lord. Through Whom the Angels praise Your Majesty, the Dominations worship it, and the Powers are in awe. The heavens and the heavenly hosts, and the blessed Seraphim join together in celebrating their joy. With these, we pray You, join our own voices also, while we say with lowly praise: Holy, Holy, Holy, Lord God of hosts. Heaven and earth are filled with Your glory. Hosanna in the highest. Blessed is He Who comes in the Name of the Lord. Hosanna in the highest.

● *Canon, page 47.*

Communion. *1 Cor. 11, 24. 25.* "This is My Body which shall be given up for you; this is the cup of the new covenant in My Blood," says the Lord; "do this as often as you receive it, in remembrance of Me."

P. The Lord be with you. *S.* And with your spirit. ⤻

Postcommunion. Be present with us, O Lord our God, and support with unceasing help, those whom You have refreshed with Your mysteries. Through our Lord, etc. *S.* Amen.

● *Final Prayers, page 73.*

"Hosanna! Blessed is He who comes in the Name of the Lord!"

HOLY WEEK: *During Holy Week the Church invites us to ascend Calvary and follow in the footsteps of Him Who chose to become the Lamb and Victim of sacrifice. She asks us to carry our cross willingly in union with Him, in a spirit of expiation and atonement, and offer our life together with Him.*

PALM SUNDAY

PURPLE VESTMENTS

THOUGHT FOR TODAY: Joy and sorrow are found closely joined in today's Mass. The triumphal entry of Jesus into Jerusalem and the sorrowful recollection of His Passion are both expressed in the Liturgy of today. The Hosannas of the people will soon yield to the "Crucify Him." It is safer for us to follow Christ along the hard way of fulfilled duties than to walk along the easy road of the world.

● *Beginning of Mass, page 19.*

The Psalm "Do me justice" and the "Glory be to the Father" are omitted as on Passion Sunday.

Introit. Ps. 21, 20. 22. O Lord, be not far from me; O my help, hasten to aid me;

save me from the lion's mouth; from the horns of the wild bulls, my wretched life. *Ps. 21, 2.* My God, my God, look upon me, why have you forsaken me? Far from my salvation are the words of my sins?——O Lord, be not far . . .

● *Kyrie, page 27. Omit Gloria.*

Prayer. Almighty and everlasting God, Who willed that our Savior should take upon Himself our flesh, and suffer on the Cross, that all mankind might have His example of humility for their imitation: grant that we may merit both to keep in mind the lesson of His patience, and to be made partakers of His Resurrection. Through the same, etc. *S.* Amen. ➤

Epistle. *Phil. 2, 5-11.* Brethren: Have this mind in you which was also in Christ Jesus, Who though He was by nature God, did not consider being equal to God a thing to be clung to, but emptied Himself, taking the nature of a slave and being made like unto men. And appearing in the form of man, He humbled Himself, becoming obedient to death, even to death on a cross. Therefore God also has exalted Him and has bestowed upon Him the Name that is above every name, (*here all genuflect*) so that at the Name of Jesus, every knee should bend of those in heaven, on earth and under the earth, and every tongue should confess that the Lord Jesus Christ is in the glory of God the Father. S. Thanks be to God. ⬎

Gradual. *Ps. 72, 24. 1-3.* You have hold of my right hand; with Your counsel You guide me; and in the end You will receive me in glory. ℣. How good God is to Israel; to those who are clean of heart! But, as for me, I almost lost my balance; my feet all but slipped, because I was envious of sinners when I saw them prosper though they were wicked. ⬎

Tract. *Ps. 21, 2-9. 18. 19. 22. 24. 32.* My God, my God, look upon me, why have You forsaken me? ℣. Far from my salvation are the words of my sins. ℣. O my God, I cry out by day, and You answer not; by night, and there is no relief. ℣. But You are enthroned in the holy place, O glory of Israel! ℣. In You our fathers trusted; they trusted, and You delivered them. ℣. To You they cried, and they escaped; in You they trusted, and they were not put to shame. ℣. But I am a worm, not a man; the scorn of men, despised by the people. ℣. All who see me, scoff at me; they mock me with parted lips, they wag their heads. ℣. "He relied on the Lord; let Him deliver him, let Him rescue him, if he loves Him." ℣. They look on and gloat over me; they divide my garments among them, and for my vesture they cast lots. ℣. Save me from the lion's mouth; from the horns of the wild bulls, my wretched life. ℣. You who fear the Lord, praise Him; all you descendants of Jacob, give glory to Him. ℣. There shall be declared to the Lord a generation to come: and the heavens shall show forth His justice. ℣. To a people that shall be born, which the Lord has made.

● *Prayer: Cleanse My Heart, page* 31.

THE PASSION OF OUR LORD
Matthew 26, 36-75; 27, 1-60

At that time, Jesus came with them to a country place called Gethsemani, and He said to His disciples, "Sit down here, while I go over yonder and pray." And He took with Him Peter and the two sons of Zebedee, and He began to be saddened and exceedingly troubled.

Then He said to them, "My soul is sad, even unto death. Wait here and watch with Me." And going forward a little, He fell prostrate and prayed, saying, "Father, if it is possible, let this cup pass away from Me; yet not as I will, but as You will." Then He came to the disciples and found them sleeping. And He said to Peter, "Could you not, then, watch one hour with Me? Watch and pray, that you may not enter into temptation. The spirit indeed is willing, but the flesh is weak." Again a second time He went away and prayed, saying, "My Father, if this cup cannot pass away unless I drink it, Your will be done." And He came again and found them sleeping, for their eyes were heavy. And leaving them He went back again, and prayed a third time, saying the same words over. Then He came to His disciples, and said to them, "Sleep on now, and take your rest! Behold, the hour is at hand when the Son of Man will be betrayed into the hands of sinners. Rise, let us go. Behold, he who betrays Me is at hand."

JESUS ARRESTED

And while He was yet speaking, behold Judas, one of the Twelve, came and with him a great crowd with swords and clubs, from the chief priests and elders of the people. Now His betrayer had given them a sign, saying, "Whomever I kiss, that is He; lay hold of Him." And he went straight up to Jesus and said, "Hail, Rabbi!" and kissed Him. And Jesus said to him, "Friend, for what purpose have you come?" Then they came forward and set hands on Jesus and took Him. And behold, one of those who were with Jesus, reached out his hand, drew his sword, and struck the servant of the high priest, cutting off his ear. Then Jesus said to him, "Put back your sword into its place; for all those who take the sword will perish by the sword. Or do you suppose that I cannot entreat My Father, and He will even now furnish Me with more than twelve legions of angels? How then are the Scriptures to be fulfilled, that thus it must take place?" In that hour Jesus said to the crowds, "As against a robber you have come out, with swords and clubs, to seize Me. I sat daily with you in the temple teaching, and you did not lay hands on Me." Now all this was done that the Scriptures of the prophets might be fulfilled. Then all the disciples left Him and fled.

JESUS BEFORE THE SANHEDRIN

Now those who had taken Jesus led Him away to Caiphas the high priest, where the Scribes and the elders had gathered together. But Peter was following Him at a distance, even to the courtyard of the high priest, and he went in and sat with the attendants to see the end. Now the chief priests and all the Sanhedrin were seeking false witness against Jesus, that they might put Him to death, but they found none, though many false witnesses came forward. But last of all two false witnesses came forward, and said, "This man said, 'I am able to destroy the temple of God, and to rebuild it after three days.'" Then the high priest, standing up, said to Him, "Do You make no answer to the things that these men prefer against You?" But Jesus kept silence. And the high priest said to Him, "I adjure You by the living God that You tell us whether You are the Christ, the Son of God." Jesus said to him, "You have said it. Nevertheless, I say to you, hereafter you shall see the Son of Man sitting at the right hand of the Power and coming upon the clouds of heaven." Then the high priest tore his garments, saying, "He has blasphemed; what further need have we of witnesses? Behold, now you have heard the blasphemy. What do you think?" And they answered and said, "He is liable to death." Then they spat in His face and buffeted Him; while others struck His face with the palms of their hands, saying, "Prophesy to us, O Christ! who is it that struck You?"

PETER'S DENIAL

Now Peter was sitting outside in the courtyard; and a maidservant came up to him and said, "You also were with Jesus the Galilean." But he denied it before them all, saying, "I do not know what you are saying." And when he had gone out to the gateway, another maid saw him, and said to those who were there, "This man also was with Jesus of Nazareth." And again he denied it with an oath, "I do not know the man!" And after a little while the bystanders came up and said to Peter, "Surely you also are one of them, for even your speech betrays you." Then he began to curse and to swear that he did not know the man. And at that moment a cock crowed. And Peter remembered the word that Jesus had said, "Before a cock crows, you will deny Me three times." And he went out and wept bitterly. Now when morning came all the chief priests and the elders of the people took counsel together against Jesus in order to put Him to death. And they bound Him and led Him away, and delivered Him to Pontius Pilate the procurator. Then Judas, who betrayed Him, when he saw that He was condemned, repented and brought back the thirty pieces of silver to the chief priests and the elders, saying, "I have sinned in betraying innocent blood." But they said, "What is that to us? See to it yourself." And he flung the pieces of silver into the temple, and withdrew; and went away and hanged himself with a halter. And the chief priests took the pieces of silver, and said, "It is not lawful to put them into the treasury, seeing that it is the price of blood." And after they had consulted together, they bought with them the potter's field, as a burial place for strangers. For this reason that field has been called even to this day, Haceldama, that is, the Field of Blood. Then what was spoken through Jeremias the prophet was fulfilled,

"And they took the thirty pieces of silver, the price of Him Who was priced, upon Whom the children of Israel set a price; and they gave them for the potter's field, as the Lord directed me."

JESUS BEFORE PILATE

Now Jesus stood before the procurator, and the procurator asked Him, saying, "Are You the king of the Jews?" Jesus said to him, "You say it." And when He was accused by the chief priests and the elders, He made no answer. Then Pilate said to Him, "Do You not hear how many things they prefer against You?" But He did not answer him a single word, so that the procurator wondered exceedingly. Now at festival time the procurator used to release to the crowd a prisoner, whomever they would. Now he had at that time a notorious prisoner called Barabbas. Therefore, when they had gathered together, Pilate said, "Whom do you wish that

I release to you? Barabbas, or Jesus Who is called Christ?" For he knew that they had delivered Him up out of envy. Now, as he was sitting on the judgment-seat, his wife sent to him, saying, "Have nothing to do with that just Man, for I have suffered many things in a dream today because of Him."

BARABBAS IS PREFERRED

But the chief priests and the elders persuaded the crowds to ask for Barabbas and to destroy Jesus. But the procurator addressed them, and said to them, "Which of the two do you wish that I release to you?" And they said, "Barabbas." Pilate said to them, "What then am I to do with Jesus Who is called Christ?" They all said, "Let Him be crucified!" The procurator said to them, "Why, what evil has He done?" But they kept crying out the more, saying, "Let Him be crucified!" Now Pilate, seeing that he was doing no good, but rather that a riot was breaking out, took water and washed his hands in sight of the crowd, saying, "I am innocent of the blood of this just Man; see to it yourselves." And all the people answered and said, "His blood be on us and our children."

THE SCOURGING AND CROWNING

Then he released to them Barabbas; but Jesus he scourged and delivered to them to be crucified. Then the soldiers of the procurator took Jesus into the praetorium, and gathered together about Him the whole cohort. And they stripped Him and put on Him a scarlet cloak; and plaiting a crown of thorns they put it upon His head, and a reed into His right hand; and bending the knee before Him they mocked Him, saying, "Hail, King of the Jews!" And they spat on Him, and took the reed and kept striking Him on the head. And when they had mocked Him, they took the cloak off Him and put His own garments on Him, and led Him away to crucify Him. Now as they went out, they found a man of Cyrene named Simon; him they forced to take up His Cross. And they came to the place called Golgotha, that is, the Place of the Skull.

THE CRUCIFIXION

And they gave Him wine to drink mixed with gall; but when He had tasted it, He would not drink. And after they had crucified Him, they divided His garments, casting lots, [to fulfill what was spoken through the prophet, "They divided My garments among them, and upon My vesture they cast lots."] And sitting down they kept watch over Him. And they put above His head the charge against Him, written, "This is Jesus, the King of the Jews." Then two robbers were crucified with Him, one on His right hand and one on His left. Now the passers-by were jeering at Him, shaking their heads, and saying, "You Who would destroy the temple, and in three days build it up again, save Yourself. If You are the Son of God, come down from the Cross!" In like manner, the chief priests with the Scribes and the elders, mocking, said, "He saved others, Himself He cannot save! If He is the King of Israel, let Him come down now from the Cross, and we will believe Him. He trusted in God; let Him deliver Him now, if He wants Him; for He said, 'I am the Son of God.'" And the robbers also, who were crucified with Him, reproached Him in the same way.

THE DEATH OF JESUS

Now from the sixth hour there was darkness over the whole land until the ninth hour. But about the ninth hour Jesus cried out with a loud voice, saying, "Eli, Eli, lamma sabacthani," that is, "My God, My God, why have You forsaken Me?" And some of the bystanders on hearing this said, "This man is calling Elias." And immediately one of them ran and, taking a sponge, soaked it in common wine, put it on a reed and offered it to Him to drink. But the rest said, "Wait, let us see whether Elias is coming to save Him." But Jesus again cried out with a loud voice, and gave up His spirit. (*Here all kneel, and pause a little while.*) And behold, the curtain of the temple was torn in two from top to bottom; and the earth quaked, and the rocks were rent, and the tombs were opened, and many bodies of the saints who had fallen asleep arose; and coming forth out of the tombs after His resurrection, they came into the Holy City, and appeared to many. Now when the centurion, and those who were with him keeping guard over Jesus, saw the earthquake and the things that were happening, they were very much afraid, and they said, "Truly He was the Son of God." And many women were there, looking on from a distance, who had followed Jesus from Galilee, ministering to Him. Among them were Mary Magdalene, and Mary the mother of James and Joseph, and the mother of the sons of Zebedee. Now when it was evening, there came a certain rich man of Arimathea, Joseph by name, who was himself a disciple of Jesus. He went to Pilate and asked for the body of Jesus. Then Pilate ordered the body to be given up. And Joseph taking the body, wrapped it in a clean linen cloth, and laid it in his new tomb, which he had hewn out in the rock. Then he rolled a large stone to the entrance of the tomb, and departed.

A Priest who celebrates a second or third Mass today is not bound to repeat the reading of the Lord's Passion; in place of it the following Gospel is read in the usual manner:

Gospel. *Matt. 27, 45-52.* After they had crucified Jesus, from the sixth hour there was darkness over the whole land until the ninth hour. But about the ninth hour Jesus cried out with a loud voice, saying, "Eli, Eli, lamma sabacthani," that is, "My God, My God, why have You forsaken Me?" And some of the bystanders on hearing this said, "This man is calling Elias." And immediately one of them ran and, taking a sponge, soaked it in common wine, put it on a

reed and offered it to Him to drink. But
the rest said, "Wait, let us see whether Elias
is coming to save Him." But Jesus again
cried out with a loud voice, and gave up
His spirit. (*Here all kneel and pause a few
moments.*) And behold, the curtain of the
temple was torn in two from top to bottom;
and the earth quaked, and the rocks were
rent, and the tombs were opened, and many
bodies of the saints who had fallen asleep
arose.

- *Creed, page 33.*

Offertory. *Ps. 68, 21-22.* Insult has broken my heart, and I am weak; I looked for
sympathy, but there was none; for comforters, and I found none; rather they put gall
in my food, and in my thirst they gave me
vinegar to drink.

- *Offertory Prayers, page 35.*

Secret. Grant, we beseech You, O Lord,
that the gift now offered in the sight of Your
Majesty, may obtain for us both the grace
of devotion, and the reward of a blessed
eternity. Through our Lord, etc. ↴

Preface of the Holy Cross

It is fitting indeed and just, right and
helpful to salvation, for us always and everywhere to give thanks to You, O Holy Lord,

Father Almighty, Everlasting God; Who set the salvation of mankind upon the tree of the Cross, so that whence came death, thence also life might rise again, and He that overcame by the tree, by the tree also might be overcome: through Christ our Lord. Through Whom the Angels praise Your Majesty, the Dominations worship it, and the Powers are in awe. The heavens and the heavenly hosts, and the blessed Seraphim join together in celebrating their joy. With these, we pray You, join our own voices also, while we say with lowly praise: Holy, Holy, Holy, Lord God of hosts. Heaven and earth are filled with Your glory. Hosanna in the highest. Blessed is He Who comes in the Name of the Lord. Hosanna in the highest.

● *Canon, page 47.*

Communion. *Matt. 26, 42.* Father, if this cup cannot pass away, unless I drink it, Your will be done.

P. The Lord be with you. *S.* And with your spirit. ⤵

Postcommunion. By the working of this mystery, O Lord, may our vices be cleansed and our just desires be fulfilled. Through our Lord, etc. *S.* Amen.

● *Final Prayers, page 73.*

In Low Masses the following Gospel is read at the end instead of that of St. John.

Gospel. *Matt. 21, 1-9.* At that time, when Jesus drew near to Jerusalem, and came to Bethphage, on the Mount of Olives, He sent two disciples, saying to them, "Go into the village opposite you, and immediately you will find an ass tied, and a colt with her; loose them and bring them to Me. And if anyone say anything to you, you shall say that the Lord has need of them, and immediately he will send them." Now this was done that what was spoken through the prophet might be fulfilled, "Tell the daughter of Sion: Behold, thy King comes to you, meek and seated upon an ass, and upon a colt, the foal of a beast of burden." So the disciples went and did as Jesus had directed them. And they brought the ass and the colt, laid their cloaks on them, and made Him sit thereon. And most of the crowd spread their cloaks upon the road, while others were cutting branches from the trees, and strewing them on the road. And the crowds that went before Him, and those that followed, kept crying out, saying, "Hosanna to the Son of David! Blessed is He Who comes in the Name of the Lord!" *S.* Thanks be to God.

HOLY WEEK

The last week of Lent is called Holy Week because of the holiness and greatness of the events commemorated and the mysteries which Jesus Christ accomplished during the seven days preceding His glorious Resurrection. In order to encourage the great masses of the faithful, especially workers and school children, to take part in the commemoration of the holiest mysteries of Christ's Passion and Death, the Sacred Congregation of Rites issued a Decree, dated November 16, 1955, and amended it by a set of declarations, dated February 1, 1957.

The Decree can be summarized as follows:

1. All liturgical functions on Holy Thursday, Good Friday and Holy Saturday must be held in the afternoon or evening.

2. Holy Communion may be received at the Good Friday service which may be held at any time between noon and 9 P.M.

3. The Lenten Fast and Abstinence hereafter ends at midnight of Holy Saturday rather than at noon.

4. The Easter Vigil Liturgy remains unchanged, but must be celebrated between sunset and midnight, to be followed by the Easter Vigil Mass.

With the Easter Vigil service being held in the evening, Holy Saturday becomes a day without any liturgy and in keeping with its historical significance — a day of mourning for Christ's death.

THE COMMISSION OF THE APOSTLES

THE LORD IS RISEN ALLELUIA!

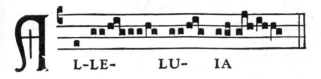

L-LE- LU- IA

EASTER TIME

Alleluia, or "Praise the Lord," is a most suitable expression of our joy at Easter Time, and the Church makes constant use of it in her liturgy.

In Latin, Easter is called "Pascha," a name taken from a Hebrew word meaning "passing over." We read in the book of Exodus (Ex. 12, 11ff) that the destroyer passed through the land of Egypt but that, seeing the blood of the lamb sprinkled on the side posts and upper door posts of the houses, he passed over. In that same night the Jews were delivered from bondage and later reached the land of promise. Since Christians have been redeemed and have "passed over" to the freedom of the children of God, they call the day of Christ's triumphant Resurrection, "Pascha" or "Passover."

The Easter Season commemorates the victory of our Divine Savior. As Christ arose from the dead so must we rise from coldness and indifference to a life of fervor and zeal. Christ offered Himself in complete holocaust on the Cross; we must offer ourselves wholeheartedly and entirely to God through our risen Savior. Risen with Christ we must "seek the things that are above."

Christ fulfilled His promise that He would rise on the third day and thus proved His Divinity giving a sure foundation to our faith. He could have ended His stay on earth with His Resurrection on

Easter Sunday. He preferred to remain among His beloved for forty days:

1. To strengthen their faith in the mystery of the Resurrection. "To them also He showed Himself alive after His Passion by many proofs, during forty days appearing to them and speaking of the kingdom of God." (Acts 1, 3.)

2. To stimulate the hope of universal resurrection as the consequence and fruit of His glorious Resurrection.

3. To console the faithful for their sorrow during His Passion and Death.

Easter is a day of gladness for all Christians, and their triumphant joy is given dramatic expression in the Sequence which follows the Gradual, the frequent alleluias, and the position of the Paschal Candle within the sanctuary throughout the Easter season.

Easter Time begins on Easter Sunday and ends on the Saturday after Pentecost.

In the Mass for Easter Sunday we find the inspiring Sequence which forms the transition from Epistle and Gradual to the Gospel. In this Christian classic the Church gives dramatic expression of her joy questioning one of the first witnesses of Christ's Resurrection.

Within the sanctuary until the Feast of the Ascension we shall see the Paschal Candle standing as a luminous witness to the risen Christ, the Light of the world.

———————◇———————

"He has risen from the dead."

EASTER SUNDAY

WHITE VESTMENTS

THOUGHT FOR TODAY: The Resurrection of Christ is a historical fact. When His enemies believed that they had destroyed Him, His real triumph began. To die to sin and to live with Christ is our way to victory and glorious resurrection.

● *Beginning of Mass, page 19.*

Introit. *Ps. 138, 18. 5. 6.* I arose, and am still with You, alleluia: You rest Your hand upon Me, alleluia: Your knowledge is too wonderful, alleluia, alleluia. *Ps. 138, 1. 2.* O Lord, You have probed Me and You know Me; You know when I sit and when I stand. ℣. Glory be.

● *Kyrie and Gloria, page 27.*

Prayer. O God, Who on this day, through Your Only-begotten Son, overcame death,

and opened to us the gate of everlasting
life: as, by Your anticipating grace, You
breathe good desires into our hearts, so also,
by Your gracious help, bring them to good
effect. Through the same, etc. S. Amen. ⸲

Epistle. *1 Cor. 5, 7-8.* Brethren: Purge
out the old leaven, that you may be a new
dough, as you really are without leaven.
For Christ, our passover, has been sacrificed. Therefore let us keep festival, not
with the old leaven, nor with the leaven
of malice and wickedness, but with the unleavened bread of sincerity and truth. S.
Thanks be to God. ⸲

Gradual. *Ps. 117, 24. 1.* This is the day
the Lord has made; let us be glad and rejoice in it. ℣. Give thanks to the Lord, for
He is good: for His mercy endures forever.

Alleluia, alleluia. ℣. *1 Cor. 5, 7.* Christ
our Passover has been sacrificed. ⸲

Sequence

O Christians, to the Paschal Victim bring:
Of praise the sacrificial Offering.
For the sheep the Lamb His Blood did
    shed:
The sinless Christ in the sinners' stead:
With God the guilty reconciling.

The Life with Death did fiercely strive:
Through dying the Leader now reigns alive.

O Mary, what did your wond'ring eyes
    adore?
"I saw the tomb of One Who dies no more!

The glorious risen Lord was shown to me:
The napkin, linen cloths there lying:
I heard the angels testifying.
Yes, Christ is ris'n and you shall see
Your Hope and mine in Galilee!"

We know that Christ rose from the grave:
O conqu'ring King, us sinners save.
Amen. Alleluia.

● *Prayer: Cleanse My Heart, page 31.*

Gospel. *Mark 16, 1-7.* At that time,
Mary Magdalene, Mary the mother of
James, and Salome, bought spices, that they
might go and anoint Jesus. And very early
on the first day of the week, they came to
the tomb, when the sun had just risen. And
they were saying to one another, "Who will
roll the stone back from the entrance of
the tomb for us?" And looking up they saw
that the stone had been rolled back, for it
was very large. But on entering the tomb,
they saw a young man sitting at the right
side, clothed in a white robe, and they were
amazed. He said to them, "Do not be terri-
fied. You are looking for Jesus of Nazareth,
Who was crucified. He has risen, He is not

here. Behold the place where they laid Him. But go, tell His disciples and Peter that He goes before you into Galilee; there you shall see Him, as He told you." *S.* Praise be to You, O Christ.

● Creed, page 33.

Offertory. *Ps. 75, 9. 10.* The earth feared and was silent, when God arose for judgment. Alleluia.

● Offertory Prayers, page 35.

Secret. Accept, we beseech You, O Lord, the prayers of Your people together with the sacrifice they offer, that what has been begun by these Easter mysteries, may, by Your working, profit us to everlasting salvation. Through our Lord, etc. ➘

Preface for Easter

P. World without end. *S.* Amen. *P.* The Lord be with you. *S.* And with your spirit. *P.* Lift up your hearts. *S.* We have lifted them up to the Lord. *P.* Let us give thanks to the Lord, our God. *S.* It is fitting and just.

It is fitting indeed and just, right and helpful to our salvation for us always to praise You, O Lord, but more gloriously *on this day** above others when Christ our Pasch was sacrificed. For He is the true Lamb Who has taken away the sins of the

---

*On Sundays after Easter, substitute: *"at this time."*

world: Who by dying has destroyed our death; and by rising again has restored us to life. And therefore with Angels and Archangels, with Thrones and Dominations, and with the whole host of the heavenly army, we sing a hymn to Your glory, saying again and again: Holy, Holy, Holy, Lord God of hosts. Heaven and earth are filled with Your glory. Hosanna in the highest. Blessed is He Who comes in the name of the Lord. Hosanna in the highest.

● *Canon, page 47.*

Communion. *1 Cor. 5, 7. 8.* Christ our passover, has been sacrificed, alleluia: therefore let us keep festival with the unleavened bread of sincerity and truth. Alleluia, alleluia, alleluia.

P. The Lord be with you. *S.* And with your spirit. ⤵

Postcommunion. Pour forth upon us, O Lord, the Spirit of Your love, that those whom You have filled with the Easter sacraments may, by Your goodness, be of one mind. Through our Lord . . . in the unity of the same, etc. *S.* Amen.

After "Go, you are dismissed," "Alleluia" is repeated twice, as also after the Response, "Thanks be to God."

● *Final Prayers, page 73.*

◇

Thomas said to Him, "My Lord and my God!"

FIRST SUNDAY AFTER EASTER

ALSO CALLED LOW SUNDAY

WHITE VESTMENTS

THOUGHT FOR TODAY: Despite all convincing proofs, many doubting Thomases are still saying, "I will not believe." We should repeat the words of the believing Thomas, "My Lord and My God," as often as we lift our eyes up to the Blessed Sacrament.

● *Beginning of Mass, page 19.*

Introt. *1 Pet. 2, 2.* Crave as newborn babes, alleluia: pure spiritual milk: alleluia, alleluia, alleluia. *Ps. 80, 2.* Sing joyfully to God our strength; acclaim the God of Jacob. ℣. Glory be.

● *Kyrie and Gloria, page 27.*

Prayer. Grant, we beseech You, almighty God, that we who have been celebrating the Paschal festivities, may, through

Your bounty, ever retain their effect, both in life and in conversation. Through our Lord, etc. S. Amen. ⇁

Epistle. *1 John 5, 4-10.* Beloved: All that is born of God overcomes the world; and this is the victory that overcomes the world, our faith. Who is there that overcomes the world if not he who believes that Jesus is the Son of God? This is He Who came in water and in blood, Jesus Christ; not in the water only, but in the water and in the blood. And it is the Spirit that bears witness that Christ is the truth. For there are three that bear witness in heaven: the Father, the Word and the Holy Spirit: and these three are one. And there are three that bear witness on earth: the Spirit, and the water, and the blood; and these three are one. If we receive the testimony of men, the testimony of God is greater; for this is the testimony of God which is greater, that He has borne witness concerning His Son. He who believes in the Son of God has the testimony of God in himself. S. Thanks be to God.

Alleluia, alleluia. ℣. *Matt. 28, 7.* "On the day of My Resurrection," says the Lord, "I will go before you into Galilee." Alleluia. ℣.

John 20, 26. After eight days, the doors being closed, Jesus stood in the midst of His disciples, and said, "Peace be to you." Alleluia.

● Prayer: Cleanse My Heart, page 31.

Gospel. *John 20, 19-31.* At that time, when it was late that same day, the first of the week, though the doors where the disciples gathered had been closed for fear of the Jews, Jesus came and stood in the midst and said to them, "Peace be to you!" And when He had said this, He showed them His hands and His side. The disciples therefore rejoiced at the sight of the Lord. He therefore said to them again, "Peace be to you! As the Father has sent Me, I also send you." When He had said this, He breathed upon them, and said to them, "Receive the Holy Spirit; whose sins you shall forgive, they are forgiven them; and whose sins you shall retain, they are retained." Now Thomas, one of the Twelve, called the Twin, was not with them when Jesus came. The other disciples therefore said to him, "We have seen the Lord." But he said to them, "Unless I see in His hands the print of the nails, and put my finger into the place of the nails, and put my hand into His side, I will not believe." And after eight days, His disciples were again inside, and Thomas with them. Jesus came, the doors being closed, and stood in their midst, and said, "Peace be to you!" Then He said to Thomas, "Bring here your finger, and see My hands; and bring here your hand, and put it into My side; and be not unbelieving, but believing." Thomas answered and said to Him, "My Lord and my God!" Jesus said to him, "Because you have seen Me, Thomas, you have believed. Blessed are they who have not seen, and yet have believed." Many other signs also Jesus worked in the sight of His disciples, which are not written in this book. But these are written that you may believe that Jesus is the Christ, the Son of God, and that believing you may have life in His Name. S. Praise be to You, O Christ.

● *Creed, page 33.*

Offertory. *Matt. 28, 2. 5. 6.* An angel of the Lord came down from heaven, and said to the women: "He Whom you seek is risen, as He said." Alleluia.

● *Offertory Prayers, page 35.*

Secret. Receive, we beseech You, O Lord, the offerings of Your exulting Church; and to her, to whom You have given cause for so great a joy, grant the fruit of perpetual gladness. Through our Lord, etc.

● *Preface for Easter, page 214.*

Communion. *John 20, 27.* Put in your hand, and know the place of the nails, alleluia: and be not unbelieving, but believing: alleluia.

P. The Lord be with you. *S.* And with your spirit. ↱

Postcommunion. We beseech You, O Lord our God, that the most holy rites, which You have given us for a safeguard for this new life, may become our remedy both now and for time to come. Through our Lord, etc. *S.* Amen.

● *Final Prayers, page 73.*

"There shall be one fold and one Shepherd."

SECOND SUNDAY AFTER EASTER

WHITE VESTMENTS

THOUGHT FOR TODAY: Our good example and prayers must help to bring the "sheep going astray" back to Christ, that there may be "one fold and one shepherd."

● *Beginning of Mass, page 19.*

Introit. *Ps. 32, 5. 6.* Of the kindness of the Lord the earth is full, alleluia; by the word of the Lord the heavens were made, alleluia, alleluia. *Ps. 32, 1.* Exult, you just, in the Lord; praise from the upright is fitting. ℣. Glory be.

● *Kyrie and Gloria, page 27.*

Prayer. O God, Who by the humility of Your Son have raised up a fallen world, grant everlasting joy to Your faithful people; that those whom You have rescued from the perils of endless death, You may cause to enjoy endless happiness. Through the same, etc. S. Amen. ↴

Epistle. *1 Pet. 2, 21-25.* Beloved: Christ has suffered for you, leaving you an example that you may follow in His steps: "Who did no sin, neither was deceit found in His mouth." Who, when He was reviled, did not revile; when He suffered, did not threaten, but yielded Himself to him who judged Him unjustly; Who Himself bore our sins in His body upon the tree, that we, having died to sin, might live to justice; and by His stripes you were healed. For you were as sheep going astray, but now you have returned to the shepherd and guardian of your souls. S. Thanks be to God.

Alleluia, alleluia. ℣. *Luke 24, 35.* The disciples recognized the Lord Jesus in the breaking of the bread. Alleluia. ℣. *John 10, 14.* I am the Good Shepherd: and I know My sheep, and Mine know Me. Alleluia.

● *Prayer: Cleanse My Heart, page* 31.

Gospel. *John 10, 11-16.* At that time, Jesus said to the Pharisees: "I am the Good Shepherd. The good shepherd lays down his life for his sheep. But the hireling, who is not a shepherd, whose own the sheep are not, sees the wolf coming and leaves the sheep and flees. And the wolf snatches and scatters the sheep; but the hireling flees because he is a hireling, and has no concern for the sheep. I am the Good Shepherd,

and I know Mine and Mine know Me, even
as the Father knows Me and I know the
Father; and I lay down My life for My
sheep. And other sheep I have that are not
of this fold. Them also I must bring, and
they shall hear My voice, and there shall
be one fold and one Shepherd." *S.* Praise
be to You, O Christ.

● Creed, page 33.

Offertory. *Ps. 62, 2. 5.* O God, my God,
to You do I watch at break of day, and in
Your Name I will lift up my hands, alleluia.

● Offertory Prayers, page 35.

Secret. May this sacred oblation, O Lord,
ever confer upon us Your salutary blessing,
that what is performed in mystery, may by
virtue thereof be fulfilled. Through our
Lord, etc.

● Preface for Easter, page 214.

Communion. *John 10, 14.* I am the Good
Shepherd, alleluia: and I know My sheep,
and Mine know Me: alleluia, alleluia.

P. The Lord be with you. *S.* And with
your spirit. ⬏

Postcommunion. Grant, we beseech You,
almighty God, that, obtaining the grace of
Your new life, we may ever glory in Your
gift. Through our Lord, etc. *S.* Amen.

● Final Prayers, page 73.

"A little while and you shall see Me no longer . . ."

THIRD SUNDAY AFTER EASTER
WHITE VESTMENTS

THOUGHT FOR TODAY: All those who resolve to live up to their Christian principles will meet with opposition and persecution. But our life on earth is only "a little while," and our "sorrow shall be turned into joy."

● *Beginning of Mass, page 19.*

Introit. *Ps. 65, 1. 2.* Shout joyfully to God, all you on earth, alleluia; sing praise to the glory of His Name, alleluia; proclaim His glorious praise, alleluia, alleluia, alleluia. *Ps. 65, 3.* Say to God, "How tremendous are Your deeds, Lord! For Your great strength Your enemies fawn upon You." ℣. Glory be.

● *Kyrie and Gloria, page 27.*

Prayer. O God, to those who go astray, You display the light of Your truth that they may return into the way of righteousness; grant to all those who profess themselves Christians, both to avoid the things which are contrary to that Name, and to follow those which are agreeable thereto. Through our Lord, etc. S. Amen. ⮌

Epistle. *1 Pet. 2, 11-19.* Beloved: I exhort you as strangers and pilgrims to abstain from carnal desires which war against the soul. Behave yourselves honorably among the pagans; that, whereas they slander you as evildoers, they may, through observing you, by reason of your good works glorify God in the day of visitation. Be subject therefore to every human creature for God's sake, whether to the king as supreme, or to governors as sent through him for vengeance on evildoers and for the praise of the good. For such is the will of God, that by doing good you should put to silence the ignorance of foolish men. Live as freemen, yet not using your freedom as a cloak for malice but as servants of God. Honor all men; love the brotherhood; fear God; honor the king. Servants, be subject to your masters in all fear, not only to the good and moderate, but also to the severe. This is indeed a grace, in Christ Jesus our Lord. S. Thanks be to God.

Alleluia, alleluia. ℣. *Ps. 110, 9.* The Lord has sent deliverance to His people. Alleluia.

℣. *Luke 24, 46.* It behooved Christ to suffer and to rise again from the dead, and so to enter into His glory, alleluia.

● *Prayer: Cleanse My Heart, page* 31.

Gospel. *John 16, 16-22.* At that time, Jesus said to His disciples: "A little while and you shall see Me no longer; and again a little while and you shall see Me, because I go to the Father." Some of His disciples therefore said to one another, "What is this He says to us, 'A little while and you shall not see Me, and again a little while and you shall see Me'; and, 'I go to the Father'?" They kept saying therefore, "What is this 'little while' of which He speaks? We do not know what He is saying." But Jesus knew that they wanted to ask Him, and He said to them, "You inquire about this among yourselves because I said, 'A little while and you shall not see Me, and again a little while and you shall see Me.' Amen, amen, I say to you, that you shall weep and lament, but the world shall rejoice; and you shall be sorrowful, but your sorrow shall be turned into joy. A woman about to give birth has sorrow, because her hour has come. But when she has brought forth the child, she no longer remembers the anguish for her joy that a man is born into the world.

And you therefore have sorrow now; but I will see you again, and your heart shall rejoice, and your joy no one shall take from you." *S.* Praise be to You, O Christ.

● Creed, page 33.

Offertory. *Ps. 145, 2.* Praise the Lord, O my soul; I will praise the Lord all my life; I will sing praise to my God while I live. Alleluia.

● Offertory Prayers, page 35.

Secret. Through these mysteries may grace be given us, O Lord, that moderating our earthly desires, we may learn to love the things of heaven. Through our Lord, etc.

● Preface for Easter, page 214.

Communion. *John 16, 16.* A little while, and you shall not see Me, alleluia: and again a little while, and you shall see Me: because I go to the Father, alleluia, alleluia.

P. The Lord be with you. *S.* And with your spirit. ↰

Postcommunion. May the sacrament which we have received, we beseech You, O Lord, both strengthen us with spiritual food, and protect us with bodily help. Through our Lord, etc. *S.* Amen.

● Final Prayers, page 73.

———— ◇ ————

"When He, the Spirit of Truth, has come . . ."

FOURTH SUNDAY AFTER EASTER

WHITE VESTMENTS

THOUGHT FOR TODAY: The Holy Spirit, promised by Christ to His Church, continues to convict the world of sin, of justice, and that there will be a judgment. Only among those people who follow this teaching, can a lasting peace be secured.

● *Beginning of Mass, page 19.*

Introit. *Ps. 97, 1. 2.* Sing to the Lord a new song, alleluia; for the Lord has done wondrous deeds, alleluia; in the sight of the nations, He has revealed His justice, alleluia, alleluia. *Ps. 97, 1.* His right hand has won victory for Him, His holy arm. ℣. Glory be.

● *Kyrie and Gloria, page 27.*

Prayer. O God, You make the minds of the faithful to be of one will; grant to Your people to love that which You command, and to desire that which You promise; that amidst the changes of this world, our hearts may be fixed where there are true joys. Through our Lord, etc. S. Amen. ⌐

Epistle. *James 1, 17-21.* Beloved: Every good gift and every perfect gift is from above, coming down from the Father of Lights, with Whom there is no change, nor shadow of alteration. Of His own will He has begotten us by the word of truth, that we might be, as it were, the first-fruits of His creatures. You know this, my beloved brethren. But let every man be swift to hear, slow to speak, and slow to wrath. For the wrath of man does not work the justice of God. Therefore, casting aside all uncleanness and abundance of malice, with meekness receive the ingrafted word, which is able to save your souls. S. Thanks be to God.

Alleluia, alleluia. ℣. *Ps. 117, 16.* The right hand of the Lord has struck with power; the right hand of the Lord has exalted me. Alleluia. ℣. *Rom. 6, 9.* Christ, having risen from the dead, dies now no more; death shall no longer have dominion over Him. Alleluia.

❯ *Prayer: Cleanse My Heart, page* 31.

Gospel. *John 16, 5-14.* At that time, Jesus said to His disciples: "I am going to Him Who sent Me, and no one of you asks Me, 'Where are You going?' But because I have spoken to you these things, sorrow has filled your heart. But I speak the truth to you; it is expedient for you that I depart. For if I do not go, the Advocate will not come to you; but if I go, I will send Him to you. And when He has come He will convict the world of sin, and of justice, and of judgment: of sin, because they do not believe in Me; of justice, because I go to the Father, and you will see Me no more; and of judgment, because the prince of this world has already been judged. Many things yet I have to say to you, but you cannot bear them now. But when He, the Spirit of truth, has come, He will teach you all the truth. For He will not speak on His own authority, but whatever He will hear He will speak, and the things that are to come He will declare to you. He will glorify Me, because He will receive of what is Mine and declare it to you." *S.* Praise be to You, O Christ.

● *Creed, page* 33.

Offertory. *Ps. 65, 1. 2. 16.* Shout joyfully to God, all you on earth, sing praise to the glory of His Name; hear now, all you who fear God, while I declare what the Lord has done for me. Alleluia.

● *Offertory Prayers, page 35.*

Secret. O God, by the adorable Communion of this sacrifice You make us partakers of the one Supreme Godhead; grant, we beseech You, that even as we recognize Your truth, so we may attain to it by a worthy life. Through our Lord, etc.

● *Preface for Easter, page 214.*

Communion. *John 16, 8.* When the Paraclete has come, the Spirit of truth, He will convict the world of sin, and of justice, and of judgment, alleluia, alleluia.

P. The Lord be with you. *S.* And with your spirit. ↴

Postcommunion. Be with us, O Lord, our God: that by these mysteries which we have faithfully received, we may both be purified from vice, and delivered from all dangers. Through our Lord, etc. *S.* Amen.

● *Final Prayers, page 73.*

———◇———

"The hour is coming when I will no longer speak to you in parables . . ."

FIFTH SUNDAY AFTER EASTER

WHITE VESTMENTS

THOUGHT FOR TODAY: At the opening of the Rogation-Week we are reminded of Christ's promise that our petitions will be granted if we ask anything in His Name. To speak in His Name we must be "doers," not "hearers" only, of the word of God.

● *Beginning of Mass, page* 19.

Introit. *Isa. 48, 20.* Declare the word of joy, and let it be heard, alleluia: declare it even to the ends of the earth; the Lord has delivered His people: alleluia, alleluia. *Ps. 65, 1. 2.* Shout joyfully to God, all you on earth, sing praise to the glory of His Name; proclaim His glorious praise. ℣. Glory be.

● *Kyrie and Gloria, page* 27.

Prayer. O God, from Whom all good things proceed, grant to Your suppliants, that by Your inspiration we may think those things that are right, and under Your guidance perform them. Through our Lord, etc. *S.* Amen. ↴

Epistle. *James 1, 22-27.* Beloved: Be doers of the word, and not hearers only, deceiving yourselves. For if anyone is a hearer of the word, and not a doer, he is like a man looking at his natural face in a mirror: for he looks at himself and goes away, and presently he forgets what kind of man he is. But he who has looked carefully into the perfect law of liberty and has remained in it, not becoming a forgetful hearer but a doer of the word, shall be blessed in his deed. And if anyone thinks himself to be religious, not restraining his tongue but deceiving his own heart, that man's religion is vain. Religion pure and undefiled before God the Father is this: to give aid to orphans and widows in their tribulation, and to keep oneself unspotted from this world. *S.* Thanks be to God.

Alleluia, alleluia. ℣. Christ is risen, and has shone upon us, whom He redeemed with His Blood. Alleluia. ℣. *John 16, 28.* I came forth from the Father, and have come into the world. Again I leave the world, and go to the Father. Alleluia.

● *Prayer: Cleanse My Heart, page* **31.**

Gospel. *John 16, 23-30.* At that time, Jesus said to His disciples: "Amen, amen, I say to you, if you ask the Father anything in My Name, He will give it to you. Hitherto you have not asked anything in My Name. Ask, and you shall receive, that your joy may be full. These things I have spoken to you in parables. The hour is coming when I will no longer speak to you in parables, but will speak to you plainly of the Father. In that day you shall ask in My Name; and I do not say to you that I will ask the Father for you, for the Father Himself loves you because you have loved Me, and have believed that I came forth from God. I came forth from the Father and have come into the world. Again I leave the world and go to the Father." His disciples said to Him, "Behold, now You speak plainly, and utter no parable. Now we know that You know all things, and do not need that anyone should question You. For this reason we believe that You came forth from God." *S.* Praise be to You, O Christ.

● *Creed, page* 33.

Offertory. *Ps. 65, 8. 9. 20.* Bless the Lord our God, you peoples, loudly sound His praise; He has given life to our souls, and has not let our feet slip; blessed be the

Lord, Who refused me not my prayer or His kindness. Alleluia.

● *Offertory Prayers, page 35.*

Secret. Receive, we beseech You, O Lord, the prayers of the faithful with this offering of sacrifice, that by these acts of a pious devotion we may pass to the glory of heaven. Through our Lord, etc.

● *Preface for Easter, page 214.*

Communion. *Ps. 95, 2.* Sing to the Lord, alleluia; sing to the Lord; bless His Name; announce His salvation day after day, alleluia, alleluia.

P. The Lord be with you. *S.* And with your spirit. ⮌

Postcommunion. O Lord, grant to us, who have been satisfied with the strength of the heavenly table, both to desire those things which are right and to obtain what we desire. Through our Lord, etc. *S.* Amen.

● *Final Prayers, page 73.*

"So then the Lord Jesus . . . was taken up into Heaven."

ASCENSION DAY

WHITE VESTMENTS

THOUGHT FOR TODAY: Our Lord ascended into heaven to prepare a place for us. His apostles were sent to teach all nations what He had commanded them. We must now cleanse our hearts from sin, which cannot enter heaven, and store up good deeds, performed in the state of grace. These will speak for us when we appear before God.

● *Beginning of Mass, page* 19.

Introit. *Acts 1, 11.* Men of Galilee, why do you stand looking up to heaven? Alleluia. He shall come in the same way as you have seen Him going up to heaven: alleluia, alleluia, alleluia. *Ps. 46, 2.* All you peoples, clap your hands, shout to God with cries of gladness. ℣. Glory be.

● *Kyrie and Gloria, page* 27.

Prayer. Grant, we beseech You, almighty God, that we who believe Your Only-begotten Son, our Redeemer, to have this day ascended into heaven, may ourselves also in mind dwell amid heavenly things. Through the same, etc. S. Amen. ⮐

Epistle. *Acts 1, 1-11.* In the former book, O Theophilus, I spoke of all that Jesus did and taught from the beginning until the day on which He was taken up, after He had given commandments through the Holy Spirit to the apostles whom He had chosen. To them also He showed Himself alive after His passion by many proofs, during forty days appearing to them and speaking of the kingdom of God. And while eating with them, He charged them not to depart from Jerusalem, but to wait for the promise of the Father, "of which you have heard," said He, "by My mouth; for John indeed baptized with water, but you shall be baptized with the Holy Spirit not many days hence." They therefore who had come together began to ask Him, saying, "Lord, will You at this time restore the kingdom to Israel?" But He said to them, "It is not for you to know the times or dates which the Father has fixed by His own authority; but you shall receive power when the Holy Spirit comes upon you, and you shall be witnesses for Me in Jerusalem and in all Judea and Samaria and even to the very ends of the earth." And when He had said this, He was lifted up before their eyes, and a cloud took Him out of their sight. And while they were gazing up to heaven as He went, behold, two men stood by them in white garments, and said to them, "Men of Galilee, why do you stand looking up to heaven? This Jesus Who has been taken up from you into heaven, shall come in the same way as you have seen Him going up to heaven." S. Thanks be to God.

Alleluia, alleluia. V̌. *Ps. 46, 6.* God mounts His throne amid shouts of joy; the Lord, amid trumpet blasts. Alleluia. V̌. *Ps. 67, 18. 19.* The Lord advances from Sinai to the sanctuary; ascending on high, He has led captivity captive. Alleluia.

● *Prayer: Cleanse My Heart, page* 31.

Gospel. *Mark 16, 14-20.* At that time, Jesus appeared to the eleven disciples as they were at table; and He upbraided them for their lack of faith and hardness of heart, in that they had not believed those who had seen Him after He had risen. And He said to them, "Go into the whole world and preach the gospel to every creature. He who believes and is baptized shall be saved, but he who does not believe shall be condemned. And these signs shall attend those who believe: in My Name they shall cast out devils;

they shall speak in new tongues; they shall take up serpents; and if they drink any deadly thing, it shall not hurt them; they shall lay hands upon the sick and they shall get well." So then the Lord Jesus, after He had spoken to them, was taken up into heaven, and sits at the right hand of God. But they went forth and preached everywhere, while the Lord worked with them and confirmed the preaching by the signs that followed. *S.* Praise be to You, O Christ.

● *Creed, page 33.*

Offertory. *Ps. 46. 6.* God mounts His throne amid shouts of joy; the Lord, amid trumpet blasts. Alleluia.

● *Offertory Prayers, page 35.*

Secret. Receive, O Lord, the gifts which we lay before You in honor of the glorious Ascension of Your Son, and mercifully grant that we may be delivered from present dangers, and arrive at everlasting life. Through the same, etc. ➔

Preface for Ascension

P. World without end. *S.* Amen. *P.* The Lord be with you. *S.* And with your spirit. *P.* Lift up your hearts. *S.* We have lifted them up to the Lord. *P.* Let us give thanks to the Lord, our God. *S.* It is fitting and just.

It is fitting indeed and just, right and helpful to salvation, for us always and everywhere to give thanks to You, O Holy Lord, Father Almighty, Everlasting God; through Christ our Lord. Who, after His Resurrection, appeared openly to all His disciples, and, while they looked on, was taken up into heaven, that He might grant unto us to be sharers in His own divinity. And therefore, with Angels and Archangels, with Thrones and Dominations, and with the whole host of the heavenly army, we sing a hymn to Your glory, saying again and again: Holy, Holy, Holy, Lord God of hosts. Heaven and earth are filled with Your glory. Hosanna in the highest. Blessed is He Who comes in the Name of the Lord. Hosanna in the highest.

● *Canon, page 47.*

Communion. *Ps. 67, 33. 34.* Chant praise to the Lord, Who rides on the heights of the heavens to the East. Alleluia.

P. The Lord be with you. *S.* And with your spirit. ➜

Postcommunion. Grant, we beseech You, almighty and merciful God, that what we have received in visible mysteries we may obtain by an invisible effect. Through our Lord, etc. *S.* Amen.

● *Final Prayers, page 73.*

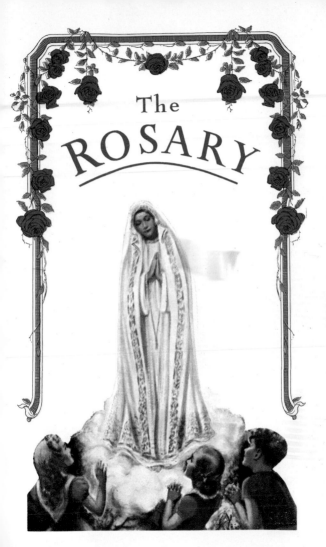

The
ROSARY

FIRST JOYFUL MYSTERY

THE ANNUNCIATION — The Angel Gabriel greeted Mary as "Full of Grace," and she humbly consented to be God's Mother.

1 Our Father. 10 Hail Marys. 1 Glory be.

SECOND JOYFUL MYSTERY

THE VISITATION — Mary visited her cousin Elizabeth and remained with her for three months to care for her.

1 Our Father. 10 Hail Marys. 1 Glory be.

THIRD JOYFUL MYSTERY

THE NATIVITY — Mary brought forth our Redeemer Jesus Christ, and laid Him in a manger in a stable at Bethlehem.

1 Our Father. 10 Hail Marys. 1 Glory be.

FOURTH JOYFUL MYSTERY

THE PRESENTATION — Mary obeyed the law of God in presenting the child Jesus to the Prophet Simeon in the Temple.

1 Our Father. 10 Hail Marys. 1 Glory be.

FIFTH JOYFUL MYSTERY

CHILD JESUS IN THE TEMPLE — After three days, Mary found the child Jesus in the Temple, in the midst of the doctors.

1 Our Father. 10 Hail Marys. 1 Glory be.

FIRST SORROWFUL MYSTERY

AGONY IN THE GARDEN — Our Lord Jesus knelt in the Garden of Gethsemani, suffering a bitter agony for our sins.

1 Our Father. 10 Hail Marys. 1 Glory be.

SECOND SORROWFUL MYSTERY

SCOURGING AT THE PILLAR — Our Lord suffered a cruel scourging at the pillar, and was struck heavy blows that tore His flesh.

1 Our Father. 10 Hail Marys. 1 Glory be.

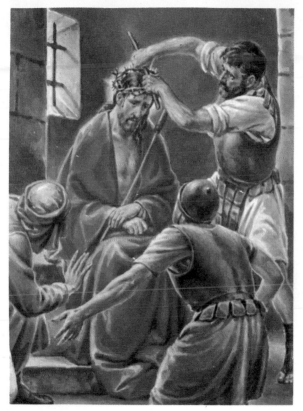

CROWNING WITH THORNS — The soldiers made a crown of sharp thorns and cruelly forced it on the sacred head of Our Lord.

1 Our Father. 10 Hail Marys. 1 Glory be.

FOURTH SORROWFUL MYSTERY

CARRYING THE CROSS — Our Lord Jesus Christ carried the heavy Cross, laid on His sacred shoulders for His greater suffering.

1 Our Father. 10 Hail Marys. 1 Glory be.

FIFTH SORROWFUL MYSTERY

THE CRUCIFIXION — Our Lord Jesus Christ was stripped of His garments, and His hands and feet were nailed to the Cross.

1 Our Father. 10 Hail Marys. 1 Glory be.

FIRST GLORIOUS MYSTERY

THE RESURRECTION—Our Lord Jesus Christ, gloriously triumphed over death, by rising again on the third day.

1 Our Father. 10 Hail Marys. 1 Glory be.

SECOND GLORIOUS MYSTERY

THE ASCENSION — Our Lord ascended into Heaven, in the presence of Mary and His disciples, forty days after His Resurrection.

1 Our Father. 10 Hail Marys. 1 Glory be.

THIRD GLORIOUS MYSTERY

THE DESCENT OF THE HOLY SPIRIT — The Holy Spirit, sent by Our Lord Jesus Christ, descended upon the Apostles.

1 Our Father. 10 Hail Marys. 1 Glory be.

FOURTH GLORIOUS MYSTERY

THE ASSUMPTION — Mary was gloriously assumed into Heaven, accompanied by angels, to be united with her Divine Son.

1 Our Father. 10 Hail Marys. 1 Glory be.

FIFTH GLORIOUS MYSTERY

CORONATION OF THE BLESSED VIRGIN —
Mary was crowned Queen of Heaven, to
the joy and glory of all the Saints.

1 Our Father. 10 Hail Marys. 1 Glory be.

"He will bear witness concerning Me."

SUNDAY AFTER THE ASCENSION

WHITE VESTMENTS

THOUGHT FOR TODAY: Fervent prayers are being said during this week in preparation for Pentecost. To make these prayers more acceptable to God, "have a constant mutual charity among yourselves; for charity covers a multitude of sins."

● *Beginning of Mass, page 19.*

Introit. *Ps. 26, 7. 8. 9.* Hear, O Lord, the sound of my call, alleluia; to You my heart speaks, Your glance I seek; Your presence, O Lord, I seek; hide not Your face from me, alleluia, alleluia. *Ps. 26, 1.* The Lord is my light and my salvation; whom should I fear? ℣. Glory be.

● *Kyrie and Gloria, page 27.*

Prayer. Almighty and everlasting God, grant us both ever to have a will devoted to You, and to serve Your Majesty with a sincere heart. Through our Lord, etc. *S.* Amen. ⇘

Epistle. *1 Pet. 4, 7-11.* Beloved: Be prudent and watchful in prayers. But above all things have a constant mutual charity among yourselves; for charity covers a multitude of sins. Be hospitable to one another without murmuring. According to the gift that each has received, administer it to one another as good stewards of the manifold grace of God. If anyone speaks, let it be as with words of God. If anyone ministers, let it be as from the strength that God furnishes; that in all things God may be honored through Jesus Christ our Lord. *S.* Thanks be to God.

Alleluia, alleluia. ℣. *Ps. 46, 9.* The Lord reigns over all the nations, God sits upon His holy throne. Alleluia. ℣. *John 14, 18.* I will not leave you orphans; I go away and I come to you, and your heart shall rejoice. Alleluia.

● *Prayer: Cleanse My Heart, page* 31.

Gospel. *John 15, 26. 27; 16, 1-4.* At that time, Jesus said to His disciples: "When the Advocate has come, Whom I will send you from the Father, the Spirit of truth Who proceeds from the Father, He will bear witness concerning Me. And you also bear witness, because from the beginning you are with Me. These things I have spoken to you that you may not be scandalized. They will expel you from the synagogues. Yes, the hour is coming for everyone who kills you to think he is offering worship to God. And these things they will do because they have not known the Father nor Me. But these things I have spoken to you, that when the time for them has come you may remember that I told you." S. Praise be to You, O Christ.

● Creed, page 33.

Offertory. *Ps. 46, 6.* God mounts His throne amid shouts of joy; the Lord, amid trumpet blasts. Alleluia.

● Offertory Prayers, page 35.

Secret. May this spotless sacrifice purify us, O Lord, and infuse into our minds the vigor of heavenly grace. Through our Lord, etc.

● Preface for Ascension, page 239.

Communion. *John 17, 12. 13. 15.* Father, while I was with them, I kept them whom You have given Me, alleluia; but now I am coming to You: I do not pray that You take them out of the world, but that You keep them from evil, alleluia, alleluia.

P. The Lord be with you. *S.* And with your spirit. ⮑

Postcommunion. Being replenished with the sacred gifts, grant us, we beseech You, O Lord, always to continue in thanksgiving. Through our Lord, etc. *S.* Amen.

● *Final Prayers, page 73.*

"And they were all filled with the Holy Spirit."

PENTECOST SUNDAY

RED VESTMENTS

THOUGHT FOR TODAY: Jesus had instructed His disciples on several occasions about the coming of the Holy Spirit. The marvelous events which accompanied His arrival were signs of the far greater effects of grace He produces in the souls of those who receive Him. We pray with the Church: "Come, O Holy Spirit, fill the hearts of Your faithful, and kindle in them the fire of Your love."

● *Beginning of Mass, page 19.*

Introit. *Wis. 1, 7.* The Spirit of the Lord fills the world, alleluia; is all-embracing, and knows man's utterance, alleluia, alleluia, alleluia. *Ps. 67, 2.* God arises; His enemies are scattered, and those who hate Him, flee before Him. ℣. Glory be.

● *Kyrie and Gloria, page 27.*

Prayer. O God, Who on this day by the light of the Holy Spirit taught the hearts of the faithful, grant us by the same Spirit to relish what is right, and always to rejoice in His comfort. Through our Lord Jesus Christ, Your son... in the unity of the same, etc. S. Amen. ⟩

Epistle. *Acts 2, 1-11.* When the days of Pentecost were drawing to a close, they were all together in one place. And suddenly there came a sound from heaven, as of a violent wind blowing, and it filled the whole house where they were sitting. And there appeared to them parted tongues as of fire, which settled upon each of them. And they were all filled with the Holy Spirit and began to speak in foreign tongues, even as the Holy Spirit prompted them to speak. Now there were staying at Jerusalem devout Jews, from every nation under heaven. And when this sound was heard, the multitude gathered and were bewildered in mind, because each heard them speaking in his own language. But they were all amazed and marvelled, saying, "Behold, are not all these that are speaking Galileans? And how have we heard each his own language in which he was born? Parthians and Medes and Elamites, and inhabitants of Mesopotamia,

Judea, and Cappadocia, Pontus and Asia, Phrygia and Pamphilia, Egypt and the parts of Libya about Cyrene, and visitors from Rome, Jews also and proselytes, Cretans and Arabians, we have heard them speaking in our own languages of the wonderful works of God." *S.* Thanks be to God.

Alleluia, alleluia. ℣. *Ps. 103, 30.* Send forth Your Spirit, and they shall be created; and You shall renew the face of the earth. Alleluia. (*Here genuflect.*) ℣. Come, O Holy Spirit, fill the hearts of Your faithful; and kindle in them the fire of Your love. ➔

Sequence

Come, O Holy Spirit, come!
From Your bright and blissful Home
Rays of healing light impart.

Come, O Father of the poor,
Source of gifts that will endure,
Light of ev'ry human heart.

You of all consolers best,
Of the soul most kindly Guest,
Quick'ning courage do bestow.

In hard labor You are rest,
In the heat You refresh best,
And solace give in our woe.

O most blessed Light divine,
Let Your radiance in us shine,
And our inmost being fill.

Nothing good by man is thought,
Nothing right by him is wrought,
When he spurns Your gracious Will.

Cleanse our souls from sinful stain,
Leave our dryness with Your rain,
Heal our wounds and mend our way.

Bend the stubborn heart and will,
Melt the frozen, warm the chill,
Guide the steps that go astray.

On the faithful who in You,
Trust with childlike piety,
Deign Your sevenfold gift to send.

Give them virtue's rich increase,
Saving grace to die in peace,
Give them joys that never end.
Amen. Alleluia.

● Prayer: Cleanse My Heart, page 31.

Gospel. *John 14, 23-31.* At that time, Jesus said to His disciples: "If anyone love Me, he will keep My word, and My Father will love him, and We will come to him and make Our abode with him. He who does not love Me, does not keep My words.

And the word that you have heard is not Mine, but the Father's Who sent Me. These things I have spoken to you while yet dwelling with you. But the Advocate, the Holy Spirit, Whom the Father will send in My Name, He will teach you all things, and bring to your mind whatever I have said to you. Peace I leave with you, My peace I give to you; not as the world gives do I give to you. Do not let your heart be troubled, or be afraid. You have heard Me say to you, 'I go away and I am coming to you.' If you loved Me, you would indeed rejoice that I am going to the Father, for the Father is greater than I. And now I have told you before it comes to pass, that when it has come to pass you may believe. I will no longer speak much with you, for the Prince of the world is coming, and in Me he has nothing. But he comes that the world may know that I love the Father, and that I do as the Father has commanded Me." S. Praise be to You, O Christ.

● Creed, page 33.

Offertory. *Ps. 67, 29. 30.* Confirm, O God, what You have wrought in us; from Your temple, which is in Jerusalem, kings shall offer gifts to You. Alleluia.

● Offertory Prayers, page 35.

Secret. Sanctify, we beseech You, O Lord, the gifts we offer, and purify our hearts by the light of the Holy Spirit. Through our Lord . . . in the unity of the same, etc. ➘

Preface for Pentecost

P. World without end. *S.* Amen. *P.* The Lord be with you. *S.* And with your spirit. *P.* Lift up your hearts. *S.* We have lifted them up to the Lord. *P.* Let us give thanks to the Lord, our God. *S.* It is fitting and just.

It is fitting indeed and just, right and helpful to salvation, for us always and everywhere to give thanks to You, O Holy Lord, Father Almighty, Everlasting God: through Christ our Lord. Who ascending above all the heavens, and sitting at Your right hand, on this day sent forth the Holy Spirit, as He had promised, on the children of adoption. Wherefore does the whole world rejoice with exceeding great joy; and the hosts above and the angelic powers also join in singing a hymn to Your glory, saying again and again: Holy, Holy, Holy, Lord God of hosts. Heaven and earth are filled with Your glory. Hosanna in the highest. Blessed is He Who comes in the name of the Lord. Hosanna in the highest.

● *Canon, page 47.*

Communion. *Acts 2, 2. 4.* Suddenly there came a sound from heaven, as of a violent wind blowing, where they were sitting, alleluia: and they were all filled with the Holy Spirit, speaking of the wonderful works of God, alleluia, alleluia.

P. The Lord be with you. *S.* And with your spirit. ↰

Postcommunion. May the inpouring of the Holy Spirit cleanse our hearts, O Lord, and render them fertile by the inward sprinkling of His heavenly dew. Through our Lord . . . in the unity of the same, etc. *S.* Amen.

● *Final Prayers, page 73.*

"Blessed be the Holy Trinity and undivided Unity!"

TRINITY SUNDAY
WHITE VESTMENTS

THOUGHT FOR TODAY: Our intellect is too limited to comprehend the inner life of the infinite God, the Mystery of One God in three Divine Persons. But we know that everything in our Christian Religion is related to the Holy Trinity: Creation, Sanctification and Salvation. The "Glory be to the Father, and to the Son, and to the Holy Spirit" is an expression of our reverence and gratitude.

● *Beginning of Mass, page 19.*

Introit. *Tob. 12, 6.* Blessed be the Holy Trinity and undivided Unity: we will give glory to Him, because He has shown His mercy to us. *Ps. 8, 2.* O Lord, our Lord: how glorious is Your Name over all the earth! ℣. Glory be.

● *Kyrie and Gloria, page 27.*

Prayer. Almighty and everlasting God, You have given Your servants, in the confession of the true faith, to acknowledge the glory of the Eternal Trinity, and to adore the unity in the power of Your Majesty; grant that by steadfastness in this faith we may ever be defended from all adversities. Through our Lord, etc. S. Amen. ➤

Epistle. *Rom. 11, 33-36.* Oh, the depth of the riches of the wisdom and of the knowledge of God! How incomprehensible are His judgments and how unsearchable His ways! For "Who has known the mind of the Lord, or who has been His counsellor? Or who has first given to Him, that recompense should be made him?" For from Him and through Him and unto Him are all things. To Him be the glory forever, amen. S. Thanks be to God. ➤

Gradual. *Dan. 3, 55. 56.* Blessed are You, O Lord, Who look into the depths from Your throne upon the Cherubim. ℣. Blessed are You, O Lord, in the firmament of heaven, and praiseworthy forever.

Alleluia, alleluia. ℣. *Dan. 3, 52.* Blessed are You, O Lord, the God of our fathers, and praiseworthy forever. Alleluia.

● *Prayer: Cleanse My Heart, page* 31.

Gospel. *Matt. 28, 18-20.* At that time, Jesus said to His disciples: "All power in heaven and on earth has been given to Me. Go, therefore, and make disciples of all nations, baptizing them in the Name of the Father, and of the Son, and of the Holy Spirit, teaching them to observe all that I have commanded you; and behold, I am with you all days, even unto the consummation of the world." *S.* Praise be to You, O Christ.

● *Creed, page 33.*

Offertory. *Tob. 12, 6.* Blessed be God the Father, and the Only-begotten Son of God, and also the Holy Spirit: because He has shown His mercy to us.

● *Offertory Prayers, page 35.*

Secret. Sanctify the victim of this offering, we beseech You, O Lord, our God, by the invocation of Your holy Name; and through the same render us an everlasting offering to You. Through our Lord, etc.

● *Preface, page 43.*

Communion. *Tob. 12, 6.* We bless the God of heaven, and before all living we will praise Him; because He has shown His mercy to us.

P. The Lord be with you. *S.* And with your spirit. ⤷

Postcommunion. May the reception of this sacrament, O Lord, our God, as also the confession of our faith in the holy and everlasting Trinity, and its undivided Unity, profit us for the health of body and soul. Through our Lord, etc. S. Amen.

● *Final Prayers, page 73.*

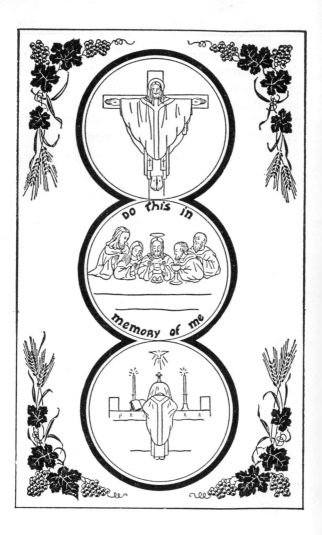

Do this in

memory of me

"Hail! Bread of Angels, broken for us . . . "

FEAST OF CORPUS CHRISTI

THURSDAY AFTER TRINITY SUNDAY

WHITE VESTMENTS

THOUGHT FOR TODAY: The joy of the institution of the Holy Eucharist is not fully expressed on Holy Thursday because of the nearness of Good Friday. Hence wherever possible, public homage and adoration are paid to Jesus in the Blessed Sacrament on this Feast of Corpus Christi, and the faithful accompany Christ in a colorful procession.

● *Beginning of Mass, page* 19.

Introit. *Ps. 80, 17.* He fed them with the best of wheat, alleluia; and filled them with honey from the rock, alleluia, alleluia, alleluia. *Ps. 80, 2.* Sing joyfully to God our strength; acclaim the God of Jacob. ℣. Glory be.

● *Kyrie and Gloria, page* 27.

Prayer. O God, under a marvelous sacrament You have left us the memorial of Your

Passion; grant, we beseech You, so to venerate the sacred mysteries of Your Body and Blood, that we may ever perceive within us the fruit of Your Redemption. Who live, etc. *S.* Amen. ↝

Epistle. *1 Cor. 11, 23-29.* Brethren: I myself have received from the Lord (what I also delivered to you), that the Lord Jesus, on the night in which He was betrayed, took bread, and giving thanks broke, and said, "Take and eat. This is My Body which shall be given up for you; do this in remembrance of Me." In like manner also the cup, after He had supped, saying, "This cup is the new covenant in My Blood; do this as often as you drink it, in remembrance of Me. For as often as you shall eat this bread and drink the cup, you proclaim the death of the Lord, until He comes." Therefore whoever eats this bread or drinks the cup of the Lord unworthily, will be guilty of the Body and the Blood of the Lord. But let a man prove himself, and so let him eat of that bread and drink of the cup; for he who eats and drinks unworthily, without distinguishing the Body of the Lord, eats and drinks judgment to himself. *S.* Thanks be to God. ↝

Gradual. *Ps. 144, 15-16.* The eyes of all look hopefully to You, O Lord; and You give them their food in due season. ℣. You open Your hand; and satisfy the desire of every living thing.

Alleluia, alleluia. *John 6, 56-57.* My Flesh is food indeed, and My Blood is drink indeed. He who eats My Flesh and drinks My Blood, abides in Me, and I in him.

At Low Mass apart from the Feast Day, if the Sequence is omitted, Alleluia is said here.

Sequence
(Extract)

Sion, to Your Savior sing,
To Your Shepherd and Your King!
Let the air with praises ring!

Words a nature's course derange,
That in Flesh the bread may change
And the wine in Christ's own Blood.

Does it pass your comprehending?
Faith, the law of light transcending,
Leaps to things not understood.

Here beneath these signs are hidden
Priceless things, to sense forbidden;
Signs, not things, are all we see.

Flesh from bread, and Blood from wine,
Yet is Christ in either sign,
All entire confessed to be.

And whoe'er of Him partakes,
Severs not, nor rends, nor breaks:
All entire, their Lord receive.

Whether one or thousand eat,
All receive the self-same meat,
Nor do less for others leave.

Both the wicked and the good
Eat of this celestial Food:
But with ends how opposite!

With this most substantial Bread,
Unto life or death they're fed,
In a difference infinite.

Nor a single doubt retain,
When they break the Host in twain,
But that in each part remain
What was in the whole before;

For the outward sign alone
May some change have undergone,
While the Signified stays one,
And the same forevermore.

Hail! Bread of Angels, broken,
For us pilgrims food, and token
Of the promise by Christ spoken,
Children's meat, to dogs denied!

Jesus, Shepherd mild and meek,
Shield the poor, support the weak,
Pity all who pardon seek,
And who place all trust in You,
Fill them with Your Charity!

Source of all we have or know,
Feed and lead us here below.
Grant that with Your Saints above,
Sitting at the feast of love,
We may see You face to face.
Amen. Alleluia.

● Prayer: Cleanse My Heart, page 31.

Gospel. *John 6, 56-59.* At that time, Jesus said to the crowds of the Jews: "My Flesh is food indeed, and My Blood is drink indeed. He who eats My Flesh, and drinks My Blood, abides in Me and I in him. As the living Father has sent Me, and as I live because of the Father, so he who eats Me, he also shall live because of Me. This is the bread that has come down from heaven; not as your fathers ate the manna, and died. He who eats this bread shall live forever." *S.* Praise be to You, O Christ.

● *Creed, page 33.*

Offertory. *Lev. 21, 6.* The priests of the Lord offer incense and loaves to God, and therefore they shall be sacred to their God and not profane His Name. Alleluia.

● *Offertory Prayers, page 35.*

Secret. We beseech You, O Lord, graciously grant to Your Church the gifts of unity and peace, which, in the gifts offered, are mystically signified. Through, etc. ➐

Preface for Weekdays

P. World without end. *S.* Amen. *P.* The Lord be with you. *S.* And with your spirit. *P.* Lift up your hearts. *S.* We have lifted them up to the Lord. *P.* Let us give thanks to the Lord, our God. *S.* It is fitting and just.

It is fitting indeed and just, right and helpful to salvation, for us always and everywhere to give thanks to You, O Holy Lord, Father Almighty, Everlasting God, through Christ our Lord. Through Him the Angels praise Your Majesty, the Dominations adore, the Powers are in awe. The heavens and the heavenly hosts, and the blessed Seraphim join together in celebrating their joy. With these, we pray You, join our own voices also, while we say with lowly praise: Holy, Holy, Holy, Lord God of hosts. Heaven and earth are filled with Your glory. Hosanna in the highest. Blessed is He Who comes in the name of the Lord. Hosanna in the highest.

● *Canon, page 47.*

Communion. *1 Cor. 11, 26-27.* As often as you shall eat this bread and drink the cup, you proclaim the death of the Lord, until He comes. Therefore whoever eats this bread or drinks the cup of the Lord unworthily, will be guilty of the Body and Blood of the Lord, alleluia.

P. The Lord be with you. *S.* And with your spirit. ⌐

Postcommunion. Grant us, we beseech You, O Lord, to be filled with the eternal enjoyment of Your Divinity, which is prefigured by the reception of Your precious Body and Blood in this life. Who live, etc. *S.* Amen.

● *Final Prayers, page 73.*

"Bring in here the poor, and the crippled . . . "

SECOND SUNDAY AFTER PENTECOST

GREEN VESTMENTS

THOUGHT FOR TODAY: The Communion-Banquet to which we are invited is not only for the just, but for all who acknowledge that they are poor, feeble, blind, and lame in their religious life and sincerely desire to be cured. We must, however, first, pass from the death of sin to the life of grace through the Sacrament of Penance before Christ can welcome us at the Eucharistic Table.

● *Beginning of Mass, page* 19.

Introit. *Ps. 17, 19. 20.* The Lord came to my support; He set me free in the open, and rescued me, because He loves me. *Ps. 17, 2. 3.* I love You, O Lord, my strength: O Lord, my rock, my fortress, my deliverer. ℣. Glory be.

● *Kyrie and Gloria, page 27.*

Prayer. Grant, O Lord, that we may have a constant fear and love of Your holy Name; for You never cease to direct and govern by Your grace those whom You solidly establish in Your love. Through our Lord, etc. S. Amen. ⤵

Epistle. *1 John 3, 13-18.* Beloved: Do not be surprised if the world hates you. We know that we have passed from death to life, because we love the brethren. He who does not love abides in death. Everyone who hates his brother is a murderer. And you know that no murderer has eternal life abiding in him. In this we have come to know His love, that He laid down His life for us; and we likewise ought to lay down our life for the brethren. He who has the goods of this world and sees his brother in need and closes his heart to him, how does the love of God abide in Him? My dear children, let us not love in word, neither with the tongue, but in deed and in truth. S. Thanks be to God. ⤵

Gradual. *Ps. 119, 1-2.* In my distress I called to the Lord, and He answered me. ℣. O Lord, deliver me from lying lip, from treacherous tongue.

Alleluia, alleluia. ℣. *Ps. 7, 2.* O Lord, my God, in You I take refuge; save me from all my pursuers and rescue me. Alleluia.

● Prayer: Cleanse My Heart, page 31.

Gospel. *Luke 14, 16-24.* At that time, Jesus spoke to the Pharisees this parable: "A certain man gave a great supper, and he invited many. And he sent his servant at supper time to tell those invited to come, for everything is now ready. And they all with one accord began to excuse themselves. The first said to him, 'I have bought a farm, and I must go out and see it; I pray you hold me excused.' And another said, 'I have bought five yoke of oxen, and I am on my way to try them; I pray you hold me excused.' And another said, 'I have married a wife, and therefore I cannot come.' And the servant returned, and reported these things to his master. Then the master of the house was angry and said to his servant, 'Go out quickly into the streets and lanes of the city, and bring in here the poor, and the crippled, and the blind, and the lame.' And the servant said, 'Sir, your order has been carried out, and still there is room.' Then the master said to the servant, 'Go out into the highways and hedges, and make them come in, so that my house may be filled.

For I tell you that none of those who were invited shall taste of my supper.'" S. Praise be to You, O Christ.

● *Creed, page 33.*

Offertory. *Ps. 6, 5.* Return, O Lord, save my life; rescue me because of Your kindness.

● *Offertory Prayers, page 35.*

Secret. May the offering about to be dedicated to Your Name purify us, O Lord, so that from day to day it may carry us on to the reality of heavenly life. Through our Lord, etc.

● *Preface, page 43.*

Communion. *Ps. 12, 6.* I will sing of the Lord, "He has been good to me"; and I will sing to the Name of the Lord the Most High.

P. The Lord be with you. *S.* And with your spirit. ↱

Postcommunion. Having received Your sacred gifts, we beseech You, O Lord, that our assistance at these mysteries may result in an increase of our salvation. Through our Lord, etc. *S.* Amen.

● *Final Prayers, page 73.*

———◇———

"The thoughts of His Heart are to all generations."

FEAST OF THE SACRED HEART OF JESUS

THIRD FRIDAY AFTER PENTECOST

WHITE VESTMENTS

The Feast of the Sacred Heart of Jesus is a reminder of all that we owe to the love of our Divine Redeemer. Appearing to St. Margaret Mary Alacoque during the Octave of Corpus Christi in the year 1675, Jesus said to her: "This is the heart which has loved men so much and in turn is so little loved by them." Let us consecrate our good will to the Sacred Heart and offer to Him the sacrifice of a holy life.

THOUGHT FOR TODAY: The Sacred Heart of Jesus is always eager to forgive whenever a sinner sincerely repents, and desires to return to God, the source of joy and peace. Why then hesitate? "Cast your care upon the Lord, and He will support you."

● *Beginning of Mass, page 19.*

Introit. *Ps. 32, 11. 19.* The thoughts of His Heart are to all generations: to deliver them from death and preserve them in spite of famine. (P.T. Alleluia, alleluia.) *Ps. 32, 1.* Exult, you just, in the Lord; praise from the upright is fitting. ℣. Glory be.

● *Kyrie and Gloria, page* 27.

Prayer. O God, You mercifully deign to bestow on us in the Heart of Your Son, wounded by our sins, an infinite treasure of love; grant, we beseech You, that rendering It the devout homage of our affection, we may also make a worthy reparation for our sins. Through the same, etc. *S.* Amen. ➤

Epistle. *Eph. 3, 8-19.* Brethren: To me, the very least of all saints, there was given this grace, to announce among the Gentiles the good tidings of the unfathomable riches of Christ, and to enlighten all men as to what is the dispensation of the mystery which has been hidden from eternity in God, Who created all things; in order that through the Church there be made known to the Principalities and the Powers in the heavens the manifold wisdom of God according to the eternal purpose which He accomplished in Christ Jesus our Lord. In Him we have assurance and confident access through faith in Him. For this reason

I bend my knees to the Father of our Lord Jesus Christ, from Whom all fatherhood in heaven and on earth receives its name, that He may grant you from His glorious riches to be strengthened with power through His Spirit unto the progress of the inner man; and to have Christ dwelling through faith in your hearts: so that, being rooted and grounded in love, you may be able to comprehend with all the saints what is the breadth and length and height and depth, and to know Christ's love which surpasses knowledge, in order that you may be filled unto all the fullness of God. S. Thanks be to God. ⸮

Gradual. *Ps. 24, 8-9.* Good and upright is the Lord; thus He shows sinners the way. ℣. He guides the humble to justice; He teaches the humble His way.

Alleluia, alleluia. *Matt. 11, 29.* Take My yoke upon you, and learn from Me, for I am meek, and humble of heart: and you will find rest for your souls. Alleluia.

In Votive Masses after Septuagesima, the Alleluia and versicle are omitted and the following Tract is said:

Tract. *Ps. 102, 8-10.* Merciful and gracious is the Lord, slow to anger and abounding in kindness. ℣. He will not always chide, nor does He keep His wrath forever. ℣. Not according to our sins does He deal with us, nor does He requite us according to our crimes.

During Paschaltime, the Gradual and the Tract are omitted and the following Alleluia is said:

Alleluia, alleluia. ℣. *Matt. 11, 28.* Take My yoke upon you, and learn from Me, for I am meek, and humble of heart: and you will find rest for your souls. Alleluia. ℣. *Matt. 11, 29.* Come to Me, all you who labor and are burdened, and I will give you rest. Alleluia.

● *Prayer: Cleanse My Heart, page* 31.

Gospel. *John 19, 31-37.* At that time, the Jews, since it was the Preparation Day, in order that the bodies might not remain upon the Cross on the Sabbath (for that Sabbath was a solemn day), besought Pilate that their legs might be broken, and that they might be taken away. The soldiers therefore came and broke the legs of the first, and of the other, who had been crucified with Him. But when they came to Jesus, and saw that He was already dead, they did not break His legs; but one of the soldiers opened His side with a lance, and immediately there came out blood and water. And he who saw it has borne witness, and his witness is true; and he knows that he tells the truth, that you also may believe. For these things came to pass that the Scripture might be fulfilled, "Not a bone of Him shall you break." And again another Scripture says, "They shall look upon Him Whom they have pierced." S. Praise be to You, O Christ.

- Creed, page 33.

Offertory. *Ps. 68, 21.* My heart expected reproach and misery; I looked for sympathy, but there was none; for comforters, and I found none.

In Votive Masses during Paschaltime, the Offertory is as follows:

Offertory. *Ps. 39, 7-9.* Holocausts or sin-offerings You sought not; then said I: "Behold I come; in the written scroll it is prescribed for Me; to do Your will, O My God, is My delight, and Your law is within My Heart." Alleluia.

- Offertory Prayers, page 35.

Secret. Regard, we beseech You, O Lord, the ineffable charity of the Heart of Your beloved Son, that what we offer may be an acceptable gift and an atonement for our sins. Through the same, etc. ↝

Preface of the Sacred Heart

P. World without end. *S.* Amen. *P.* The Lord be with you. *S.* And with your spirit. *P.* Lift up your hearts. *S.* We have lifted them up to the Lord. *P.* Let us give thanks to the Lord, our God. *S.* It is fitting and just.

It is fitting indeed and just, right and helpful to salvation, for us always and everywhere to give thanks to You, O Holy Lord, Father Almighty, Everlasting God, Who willed that Your Only-begotten Son should be pierced by the soldier's lance as He hung upon the Cross; that the Heart thus opened, the sanctuary of divine bounty, should pour out on us an abundance of mercy and grace, and as it never ceases to burn with love for us, it may be for the devout a haven of rest, and for the penitent an ever-open refuge of salvation. And therefore, with Angels and Archangels, with Thrones and Dominations, and with the whole host of the heavenly army, we sing a hymn to Your glory, saying again and again: Holy, Holy, Holy, Lord God of hosts. Heaven and earth are filled with Your glory. Hosanna in the highest. Blessed is He Who

THE SACRED HEART OF JESUS

HAIL MARY, FULL OF GRACE!

comes in the name of the Lord. Hosanna in the highest.

● *Canon, page 47.*

Communion. *John 19, 34.* One of the soldiers opened His side with a lance, and immediately there came out blood and water.

In Votive Masses during Paschaltime, the Communion is as follows:

Communion. *John 7, 37.* If anyone thirst, let him come to Me and drink, alleluia, alleluia.

P. The Lord be with you. *S.* And with your spirit. ⮑

Postcommunion. May Your holy mysteries, O Lord Jesus, impart to us a divine fervor, whereby, having known the sweetness of Your most tender Heart, we may learn to despise what is earthly and to love what is heavenly. Who live, etc. *S.* Amen.

● *Final Prayers, page 73.*

*"Rejoice with me because I have found
my sheep that was lost."*

THIRD SUNDAY AFTER
PENTECOST

GREEN VESTMENTS

THOUGHT FOR TODAY: The Catholic Church is
a hospice for souls that are spiritually ill. Some
people are scandalized because She is kind to
sinners and forgives them over and over again.
They forget that She obeys the merciful Heart
of the Physician of souls.

● *Beginning of Mass, page 19.*

Introit. *Ps. 24, 16. 18.* Look toward me,
and have pity on me, O Lord; for I am
alone and afflicted; put an end to my affliction and my suffering; and take away all
my sins, O my God. *Ps. 24, 1. 2.* To You, I
lift up my soul, O Lord; in You, O my God,
I trust; let me not be put to shame. ℣. Glory
be.

● *Kyrie and Gloria, page 27.*

Prayer. O God, the Protector of those who hope in You, without Whom nothing is strong, nothing holy: multiply upon us Your mercy, that with You as our ruler and guide, we may so pass through good things of this life as not to lose those which are eternal. Through our Lord, etc. S. Amen. ⤷

Epistle. *1 Pet. 5, 6-11.* Beloved: Humble yourselves under the mighty hand of God, that He may exalt you in the time of visitation; cast all your anxiety upon Him, because He cares for you. Be sober, be watchful! For your adversary the devil, as a roaring lion, goes about seeking someone to devour. Resist him, steadfast in the faith, knowing that the same suffering befalls your brethren all over the world. But the God of all grace, Who has called us unto His eternal glory in Christ Jesus, will Himself, after we have suffered a little while, perfect, strengthen and establish us. To Him is the glory and the dominion forever and ever. Amen. S. Thanks be to God. ⤷

Gradual. *Ps. 54, 23. 17. 19.* Cast your care upon the Lord, and He will support you. ℣. When I called upon the Lord, He heard my voice, from those who war against me.

Alleluia. alleluia. ℣. *Ps. 7, 12.* A just judge is God, strong and patient; is He angry every day? Alleluia.

● *Prayer: Cleanse My Heart, page* 31.

Gospel. *Luke 15, 1-10.* At that time, the publicans and sinners were drawing near to Jesus to listen to Him. And the Pharisees and the Scribes murmured, saying, "This man welcomes sinners and eats with them." But He spoke to them this parable, saying, "What man of you having a hundred sheep, and losing one of them, does not leave the ninety-nine in the desert, and go after that which is lost, until he finds it? And when he has found it, he lays it upon his shoulders rejoicing. And on coming home he calls together his friends and neighbors, saying to them, 'Rejoice with me, because I have found my sheep that was lost.' I say to you that, even so, there will be joy in heaven over one sinner who repents, more than over ninety-nine just who have no need of repentance. Or what woman, having ten drachmas, if she loses one drachma, does not light a lamp and sweep the house and search carefully until she finds it? And when she has found it, she calls together her friends and neighbors, saying, 'Rejoice with me, for I have found the drachma that I had lost.' Even so, I say to you, there will be joy among the angels of God over one sinner who repents." S. Praise be to You, O Christ.

● *Creed, page 33.*

Offertory. *Ps. 9, 11. 12. 13.* They trust in You who cherish Your Name, O Lord, for You forsake not those who seek You; sing praise to the Lord enthroned in Sion; for He has not forgotten the cry of the afflicted.

● *Offertory Prayers, page 35.*

Secret. Regard with favor, O Lord, the gifts of Your suppliant Church, and grant that they may avail to the salvation of the faithful who partake of them. Through our Lord, etc.

● *Preface, page 43.*

Communion. *Luke 15, 10.* I say to you: there is joy among the angels of God over one sinner who repents.

P. The Lord be with you. *S.* And with your spirit. ⤵

Postcommunion. May Your sacrament which we have received quicken us, O Lord; and having cleansed us from sin, prepare us for Your everlasting mercy. Through our Lord, etc. *S.* Amen.

● *Final Prayers, page 73.*

———◆———

"They enclosed a great number of fishes . . ."

FOURTH SUNDAY AFTER PENTECOST

GREEN VESTMENTS

THOUGHT FOR TODAY: Let us always work as Christians laboring in union with, and for, the honor of Christ. We must also be fishers of men, eager to draw them into the boat of Peter, the Catholic Church.

● *Beginning of Mass, page 19.*

Introit. *Ps. 26, 1. 2.* The Lord is my light and my salvation; whom should I fear? The Lord is my life's refuge; of whom should I be afraid? My foes and my enemies themselves stumble and fall. *Ps. 26, 3.* Though an army encamp against me; my heart will not fear. ℣. Glory be.

● *Kyrie and Gloria, page 27.*

Prayer. Grant, we beseech You, O Lord, that the course of the world may, by Your governance, be peaceably ordered for us, and that Your Church may rejoice in quiet devotion. Through our Lord, etc. S. Amen. ⤵

Epistle. *Rom. 8, 18-23.* Brethren: I reckon that the sufferings of the present time are not worthy to be compared with the glory to come that will be revealed in us. For the eager longing of creation awaits the revelation of the sons of God. For creation was made subject to vanity — not by its own will but by reason of Him Who made it subject — in hope, because creation itself also will be delivered from its slavery to corruption into the freedom of the glory of the sons of God. For we know that all creation groans and travails in pain until now. And not only it, but we ourselves also who have the first-fruits of the Spirit — we ourselves groan within ourselves, waiting for the adoption as sons of God, the redemption of our body, in Christ Jesus our Lord. S. Thanks be to God. ⤵

Gradual. *Ps. 78, 9. 10.* Pardon our sins, O Lord; why should the nations say, "Where is their God?" ℣. Help us, O God our Savior; for the glory of Your Name, O Lord, deliver us.

Alleluia, alleluia. ℣. *Ps. 9, 5. 10.* O God, seated on Your throne, judging justly: be a stronghold for the oppressed in times of distress. Alleluia.

● Prayer: Cleanse My Heart, page 31.

Gospel. *Luke 5, 1-11.* At that time, while the crowds were pressing upon Jesus to hear the word of God, He was standing by Lake Genesareth. And He saw two boats moored by the lake, but the fishermen had left them and were washing their nets. And getting into one of the boats, the one that was Simon's, He asked them to put out a little from the land. And sitting down, He began to teach the crowds from the boat. But when He had ceased speaking, He said to Simon, "Put out into the deep, and lower your nets for a catch." And Simon answered and said to Him, "Master, the whole night through we have toiled and have taken nothing; but at Your word I will lower the net." And when they had done so, they enclosed a great number of fishes, but their net was breaking. And they beckoned to their comrades in the other boat to come and help them. And they came and filled both the boats, so that they began to sink. But when Simon Peter saw this, he fell down at Jesus' knees, saying, "Depart from me, for I am a sinful man, O Lord." For he and all who were with him were amazed at the catch of fish they had made; and so were also James and John, the sons of Zebedee, who were partners with Simon. And Jesus said to Simon, "Do not be afraid; henceforth you shall catch men." And when they had brought their boats to land, they left all and followed Him. *S.* Praise be to You, O Christ.

● *Creed, page* 33.

Offertory. *Ps. 12, 4. 5.* Give light to my eyes, that I may not sleep in death; lest my enemy say, "I have overcome him."

● *Offertory Prayers, page* 35.

Secret. Be appeased, we pray, O Lord, by the acceptance of our offerings, and graciously compel our wills, even though rebellious, to turn to You. Through, etc.

● *Preface, page* 43.

Communion. *Ps. 17, 3.* O Lord, my rock, my fortress, my deliverer: my God, my rock of refuge!

P. The Lord be with you. *S.* And with your spirit. ↱

Postcommunion. May the mysteries which we have received purify us, we beseech You, O Lord, and by their power defend us. Through our Lord, etc. *S.* Amen.

● *Final Prayers, page* 73.

———◆———

"Go first to be reconciled with your brother . . . "

FIFTH SUNDAY AFTER PENTECOST

GREEN VESTMENTS

THOUGHT FOR TODAY: Purely external practices of devotion like those of the Pharisees have no value in God's eyes. We must first "hallow the Lord Christ in (our) hearts." From this inner grace and pure intention will spring patience and readiness to help and forgive even an offending neighbor.

● *Beginning of Mass, page 19.*

Introit. *Ps. 26, 7. 9.* Hear, O Lord, the sound of my call; be my helper; forsake me not; despise me not, O God my Savior. *Ps. 26, 1.* The Lord is my light and my salvation; whom should I fear? ℣. Glory be.

● *Kyrie and Gloria, page 27.*

Prayer. O God, You have prepared invisible good things for those who love You; pour into our hearts an ardent love of You, that loving You in all things, and above all things, we may obtain Your promises, which exceed all that we can desire. Through our Lord, etc. S. Amen. ↴

Epistle. *1 Pet. 3, 8-15.* Beloved: Be all like-minded in prayer, compassionate, lovers of the brethren, merciful, reserved, humble; not rendering evil for evil, or abuse for abuse, but contrariwise, blessing; for unto this were you called that you might inherit a blessing. For, "He who would love life, and see good days, let him refrain his tongue from evil, and his lips that they speak no deceit. Let him turn away from evil and do good, let him seek after peace and pursue it. For the eyes of the Lord are upon the just, and His ears unto their prayers; but the face of the Lord is against those who do evil." And who is there to harm you, if you are zealous for what is good? But even if you suffer anything for justice' sake, blessed are you. So have no fear of their fear and do not be troubled. But hallow the Lord Christ in your hearts. S. Thanks be to God. ↴

Gradual. *Ps. 83, 10. 9.* Behold, O God, our protector, and look on Your servants. ℣. O Lord God of hosts, hear the prayers of Your servants.

Alleluia, alleluia. ℣. *Ps. 20, 1.* O Lord, in Your strength the king is glad; in Your victory how greatly he rejoices. Alleluia.

● Prayer: Cleanse My Heart, page 31.

Gospel. *Matt. 5, 20-24.* At that time, Jesus said to His disciples: "Unless your justice exceeds that of the Scribes and Pharisees, you shall not enter the kingdom of heaven. You have heard that it was said to the ancients, 'You shall not kill'; and that whoever shall kill shall be liable to judgment. But I say to you that everyone who is angry with his brother shall be liable to judgment; and whoever says to his brother, 'Raca,' shall be liable to the Sanhedrin; and whoever says, 'You fool!' shall be liable to the fire of Gehenna. Therefore, if you are offering your gift at the altar, and there remember that your brother has anything against you, leave your gift before the altar and go first to be reconciled to your brother, and then come and offer your gift." *S.* Praise be to You, O Christ.

● Creed, page 33.

Offertory. *Ps. 15, 7. 8.* I bless the Lord, Who counsels me; I set God ever before me; with Him at my right hand I shall not be disturbed.

● *Offertory Prayers, page* 35.

Secret. Be propitious to our supplications, O Lord, and graciously receive these oblations of Your servants and handmaids, that what each one offered to the glory of Your name, may profit all to salvation. Through our Lord, etc.

● *Preface, page* 43.

Communion. *Ps. 26, 4.* One thing I ask of the Lord; this I seek: to dwell in the house of the Lord all the days of my life.

P. The Lord be with you. *S.* And with your spirit. ↰

Postcommunion. Grant, we beseech You, O Lord, that we, whom You have fed with Your heavenly Gift, may both be cleansed from our hidden sins, and delivered from the snares of our enemies. Through our Lord, etc. *S.* Amen.

● *Final Prayers, page* 73.

"Taking the seven loaves, He . . . gave them to His disciples . . ."

SIXTH SUNDAY AFTER PENTECOST

GREEN VESTMENTS

THOUGHT FOR TODAY: Easter time has passed but its spirit should never pass. Christ died once and now lives His glorious unending life. Having risen from sin let us strive to live in union with Christ the new life of holiness, sustaining ourselves by the Holy Eucharist prefigured in the miracle of the multiplication of the loaves.

● *Beginning of Mass, page 19.*

Introit. *Ps. 27, 8. 9.* The Lord is the strength of His people, the saving refuge of His anointed; save Your people, O Lord, and bless Your inheritance; and rule them forever. *Ps. 27, 1.* To You, O Lord, I call; O my God, be not deaf to me; lest, if You heed me not, I become one of those going down into the pit. ℣. Glory be.

● *Kyrie and Gloria, page 27.*

Prayer. O God of hosts, to Whom belongs all that is perfect, engraft in our hearts the love of Your Name, and grant us an increase of religion; that what in us is good, You may nourish, and, in Your lovingkindness, preserve in us what You have nourished. Through our Lord, etc. S. Amen. ➔

Epistle. *Rom. 6, 3-11.* Brethren: All we who have been baptized into Christ Jesus have been baptized into His death. For we were buried with Him by means of Baptism into death, in order that, just as Christ has risen from the dead through the glory of the Father, so we also may walk in newness of life. For if we have been united with Him in the likeness of His death, we shall be so in the likeness of His resurrection also. For we know that our old self has been crucified with Him, in order that the body of sin may be destroyed, that we may no longer be slaves to sin; for he who is dead is acquitted of sin. But if we have died with Christ, we believe that we shall also live together with Christ; for we know that Christ, having risen from the dead, dies now no more, death shall no longer have dominion over Him. For the death that He died, He died to sin once for all, but the life that He lives, He lives unto God. Thus do you consider yourselves also as dead to sin, but alive to God in Christ Jesus our Lord. S. Thanks be to God. ⤶

Gradual. *Ps. 89, 13. 1.* Return, O Lord! How long? Have pity on Your servants. ℣. Lord, You have been our refuge through all generations.

Alleluia, alleluia. ℣. *Ps. 30, 2. 3.* In You, O Lord, I take refuge; let me never be put to shame; in Your justice rescue me and release me; incline Your ear to me, make haste to deliver me. Alleluia.

● *Prayer: Cleanse My Heart, page* 31.

Gospel. *Mark 8, 1-9.* At that time, when there was a great crowd with Jesus, and they had nothing to eat, He called His disciples together and said to them, "I have compassion on the crowd, for behold, they have now been with Me three days, and have nothing to eat; and if I send them away to their homes fasting, they will faint on the way, for some of them have come from a distance." And His disciples answered Him, "How will anyone be able to satisfy these with bread, here in a desert?" And He asked them, "How many loaves have you?" And they said, "Seven." And He bade the crowd recline on the ground. Then taking the seven loaves, He gave thanks, broke them and gave them to His disciples to distribute; and they set them before the crowd. And they had a few little fishes; and He blessed them, and ordered them to be distributed. And they ate and were satisfied; and they took up what was left of the fragments, seven baskets. Now those who had eaten were about four thousand. And He dismissed them. S. Praise be to You, O Christ.

● Creed, page 33.

Offertory. *Ps. 16, 5. 6. 7.* Make my steps steadfast in Your paths, that my feet may not falter; incline Your ear to me; hear my word; show Your wondrous kindness, O Lord, Savior of those who trust in You.

● Offertory Prayers, page 35.

Secret. Be propitious, O Lord, to our supplications, and graciously receive these oblations of Your people; and that the prayer of none be in vain nor the petition of any without effect, grant that what we ask with faith, we may efficaciously obtain. Through our Lord, etc.

● Preface, page 43.

Communion. *Ps. 26, 6.* I will go round and offer in His tent sacrifices with shouts of gladness; I will sing and chant praise to the Lord.

P. The Lord be with you. *S.* And with your spirit. ↲

Postcommunion. We have been filled with Your gifts, O Lord, and beseech You to grant that we may both be cleansed by their virtue, and strengthened by their help. Through our Lord, etc. *S.* Amen.

● *Final Prayers, page 73.*

"By their fruits you will know them."

SEVENTH SUNDAY AFTER PENTECOST

GREEN VESTMENTS

THOUGHT FOR TODAY: "The grace of God is life everlasting." As good trees we must bring forth good fruit. We hear enough pious words, but we do not see enough good deeds. Thus, we pray, "O Lord, lead us to do that which is right before You."

● *Beginning of Mass, page 19.*

Introit. *Ps. 46, 2.* All you peoples, clap your hands, shout to God with cries of gladness. *Ps. 46, 3.* For the Lord, the Most High, the awesome, is the great King over all the earth. ℣. Glory be.

● *Kyrie and Gloria, page 27.*

Prayer. O God, Whose providence never fails in what it ordains, we humbly beseech You to put away from us all things harmful, and to give all things profitable to us. Through our Lord, etc. S. Amen. ↱

Epistle. *Rom. 6, 19-23.* Brethren: I speak in a human way because of the weakness of your flesh; for as you yielded your members as slaves of uncleanness and iniquity unto iniquity, so now yield your members as slaves of justice unto sanctification. For when you were the slaves of sin, you were free as regards justice. But what fruit had you then from those things of which you are now ashamed? For the end of these things is death. But now set free from sin and become slaves to God, you have your fruit unto sanctification, and as your end, life everlasting. For the wages of sin is death, but the gift of God is life everlasting in Christ Jesus our Lord. S. Thanks be to God. ↱

Gradual. *Ps. 33, 12. 6.* Come, children, hear me; I will teach you the fear of the Lord. ℣. Look to Him that you may be radiant with joy, and your faces may not blush with shame.

Alleluia, alleluia. ℣ *Ps. 46, 2.* All you peoples, clap your hands, shout to God with cries of gladness. Alleluia.

● *Prayer: Cleanse My Heart, page 31.*

Gospel. *Matt. 7, 15-21.* At that time, Jesus said to His disciples: "Beware of false prophets, who come to you in sheep's clothing, but inwardly are ravenous wolves. By their fruits you will know them. Do men gather grapes from thorns, or figs from thistles? Even so, every good tree bears good fruit, but the bad tree bears bad fruit. A good tree cannot bear bad fruit, nor can a bad tree bear good fruit. Every tree that does not bear good fruit is cut down and thrown into the fire. Therefore, by their fruits you will know them. Not everyone who says to Me, 'Lord, Lord,' shall enter the kingdom of heaven; but he who does the will of My Father in heaven shall enter the kingdom of heaven." S. Praise be to You, O Christ.

- *Creed, page 33.*

Offertory. *Dan. 3, 40.* As in holocausts of rams and bullocks, and as in thousands of fat lambs, so let our sacrifice be made in Your sight this day, that it may please You: for there is no confusion to those who trust in You, O Lord.

- *Offertory Prayers, page 35.*

Secret. O God, Who, in the one perfect sacrifice, have ratified the variety of victims prescribed by the law, receive this sacrifice from Your devoted servants, and sanctify it with a blessing like that wherewith You blessed the gifts of Abel: that what is offered individually to the honor of Your Majesty, may profit for the salvation of all. Through our Lord, etc.

● *Preface, page 43.*

Communion. *Ps. 30, 3.* Incline Your ear to me, make haste to deliver me.

P. The Lord be with you. *S.* And with your spirit. ↰

Postcommunion. May Your health-giving operation, O Lord, both mercifully free us from our evil inclinations, and lead us to do that which is right before You. Through our Lord, etc. *S.* Amen.

● *Final Prayers, page 73.*

"Make an accounting of your stewardship . . ."

EIGHTH SUNDAY AFTER PENTECOST

GREEN VESTMENTS

THOUGHT FOR TODAY: The parable of the steward shows how "the children of the light" neglected so many opportunities to gain a happy eternity by not participating in the Holy Sacrifice of the Mass and letting other means of sanctification go by unused.

● *Beginning of Mass, page 19.*

Introit. *Ps. 47, 10. 11.* O God, we ponder Your kindness within Your temple; as Your Name, O God, so also Your praise reaches to the ends of the earth; of justice Your right hand is full. *Ps. 47, 2.* Great is the Lord, and wholly to be praised; in the city of our God, His holy mountain. ℣. Glory be.

● *Kyrie and Gloria, page 27.*

Prayer. Graciously impart to us, we beseech You, O Lord, the spirit at all times to think and to do the things that are right; that we, who cannot subsist without You, may be enabled to live according to Your will. Through our Lord, etc. S. Amen. ➤

Epistle. *Rom. 8, 12-17.* Brethren: We are debtors, not to the flesh, that we should live according to the flesh, for if you live according to the flesh you will die; but if by the spirit you put to death the deeds of the flesh, you will live. For whoever are led by the Spirit of God, they are the sons of God. Now you have not received a spirit of bondage so as to be again in fear, but you have received a spirit of adoption as sons, by virtue of which we cry, "Abba! Father!" The Spirit Himself gives testimony to our spirit that we are sons of God. But if we are sons, we are heirs also: heirs indeed of God and joint heirs with Christ. S. Thanks be to God. ➤

Gradual. *Ps. 30, 3.* Be my rock of refuge, O God, a stronghold to give me safety. ℣. *Ps. 70, 1.* In You, O God, I take refuge; O Lord, let me never be put to shame.

Alleluia, alleluia. ℣. *Ps. 47, 2.* Great is the Lord, and wholly to be praised; in the city of our God, His holy mountain. Alleluia.

● *Prayer: Cleanse My Heart, page* 31.

Gospel. *Luke 16, 1-9.* At that time, Jesus spoke to His disciples this parable: "There was a certain rich man who had a steward, who was reported to him as squandering his possessions. And he called him and said to him, 'What is this that I hear of you? Make an accounting of your stewardship, for you can be steward no longer.' And the steward said within himself, 'What shall I do, seeing that my master is taking away the stewardship from me? To dig I am not able; to beg I am ashamed. I know what I shall do, that when I am removed from my stewardship they may receive me into their houses.' And he summoned each of his master's debtors and said to the first, 'How much do you owe my master?' And he said, 'A hundred jars of oil.' He said to him, 'Take your bond and sit down at once and write fifty.' Then he said to another, 'How much do you owe?' He said, 'A hundred kors of wheat.' He said to him, 'Take your bond and write eighty.' And the master commended the unjust steward, in that he had acted prudently; for the children of this world, in relation to their own generation, are more prudent than the children of the light. And I say to you, make friends for yourselves with the mammon of wickedness, so that when you fail they may re-

ceive you into the everlasting dwellings." *S.*
Praise be to You, O Christ.

● *Creed, page 33.*

Offertory. *Ps. 17, 28. 32.* Lowly people
You save, O Lord, but haughty eyes You
bring low; for who is God except You, O
Lord?

● *Offertory Prayers, page 35.*

Secret. Accept, we beseech You, O Lord,
the gifts which, of Your bounty, we bring
to You: that, by the working of the power
of Your grace, these most sacred mysteries
may both sanctify us during the course of
this life, and bring us to everlasting joys.
Through our Lord, etc.

● *Preface, page 43.*

Communion. *Ps. 33, 9.* Taste and see
how good the Lord is; happy the man who
takes refuge in Him.

P. The Lord be with you. *S.* And with
your spirit. ↰

Postcommunion. May this heavenly mystery, O Lord, renew us in mind and body,
that we may feel the effect of what we celebrate. Through our Lord, etc. *S.* Amen.

● *Final Prayers, page 73.*

———————◇———————

"My house is a house of prayer, but you have made it a den of thieves."

NINTH SUNDAY AFTER PENTECOST

GREEN VESTMENTS

THOUGHT FOR TODAY: The Holy Scriptures prove that God rewards and punishes even here on earth. Jerusalem rejected the Savior and it was destroyed. No temptation is so strong that we cannot conquer it with the grace of God, "Who will not permit you to be tempted beyond your strength."

● *Beginning of Mass, page* 19.

Introit. *Ps. 53, 6. 7.* Behold, God is my helper; the Lord sustains my life. Turn back the evil upon my foes; in Your faithfulness destroy them, O Lord, my protector. *Ps. 53, 3.* O God, by Your Name save me, and by Your might deliver me. ℣. Glory be.

● *Kyrie and Gloria, page* 27.

Prayer. Let the ears of Your mercy, O Lord, be open to the prayers of Your suppliants, and, that You may grant them what they desire, make them ask the things that are pleasing to You. Through our Lord, etc. S. Amen. ↰

Epistle. *1 Cor. 10, 6-13.* Brethren: We should not lust after evil things even as they lusted. And do not become idolaters, even as some of them were, as it is written, "The people sat down to eat and drink, and rose up to play." Neither let us commit fornication, even as some of them committed fornication, and there fell in one day twenty-three thousand. Neither let us tempt Christ, as some of them tempted, and perished by the serpents. Neither murmur, as some of them murmured, and perished at the hands of the destroyer. Now all these things happened to them as a type, and they were written for our correction, upon whom the final age of the world has come. Therefore let him who thinks he stands take heed lest he fall. May no temptation take hold of you but such as man is equal to. God is faithful and will not permit you to be tempted beyond your strength, but with the temptation will also give you a way out that you may be able to bear it. S. Thanks be to God. ⮒

Gradual. *Ps. 8, 2.* O Lord our Lord, how glorious is Your Name over all the earth! ℣. You have elevated Your Majesty above the heavens.

Alleluia, alleluia. ℣. *Ps. 58, 2.* Rescue me from my enemies, O my God; from my adversaries defend me. Alleluia.

● *Prayer: Cleanse My Heart, page* 31.

Gospel. *Luke 19, 41-47.* At that time, when Jesus drew near to Jerusalem and saw the city, He wept over it, saying, "If you had known, in this your day, even you, the things that are for your peace! But now they are hidden from your eyes. For days will come upon you when your enemies will throw up a rampart about you, and surround you and shut you in on every side, and will dash you to the ground and your children within you, and will not leave in you one stone upon another, because you have not known the time of your visitation." And He entered the temple, and began to cast out those who were selling and buying in it, saying to them, "It is written, 'My house is a house of prayer,' but you have made it a den of thieves." And He was teaching daily in the temple. *S.* Praise be to You, O Christ.

● Creed, page 33.

Offertory. *Ps. 18, 9. 10. 11. 12.* The precepts of the Lord are right, rejoicing the heart, and His ordinances sweeter than syrup or honey from the comb; therefore Your servant is careful of them.

● Offertory Prayers, page 35.

Secret. Grant us, we beseech You, O Lord, worthily to frequent these mysteries: since as often as the remembrance of this Victim is celebrated, so often is the work of our Redemption carried on. Through our Lord, etc.

● Preface, page 43.

Communion. *John 6, 57.* "He who eats My Flesh, and drinks My Blood, abides in Me, and I in him," says the Lord.

P. The Lord be with you. *S.* And with your spirit. ↱

Postcommunion. May the communion of Your sacrament, we beseech You, O Lord, both purify us, and grant us unity in Your service. Through our Lord, etc. *S.* Amen.

● Final Prayers, page 73.

———◆———

"O God, I thank You that I am not like the rest of men . . . or even like this publican."

TENTH SUNDAY AFTER PENTECOST

GREEN VESTMENTS

THOUGHT FOR TODAY: Humility is the foundation of all Christian virtues. God reveals Himself to the humble and despises arrogance and pride. We may be aware of our capabilities and accomplishments, but we must remember that "all these things are the work of one and the same Spirit"; therefore, give glory to God.

● *Beginning of Mass, page 19.*

Introit. *Ps. 54, 17. 18. 20. 23.* When I called upon the Lord, He heard my voice, from those who war against me; and He humbled them, Who is before all ages, and remains forever; cast your care upon the Lord, and He will support you. *Ps. 54, 2.* Hearken, O God, to my prayer; turn not away from my pleading; give heed to me, and answer me. ℣. Glory be.

● *Kyrie and Gloria, page 27.*

Prayer. O God, You manifest Your almighty power most of all in sparing and showing mercy; multiply upon us Your mercy, that we, running to Your promises, may be made partakers of Your heavenly goods. Through our Lord, etc. *S.* Amen. ↴

Epistle. *1 Cor. 12, 2-11.* Brethren: You know that when you were Gentiles, you went to dumb idols according as you were led. Wherefore I give you to understand that no one speaking in the Spirit of God says "Anathema" to Jesus. And no one can say "Jesus is Lord," except in the Holy Spirit. Now there are varieties of gifts, but the same Spirit; and there are varieties of ministries, but the same Lord; and there are varieties of workings, but the same God, Who works all things in all. Now the manifestation of the Spirit is given to everyone for profit. To one through the Spirit is given the utterance of wisdom; and to another the utterance of knowledge, according to the same Spirit; to another faith, in the same Spirit; to another the gift of healing, in the one Spirit; to another the working of miracles; to another prophecy; to another the distinguishing of spirits; to another various kinds of tongues; to another interpretation of tongues. But all these things are the work of one and the same Spirit, Who

THE GOOD SHEPHERD

THE KEYS TO THE KINGDOM OF HEAVEN

allots to everyone according as He will. S.
Thanks be to God. ↰

Gradual. *Ps. 16, 8. 2.* Keep me, O Lord,
as the apple of Your eye: hide me in the
shadow of Your wings. ℣. From You let
judgment come; Your eyes behold what is
right.

Alleluia, alleluia. ℣. *Ps. 64, 2.* To You,
we owe our hymn of praise, O God, in Sion;
to You must vows be fulfilled in Jerusalem.
Alleluia.

● *Prayer: Cleanse My Heart, page* 31.

Gospel. *Luke 18, 9-14.* At that time,
Jesus spoke this parable to some who
trusted in themselves as being just and despised others. "Two men went up to the
temple to pray, the one a Pharisee and the
other a publican. The Pharisee stood and
began to pray thus within himself: 'O God,
I thank You that I am not like the rest of
men, robbers, dishonest, adulterers, or even
like this publican. I fast twice a week; I
pay tithes of all that I possess.' But the
publican, standing afar off, would not so
much as lift up his eyes to heaven, but kept
striking his breast, saying, 'O God, be merciful to me the sinner!' I tell you, this man
went back to his home justified rather than
the other; for everyone who exalts himself

shall be humbled, and he who humbles himself shall be exalted." *S.* Praise be to You, O Christ.

● Creed, page 33.

Offertory. *Ps. 24, 1-3.* To You I lift up my soul, O Lord; in You, O my God, I trust; let me not be put to shame, let not my enemies exult over me. No one who waits for You shall be put to shame.

● Offertory Prayers, page 35.

Secret. May this sacrifice become dedicated to You, O Lord: a sacrifice which, it has pleased You, should in such a manner be offered to the honor of Your Name, and at the same time become our remedy. Through our Lord, etc.

● Preface, page 43.

Communion. *Ps. 50, 21.* You shall be pleased with due sacrifices, burnt offerings and holocausts on Your altar, O Lord.

P. The Lord be with you. *S.* And with your spirit. ↱

Postcommunion. We beseech You, O Lord, our God, that in Your goodness You would not deprive of Your aid those whom You do not cease to refresh with Your divine sacraments. Through our Lord, etc. *S.* Amen.

● Final Prayers, page 73.

◆

"Ephpheta," that is, "Be opened."

ELEVENTH SUNDAY AFTER PENTECOST

GREEN VESTMENTS

THOUGHT FOR TODAY: If we would not take so many things as a matter of course, we would marvel at the beauty of our Religion, and we could speak intelligently about our religious belief to others.

● *Beginning of Mass, page 19.*

Introit. *Ps. 67, 6. 7. 36.* God is in His holy dwelling, God Who makes men of one mind to dwell in a house; He shall give power and strength to His people. *Ps. 67, 2.* God arises; His enemies are scattered, and those who hate Him flee before Him. ℣. Glory be.

● *Kyrie and Gloria, page 27.*

Prayer. Almighty and everlasting God, in the abundance of Your loving-kindness, You exceed both the merits and the desires of Your supplicants; pour forth Your mercy upon us, that You may forgive what our conscience fears and grant what we do not presume to ask. Through our Lord, etc. S. Amen. ↰

Epistle. *1 Cor. 15, 1-10.* Brethren: I recall to your minds the gospel that I preached to you, which also you received, wherein also you stand, through which also you are being saved, if you hold it fast, as I preached it to you — unless you have believed to no purpose. For I delivered to you first of all, what I also received, that Christ died for our sins according to the Scriptures, and that He was buried, and that He rose again the third day, according to the Scriptures, and that He appeared to Cephas, and after that to the Eleven. Then He was seen by more than five hundred brethren at one time, many of whom are with us still, but some have fallen asleep. After that He was seen by James, then by all the apostles. And last of all, as by one born out of due time, He was seen also by me. For I am the least of the apostles, and am not worthy to be called an apostle, because I persecuted the Church of God. But by the grace of God I am what I am, and His grace in me has not been fruitless. S. Thanks be to God. ↰

Gradual. *Ps. 27, 7. 1.* In God my heart trusts, and I find help; then my heart exults, and with my song I give Him thanks. ℣. To You, O Lord, I call; O my God, be not deaf to me; depart not from me.

Alleluia, alleluia. ℣. *Ps. 80, 2. 3.* Sing joyfully to God our strength; acclaim the God of Jacob; take up a pleasant psalm with the harp. Alleluia.

● *Prayer: Cleanse My Heart, page* 31.

Gospel. *Mark 7, 31-37.* At that time, Jesus departing from the district of Tyre came by way of Sidon to the sea of Galilee, through the midst of the district of Decapolis. And they brought to Him one deaf and dumb, and entreated Him to lay His hand upon him. And taking him aside from the crowd, He put His fingers into the man's ears, and spitting, He touched his tongue. And looking up to heaven, He sighed, and said to him, "Ephpheta," that is, "Be opened." And his ears were at once opened, and the bond of his tongue was loosed, and he began to speak correctly. And He charged them to tell no one. But the more He charged them, so much the more did they continue to publish it. And so much the more did they wonder, saying, "He has done all things well. He has made both the deaf

to hear and the dumb to speak." S. Praise
be to You, O Christ.

● Creed, page 33.

Offertory. *Ps. 29, 2-3.* I will extol You,
O Lord, for You drew me clear and did not
let my enemies rejoice over me; O Lord, I
cried out to You and You healed me.

● Offertory Prayers, page 35.

Secret. Mercifully regard our service, we
beseech You, O Lord, that the gift which we
offer may be acceptable to You, and be the
support of our frailty. Through our Lord, etc.

● Preface, page 43.

Communion. *Prov. 3, 9-10.* Honor the
Lord with your wealth, with first fruits of
all your produce; then will your barns be
filled with grain, with new wine your vats
will overflow.

P. The Lord be with you. *S.* And with
your spirit. ⮰

Postcommunion. By the reception of
Your sacrament, we beseech You, O Lord,
may we feel a support of mind and body,
that, saved in both, we may glory in the
fullness of the heavenly remedy. Through
our Lord, etc. *S.* Amen.

● Final Prayers, page 73.

———◆———

The Good Samaritan "bound up his wounds, pouring on oil and wine."

TWELFTH SUNDAY AFTER PENTECOST

GREEN VESTMENTS

THOUGHT FOR TODAY: "Blessed are the eyes that see (the things which) you see." Assisting at Mass, we see the re-presentation and continuation of the Sacrifice on Calvary. We see with the eyes of faith, Christ present in the Consecrated Host. Personally and actively to participate in the Mass makes us love God, and increases in us a spirit of kindness in dealing with others.

● *Beginning of Mass, page 19.*

Introit. *Ps. 69, 2-3.* Deign, O God, to rescue me; O Lord, make haste to help me; let them be put to shame and confounded who seek my life. *Ps. 69, 4.* Let them be turned back in disgrace who desire my ruin. ℣. Glory be.

● *Kyrie and Gloria, page 27.*

Prayer. Almighty and merciful God, of Whose gift it comes that Your faithful people do You worthy and laudable service, grant, we beseech You, that we may run without stumbling to the attainment of Your promises. Through our Lord, etc. S. Amen. ➔

Epistle. *2 Cor. 3, 4-9.* Brethren: Such is the assurance I have through Christ towards God. Not that we are sufficient of ourselves to think anything, as from ourselves, but our sufficiency is from God. He also it is Who has made us fit ministers of the new covenant, not of the letter but of the spirit; for the letter kills, but the spirit gives life. Now if the ministration of death, which was engraved in letters upon stones, was inaugurated in such glory that the children of Israel could not look steadfastly upon the face of Moses on account of the transient glory that shone upon it, shall not the ministration of the spirit be still more glorious? For if there is glory in the ministration that condemned, much more does the ministration that justifies abound in glory. S. Thanks be to God. ➔

Gradual. *Ps. 33, 2. 3.* I will bless the Lord at all times; His praise shall be ever in my mouth. ℣. Let my soul glory in the Lord; the lowly will hear me and be glad.

Alleluia, alleluia. ℣. *Ps. 87, 2.* O Lord, the God of my salvation, by day I cry out, at night I clamor in Your presence. Alleluia.

● *Prayer: Cleanse My Heart, page 31.*

Gospel. *Luke 10, 23-37.* At that time, Jesus said to His disciples: "Blessed are the eyes that see what you see! For I say to you, many prophets and kings have desired to see what you see, and they have not seen it; and to hear what you hear, and they have not heard it." And behold, a certain lawyer got up to test Him, saying, "Master, what must I do to gain eternal life?" But He said to him, "What is written in the Law? How do you read?" He answered and said, "You shall love the Lord your God with your whole heart, and with your whole soul, and with your whole strength, and with your whole mind; and your neighbor as yourself." And He said to him, "You have answered rightly; do this and you shall live." But he, wishing to justify himself, said to Jesus, "And who is my neighbor?" Jesus answered and said, "A certain man was going down from Jerusalem to Jericho, and he fell in with robbers, who after both stripping him and beating him went their way, leaving him half-dead. But, as it happened, a certain priest was going down the same way; and when he saw him, he passed by. And likewise a Levite also, when he was near the place and saw him, passed by. But a certain Samaritan as he journeyed came upon him, and seeing him, was moved with compassion. And he went up to him and bound up his wounds, pouring on oil and wine. And setting him on his own beast, he brought him to an inn and took care of him. And the next day he took out two denarii and gave them to the innkeeper and said, 'Take care of him; and whatever more you spend, I, on my way back, will repay you.' Which of these three, in your opinion, proved himself neighbor to him who fell among the robbers?" And he said, "He who took pity on him." And Jesus said to him, "Go and do you also in like manner." *S.* Praise be to You, O Christ.

● *Creed, page 33.*

Offertory. *Ex. 32, 11. 13. 14.* Moses prayed in the sight of the Lord his God, and said, "Why, O Lord, is Your indignation enkindled against Your people? Let the anger of Your mind cease; remember Abraham, Isaac, and Jacob, to whom You swore to give a land flowing with milk and honey." And the Lord was appeased from doing the evil which He had spoken of doing against His people.

● *Offertory Prayers, page 35.*

Secret. Mercifully look down, we beseech You, O Lord, upon the sacrifices which we present on Your sacred altar; that while procuring pardon for us, they may render honor to Your Name. Through our Lord, etc.

● *Preface, page 43.*

Communion. *Ps. 103, 13. 14. 15.* The earth is replete with the fruit of Your works, O Lord; You produce bread from the earth, and wine to gladden men's hearts, so that their faces gleam with oil, and bread fortifies the hearts of men.

P. The Lord be with you. *S.* And with your spirit. ↴

Postcommunion. May the holy participation of this mystery give life to us, we beseech You, O Lord, and afford us both expiation and protection. Through our Lord, etc. *S.* Amen.

● *Final Prayers, page 73.*

"Arise . . . for your faith has saved you."

THIRTEENTH SUNDAY AFTER PENTECOST

GREEN VESTMENTS

THOUGHT FOR TODAY: Ten lepers "were made clean." Only one returned to give thanks and glory to God. We send many petitions to heaven, but we often forget our prayers of thanksgiving. A grateful soul may always hope for more and greater blessings.

● *Beginning of Mass, page 19.*

Introit. *Ps. 73, 20. 19. 23.* Look to Your covenant, O Lord, forsake not forever the lives of Your afflicted ones; arise, O Lord; defend Your cause; be not unmindful of the voices of those who ask You. *Ps. 73, 1.* Why, O God, have You cast us off forever? Why does Your anger smolder against the sheep of Your pasture? ℣. Glory be.

● *Kyrie and Gloria, page 27.*

Prayer. Almighty and everlasting God, give us an increase of Faith, Hope and Charity; and that we may deserve to obtain that which You promise, make us love that which You command. Through our Lord, etc. S. Amen. ⤵

Epistle. *Gal. 3, 16-22.* Brethren: The promises were made to Abraham and to his offspring. He does not say, "And to his offsprings," as of many; but as of one, "And to your offspring," Who is Christ. Now I mean this: The Law which was made four hundred and thirty years later does not annul the covenant which was ratified by God, so as to make the promise void. For if the right to inherit be from the Law, it is no longer from a promise. But God gave it to Abraham by promise. What then was the Law? It was enacted on account of transgressions, being delivered by angels through a mediator, until the offspring should come to whom the promise was made. Now there is no intermediary where there is only one; but God is one. Is the Law then contrary to the promises of God? By no means. For if a law had been given that could give life, justice would truly be from the Law. But the Scripture shut up all things under sin, that by the faith of Jesus Christ the promise might be given to those who believe. S. Thanks be to God. ⮧

Gradual. *Ps. 73, 20. 19. 22.* Look to Your covenant, O Lord, be not forever unmindful of the lives of Your afflicted ones. ℣. Arise, O Lord; defend Your cause; remember the reproach of Your servants.

Alleluia, alleluia. ℣. *Ps. 89, 1.* Lord, You have been our refuge through all generations. Alleluia.

● *Prayer: Cleanse My Heart, page* 31.

Gospel. *Luke 17, 11-19.* At that time, as Jesus was going to Jerusalem, He was passing between Samaria and Galilee. And as He was entering a certain village, there met Him ten lepers, who stood afar off and lifted up their voice, crying, "Jesus, Master, have pity on us." And when He saw them He said, "Go, show yourselves to the priests." And it came to pass as they were on their way, that they were made clean. But one of them, seeing that he was made clean, returned, with a loud voice glorifying God, and he fell on his face at His feet, giving thanks; and he was a Samaritan. But Jesus answered and said, "Were not the ten made clean? But where are the nine? Has no one been found to return and give glory to God except this foreigner?" And He said to him, "Arise, go your way, for your faith has saved you." *S.* Praise be to You, O Christ.

● Creed, page 33.

Offertory. *Ps. 30, 15. 16.* My trust is in You, O Lord; I say, "You are my God." In Your hands is my destiny.

● Offertory Prayers, page 35.

Secret. Be merciful, O Lord, to Your people, and favorable to their offerings, that, appeased by this oblation, You may bestow upon us pardon, and grant what we ask. Through our Lord, etc.

● Preface, page 43.

Communion. *Wis. 16, 20.* You have given us, O Lord, bread from heaven, endowed with all delights and the sweetness of every taste.

P. The Lord be with you. *S.* And with your spirit. ↰

Postcommunion. We who have partaken of Your heavenly sacraments beseech You, O Lord, that we may profit to the increase of everlasting redemption. Through our Lord, etc. *S.* Amen.

● Final Prayers, page 73.

"Consider how the lilies of the field grow."

FOURTEENTH SUNDAY AFTER PENTECOST

GREEN VESTMENTS

THOUGHT FOR TODAY: We "of little faith" attend with such anxiety to our temporal affairs that we neglect our religious duties. If we seek the supernatural first, we may confidently rely on God's help in our daily affairs.

● *Beginning of Mass, page* 19.

Introit. *Ps. 83, 10. 11.* Behold, O God, our Protector, and look upon the face of Your Anointed. Better is one day in Your courts than a thousand elsewhere. *Ps. 83, 2. 3.* How lovely is Your dwelling place, O Lord of hosts! my soul yearns and pines for the courts of the Lord. ℣. Glory be.

● *Kyrie and Gloria, page* 27.

Prayer. Protect, we beseech You, O Lord, Your Church with Your perpetual mercy, and because without You human frailty goes astray, may we be ever withheld by Your grace from what is hurtful, and directed to what is profitable. Through our Lord, etc. *S.* Amen. ⤸

Epistle. *Gal 5, 16-24.* Brethren: Walk in the Spirit, and you will not fulfill the lusts of the flesh. For the flesh lusts against the spirit, and the spirit against the flesh; for these are opposed to each other, so that you do not do what you would. But if you are led by the Spirit, you are not under the Law. Now the works of the flesh are manifest, which are immorality, uncleanness, licentiousness, idolatry, witchcrafts, enmities, contentions, jealousies, anger, quarrels, factions, parties, envies, murders, drunkenness, carousings, and suchlike. And concerning these I warn you, as I have warned you, that they who do such things, will not attain the kingdom of God. But the fruit of the Spirit is: charity, joy, peace, patience, kindness, goodness, long-suffering, mildness, faith, modesty, continency, chastity. Against such things there is no law. And they who belong to Christ have crucified their flesh with its passions and desires. *S.* Thanks be to God. ⤸

Gradual. *Ps. 117, 8. 9.* It is better to take refuge in the Lord than to trust in man. ℣. It is better to take refuge in the Lord than to trust in princes.

Alleluia, alleluia. ℣. *Ps. 94, 1.* Come, let us sing joyfully to the Lord; let us acclaim the God of our salvation. Alleluia.

● *Prayer: Cleanse My Heart, page* 31.

Gospel. *Matt. 6, 24-33.* At that time, Jesus said to His disciples: "No man can serve two masters; for either he will hate the one and love the other, or else he will stand by the one and despise the other. You cannot serve God and mammon. Therefore I say to you, do not be anxious for your life, what you shall eat; nor yet for your body, what you shall put on. Is not the life a greater thing than the food, and the body than the clothing? Look at the birds of the air: they do not sow, or reap, or gather into barns; yet your heavenly Father feeds them. Are not you of much more value than they? But which of you by being anxious about it can add to his stature a single cubit? And as for clothing, why are you anxious? Consider how the lilies of the field grow; they neither toil nor spin, yet I say to you that not even Solomon in all his glory was arrayed like one of these. But if God so clothes the grass of the field, which flourishes today but tomorrow is thrown into the oven, how much more you, O you of little faith! Therefore do not be anxious, saying, 'What shall we eat?' or, 'What shall we drink?' or, 'What are we to put on?' (for after all these things the Gentiles seek); for your Father knows that you need all these things. But seek first the kingdom of God and His justice, and all these things shall be given you besides." S. Praise be to You, O Christ.

● Creed, page 33.

Offertory. *Ps. 33, 8. 9.* The Angel of the Lord encamps around those who fear Him, and delivers them. Taste and see how good the Lord is.

● Offertory Prayers, page 35.

Secret. Grant, we beseech You, O Lord, that this salutary offering may both cleanse us from our offenses, and propitiate Your power. Through our Lord, etc.

● Preface, page 43.

Communion. *Matt. 6, 33.* "Seek first the Kingdom of God; and all things shall be given you besides," says the Lord.

P. The Lord be with you. *S.* And with your spirit. ↴

Postcommunion. May Your sacraments, O God, ever purify and protect us; and lead us to the attainment of eternal salvation. Through our Lord, etc. S. Amen.

● Final Prayers, page 73.

———◆———

"And he who was dead sat up and began to speak."

FIFTEENTH SUNDAY AFTER PENTECOST

GREEN VESTMENTS

THOUGHT FOR TODAY: Physical and spiritual health are not always found together. If your conscience tells you that you are spiritually dead, do not delay to arise in sincere confession. Life is too short to be wasted. "What a man sows, that he will also reap," life or death.

● *Beginning of Mass, page 19.*

Introit. *Ps. 85, 1. 2. 3.* Incline Your ear, O Lord; answer me; save Your servant, O my God, who trusts in You. Have pity on me, O Lord, for to You I call all the day. *Ps. 85, 4.* Gladden the soul of Your servant, for to You, O Lord, I lift up my soul. ℣. Glory be.

● *Kyrie and Gloria, page 27.*

Prayer. May Your continual pity, O Lord, cleanse and defend Your Church; and because without You she cannot endure in safety, may she ever be governed by Your bounty. Through our Lord, etc. S. Amen. ➘

Epistle. *Gal. 5, 25-26; 6, 1-10.* Brethren: If we live by the Spirit, by the Spirit let us also walk. Let us not become desirous of vainglory, provoking one another, envying one another. Brethren, even if a person is caught doing something wrong, you who are spiritual instruct such a one in a spirit of meekness, considering yourself, lest you also be tempted. Bear one another's burdens, and so you will fulfill the law of Christ. For if anyone thinks himself to be something, whereas he is nothing, he deceives himself. But let everyone test his own work, and so he will have glory in himself only, and not in comparison with another. For each one will bear his own burden. And let him who is instructed in the word share all good things with his teacher. Be not deceived, God is not mocked. For what a man sows, that he will also reap. For he who sows in the flesh, from the flesh also will reap corruption. But he who sows in the spirit, from the spirit will reap life everlasting. And in doing good let us not grow tired;

for in due time we shall reap if we do not relax. Therefore, while we have time, let us do good to all men, but especially to those who are of the household of faith. S. Thanks be to God. ↰

Gradual. *Ps. 91, 2. 3.* It is good to give thanks to the Lord, to sing to Your Name, Most High. ℣. To proclaim Your kindness at dawn and Your faithfulness throughout the night.

Alleluia, alleluia. ℣. *Ps. 94, 3.* For the Lord is a great God, and a great King over all the earth. Alleluia.

● *Prayer: Cleanse My Heart, page* 31.

Gospel. *Luke 7, 11-16.* At that time, Jesus went to a town called Naim; and His disciples and a large crowd went with Him. And as He drew near the gate of the town, behold, a dead man was being carried out, the only son of his mother, and she was a widow; and a large gathering from the town was with her. And the Lord, seeing her, had compassion on her, and said to her, "Do not weep." And He went up and touched the stretcher; and the bearers stood still. And He said, "Young man, I say to you, arise." And he who was dead, sat up, and began to speak. And He gave him to his mother.

But fear seized upon all, and they began to glorify God, saying, "A great prophet has risen among us," and "God has visited His people." S. Praise be to You, O Christ.

● Creed, page 33.

Offertory. *Ps. 39, 2. 3. 4.* I have waited, waited for the Lord, and He stooped toward me and heard my cry; and He put a new song into my mouth, a hymn to our God.

● Offertory Prayers, page 35.

Secret. May Your sacraments keep us, O Lord, and ever protect us against the assaults of the devil. Through our Lord, etc.

● Preface, page 43.

Communion. *John 6, 52.* The bread that I will give is My Flesh for the life of the world.

P. The Lord be with you. S. And with your spirit. ↴

Postcommunion. May the working of this heavenly Gift, we beseech You, O Lord, possess our minds and bodies: that its effect, and not our own inclinations, have precedence within us. Through our Lord, etc. S. Amen.

● Final Prayers, page 73.

———◇———

"Everyone who exalts himself shall be humbled."

SIXTEENTH SUNDAY AFTER PENTECOST

GREEN VESTMENTS

THOUGHT FOR TODAY: The supernatural life which we receive in baptism is like a seed that must be developed. "Rooted and grounded in love," we pray that God may increase our faith and hope, and that His grace may stir up in us zeal for good works.

● *Beginning of Mass, page 19.*

Introit. *Ps. 85, 3. 5.* Have pity on me, O Lord, for to You I call all the day; for You, O Lord, are good and forgiving, abounding in kindness to all who call upon You. *Ps. 85, 1.* Incline Your ear, O Lord; answer me, for I am afflicted and poor. ℣. Glory be.

● *Kyrie and Gloria, page 27.*

Prayer. Let Your grace, we beseech You, O Lord, always go before us and follow us, and make us continually intent upon good works. Through our Lord, etc. S. Amen. ⮌

Epistle. *Eph. 3, 13-21.* Brethren: I pray you not to be disheartened at my tribulations for you, for they are your glory. For this reason I bend my knees to the Father of our Lord Jesus Christ, from Whom all fatherhood in heaven and on earth receives its name, that He may grant you from His glorious riches to be strengthened with power through His Spirit unto the progress of the inner man; and to have Christ dwelling through faith in your hearts: so that, being rooted and grounded in love, you may be able to comprehend with all the saints what is the breadth and length and height and depth, and to know Christ's love which surpasses knowledge, in order that you may be filled unto all the fullness of God. Now, to Him Who is able to accomplish all things in a measure far beyond what we ask or conceive, in keeping with the power that is at work in us — to Him be glory in the Church and in Christ Jesus down through all the ages of time without end. Amen. S. Thanks be to God. ⮌

Gradual. *Ps. 101, 16-17.* The nations shall revere Your Name, O Lord, and all the kings of the earth Your glory. ℣. For the Lord has rebuilt Sion, and He shall appear in His glory.

Alleluia, alleluia. ℣. *Ps. 97, 1.* Sing to the Lord a new song, for the Lord has done wondrous deeds. Alleluia.

● *Prayer: Cleanse My Heart, page* 31.

Gospel. *Luke 14, 1-11.* At that time, when Jesus entered the house of one of the rulers of the Pharisees on the Sabbath to take food, they watched Him. And behold, there was a certain man before Him who had the dropsy. And Jesus asked the lawyers and Pharisees, saying, "Is it lawful to cure on the Sabbath?" But they remained silent. And He took and healed him and let him go. Then addressing them, He said, "Which of you shall have an ass or an ox fall into a pit, and will not immediately draw him up on the Sabbath?" And they could give Him no answer to these things. But He also spoke a parable to those invited, observing how they were choosing the first places at table, and He said to them, "When you are invited to a wedding feast, do not recline in the first place, lest perhaps one more distinguished than you have been invited by him, and he who invited you and him come and say to you, 'Make room for this man'; and then you begin with shame to take the last place. But when you are invited, go and recline in the last place; that when he who invited you comes in, he may say to you, 'Friend, go up higher!' Then you will be honored in the presence of all who are at table with you. For everyone who exalts himself shall be humbled, and he who humbles himself shall be exalted." S. Praise be to You, O Christ.

● Creed, page 33.

Offertory. *Ps. 39, 14. 15.* Deign, O Lord, to rescue me; let all be put to shame and confusion who seek to snatch away my life. Deign, O Lord, to rescue me.

● Offertory Prayers, page 35.

Secret. Cleanse us, we beseech You, O Lord, through the effect of this sacrifice; and taking pity on us, grant that we may become worthy partakers of it. Through our Lord, etc.

● Preface, page 43.

Communion. *Ps. 70, 16. 17. 18.* O Lord, I will tell of Your singular justice; O God, You have taught me from my youth; and now that I am old and gray, O God, forsake me not.

P. The Lord be with you. *S.* And with your spirit. ↴

Postcommunion. Graciously purify our minds, we beseech You, O Lord, and renew them with these heavenly sacraments, so that our bodies may likewise receive help both for the present and the future. Through our Lord, etc. *S.* Amen.

● *Final Prayers, page 73.*

"You shall love your neighbor as yourself."

SEVENTEENTH SUNDAY AFTER PENTECOST

GREEN VESTMENTS

THOUGHT FOR TODAY: We all have "one Lord, one faith, one Baptism, one God and Father of all." This supernatural unity encourages us to "avoid every contamination of the devil," and to perform works of charity. By the grace of the Sacraments we curb our passions that they may not separate us from our holy union in the Mystical Body of Christ.

● *Beginning of Mass, page* 19.

Introit. *Ps. 118, 137. 124.* You are just, O Lord, and Your ordinance is right; deal with Your servant according to Your kindness. *Ps. 118, 1.* Happy are they whose way is blameless, who walk in the law of the Lord. ℣. Glory be.

● *Kyrie and Gloria, page* 27.

Prayer. Grant to Your people, we beseech You, O Lord, to avoid every contamination of the devil, and, with pure minds, to follow You, the only God. Through our Lord, etc. S. Amen. ⤵

Epistle. *Eph. 4, 1-6.* Brethren: I, the prisoner in the Lord, exhort you to walk in a manner worthy of the calling with which you were called, with all humility and meekness, with patience, bearing with one another in love, careful to preserve the unity of the Spirit in the bond of peace: one body and one Spirit, even as you were called in one hope of your calling; one Lord, one faith, one Baptism, one God and Father of all, Who is above all, and throughout all, and in us all, Who is blessed forever and ever. Amen. S. Thanks be to God. ⤵

Gradual. *Ps. 32, 12. 6.* Happy the nation whose God is the Lord, the people the Lord has chosen for His own inheritance. ℣. By the word of the Lord the heavens were made; by the breath of His mouth all their host.

Alleluia, alleluia. ℣. *Ps. 101, 2.* O Lord, hear my prayer, and let my cry come to You. Alleluia.

● *Prayer: Cleanse My Heart, page* **31**.

Gospel. *Matt. 22, 34-46.* At that time, the Pharisees came to Jesus and one of them, a doctor of the Law, putting Him to the test, asked Him, "Master, which is the great commandment in the Law?" Jesus said to him, " 'You shall love the Lord your God with your whole heart, and with your whole soul, and with your whole mind.' This is the greatest and first commandment. And the second is like it, 'You shall love your neighbor as yourself.' On these two commandments depend the whole Law and the Prophets." Now while the Pharisees were gathered together, Jesus questioned them, saying, "What do you think of the Christ? Whose son is He?" They said to Him, "David's." He said to them, "How then does David in the Spirit call Him Lord, saying, 'The Lord said to my Lord: Sit at My right hand, till I make Your enemies Your footstool'? If David, therefore calls Him 'Lord,' how is He his son?" And no one could answer Him a word; neither did anyone dare from that day forth to ask Him any more questions. *S.* Praise be to You, O Christ.

● *Creed, page* 33.

Offertory. *Dan. 9, 17. 18. 19.* I, Daniel, prayed to my God, saying, "Hear, O Lord, the prayers of Your servant; show Your face upon Your sanctuary, and favorably look down upon this people, upon whom Your Name is invoked, O God."

● *Offertory Prayers, page 35.*

Secret. We suppliantly beseech Your Majesty, O Lord, that the sacred mysteries which we perform, may free us both from past sins and future transgressions. Through our Lord, etc.

● *Preface, page 43.*

Communion. *Ps. 75, 12-13.* Make vows to the Lord, your God, and fulfill them; let all round about Him bring gifts to the terrible Lord Who checks the pride of princes, Who is terrible to the kings of the earth.

P. The Lord be with you. *S.* And with your spirit. ⸜

Postcommunion. O almighty God, may our vices be cured by Your sanctifying graces and may everlasting remedies be bestowed upon us. Through our Lord, etc. *S.* Amen.

● *Final Prayers, page 73.*

———◇———

"Arise, take up your pallet and go to your house."

EIGHTEENTH SUNDAY AFTER PENTECOST

GREEN VESTMENTS

THOUGHT FOR TODAY: "Your sins are forgiven you." We also hear the identical words, "I absolve you from your sins," when after due preparation, we humbly confess our sins. Let us be grateful to God for the Sacrament of Penance and use it frequently to restore or to increase the supernatural life of our souls, which is so pleasing to Him.

● *Beginning of Mass, page 19.*

Introit. *Ecclus. 36, 18.* Give peace, O Lord, to those who have hoped in You, and let Your Prophets be proved true. Hear the prayers of Your servant, and of Your people Israel. *Ps. 121, 1.* I rejoiced because they said to me: "We will go up to the house of the Lord." ℣. Glory be.

● *Kyrie and Gloria, page 27.*

– 337 –

Prayer. May the working of Your mercy direct our hearts, we beseech You, O Lord: for without You, we are not able to please You. Through our Lord, etc. *S.* Amen. ➷

Epistle. *1 Cor. 1, 4-8.* Brethren: I give thanks to my God always concerning you for the grace of God which was given you in Christ Jesus, because in everything you have been enriched in Him, in all utterance and in all knowledge; even as the witness to the Christ has been made so firm in you that you lack no grace, while awaiting the appearance of our Lord Jesus Christ, Who will also keep you secure unto the end, unimpeachable in the day of the coming of our Lord Jesus Christ. *S.* Thanks be to God. ➷

Gradual. *Ps. 121, 1. 7.* I rejoiced because they said to me: "We will go up to the house of the Lord." ℣. May peace be within your walls, prosperity in your buildings.

Alleluia, alleluia. ℣. *Ps. 101, 16.* The nations shall revere Your Name, O Lord, and all the kings of the earth Your glory. Alleluia.

● *Prayer: Cleanse My Heart, page 31.*

Gospel. *Matt. 9, 1-8.* At that time, Jesus, getting into a boat, crossed over and came to His own town. And behold, they brought to Him a paralytic lying on a pallet. And Jesus, seeing their faith, said to the paralytic, "Take courage son; your sins are forgiven you." And behold, some of the Scribes said within themselves, "This man blasphemes." And Jesus, knowing their thoughts, said, "Why do you harbor evil thoughts in your hearts? For which is easier, to say, 'Your sins are forgiven you,' or to say, 'Arise and walk'? But that you may know that the Son of Man has power on earth to forgive sins,"—then He said to the paralytic —"Arise, take up your pallet and go to your house." And he arose, and went away to his house. But when the crowds saw it, they were struck with fear, and glorified God Who had given such power to men. S. Praise be to You, O Christ.

● Creed, page 33.

Offertory. *Ex. 24, 4. 5.* Moses consecrated an altar to the Lord, offering upon it holocausts, and sacrificing victims: he made an evening sacrifice to the Lord God for an odor of sweetness, in the sight of the Israelites.

● Offertory Prayers, page 35.

Secret. O God, by the adorable Communion of this sacrifice You make us partakers of the one Supreme Godhead; grant, we beseech You, that even as we recognize Your truth, so also we may attain to it by a worthy life. Through our Lord, etc.

● *Preface, page 43.*

Communion. *Ps. 95, 8. 9.* Bring gifts and enter His courts; worship the Lord in His holy court.

P. The Lord be with you. *S.* And with your spirit. ↱

Postcommunion. Fed with this sacred gift, O Lord, we give thanks to You, beseeching Your mercy to render us worthy of our participation in it. Through our Lord, etc. *S.* Amen.

● *Final Prayers, page 73.*

"For many are called, but few are chosen."

NINETEENTH SUNDAY AFTER PENTECOST

GREEN VESTMENTS

THOUGHT FOR TODAY: Without the garment of sanctifying grace, we cannot enter the kingdom of heaven. To die in the state of grace is a special gift for which we must pray and which God will certainly not deny us if we keep His commandments.

● *Beginning of Mass, page 19.*

Introit. "I am the salvation of the people," says the Lord; "in whatever tribulation they shall cry to Me, I will hear them; and I will be their Lord forever." *Ps. 77, 1.* Hearken, My people, to My teaching; incline your ears to the words of My mouth. ℣. Glory be.

● *Kyrie and Gloria, page 27.*

Prayer. Almighty and merciful God, in Your bounty graciously defend us from all that is hurtful; that, free in mind and body, we may with ready minds carry out the things that are Yours. Through our Lord, etc. S. Amen. ↰

Epistle. *Eph. 4, 23-28.* Brethren: Be renewed in the spirit of your mind, and put on the new man, which has been created according to God in justice and holiness of truth. Wherefore, put away lying and speak truth each one with his neighbor, because we are members of one another. "Be angry and do not sin"; do not let the sun go down upon your anger; do not give place to the devil. He who was wont to steal, let him steal no longer; but rather let him labor, working with his hands at what is good, that he may have something to share with him who suffers need. S. Thanks be to God. ↰

Gradual. *Ps. 140, 2.* Let my prayer come like incense before You, O Lord. ℣. The lifting up of my hands, like the evening sacrifice.

Alleluia, alleluia. ℣. *Ps. 104, 1.* Give thanks to the Lord, invoke His Name; make known among the nations His deeds. Alleluia.

● *Prayer: Cleanse My Heart, page* 31.

Gospel. *Matt. 22, 1-14.* At that time, Jesus spoke to the chief priests and the Pharisees in parables, saying, "The kingdom of heaven is like a king who made a marriage feast for his son. And he sent his servants to call in those invited to the marriage feast, but they would not come. Again he sent out other servants, saying, 'Tell those who are invited, behold, I have prepared my dinner; my oxen and fatlings are killed, and everything is ready; come to the marriage feast.' But they made light of it, and went off, one to his farm, and another to his business; and the rest laid hold of his servants, treated them shamefully, and killed them. But when the king heard of it, he was angry; and he sent his armies, destroyed those murderers, and burnt their city. Then he said to his servants, 'The marriage feast indeed is ready, but those who were invited were not worthy; go therefore to the crossroads, and invite to the marriage feast whomever you shall find.' And his servants went out into the roads, and gathered all whom they found, both good and bad; and the marriage feast was filled with guests. Now the king went in to see the guests, and he saw there a man who had not on a wedding garment. And he said to him, 'Friend, how did you come in here without a wedding garment?' But he was speechless. Then the king said to the attendants, 'Bind his hands and feet and cast him forth into the darkness outside,

344 NINETEENTH SUNDAY AFTER PENTECOST

where there will be the weeping, and the gnashing of teeth.' For many are called, but few are chosen." S. Praise be to You, O Christ.

● *Creed, page 33.*

Offertory. *Ps. 137, 7.* Though I walk amid distress, You preserve me, O Lord; against the anger of my enemies You raise Your hand; Your right hand saves me.

● *Offertory Prayers, page 35.*

Secret. Grant, we beseech You, O Lord, that these gifts which we offer in the sight of Your Majesty may be salutary to us. Through our Lord, etc.

● *Preface, page 43.*

Communion. *Ps. 118, 4-5.* You have commanded that Your precepts be diligently kept. Oh, that I might be firm in the ways of keeping Your statutes!

P. The Lord be with you. *S.* And with your spirit. ↴

Postcommunion. May Your healing power, O Lord, mercifully free us from our perverse inclinations, and make us ever cleave to Your commandments. Through our Lord, etc. *S.* Amen.

● *Final Prayers, page 73.*

"Go your way, your son lives."

TWENTIETH SUNDAY AFTER PENTECOST

GREEN VESTMENTS

THOUGHT FOR TODAY: "The days are evil." Numberless sins, committed daily on earth, cry to heaven for punishment. Let us appease God by leading a good Christian life. The Holy Sacraments are the medicine to "cleanse away the vices of our hearts."

● *Beginning of Mass, page* 19.

Introit. *Dan. 3, 31. 29. 35.* All that You have done to us, O Lord, You have done in true judgment; because we have sinned against You, and we have not obeyed Your commandments; but give glory to Your Name, and deal with us according to the multitude of Your mercy. *Ps. 118, 1.* Happy are they whose way is blameless, who walk in the law of the Lord. ℣. Glory be.

● *Kyrie and Gloria, page* 27.

Prayer. Be appeased, O Lord, we beseech You, and grant to Your faithful people pardon and peace; that they may both be cleansed from all their offenses, and serve You with secure minds. Through our Lord, etc. S. Amen. ↰

Epistle. *Eph. 5, 15-21.* Brethren: See to it that you walk with care: not as unwise but as wise, making the most of your time, because the days are evil. Therefore, do not become foolish, but understand what the will of the Lord is. And do not be drunk with wine, for in that is debauchery; but be filled with the Spirit, speaking to one another in psalms and hymns and spiritual songs, singing and making melody in your hearts to the Lord, giving thanks always for all things in the Name of our Lord Jesus Christ to God the Father. Be subject to one another in the fear of Christ. S. Thanks be to God. ↰

Gradual. *Ps. 144, 15-16.* The eyes of all look hopefully to You, O Lord, and You give them their food in due season. ℣. You open Your hand and satisfy the desire of every living thing.

Alleluia, alleluia. ℣. *Ps. 107, 2.* My heart is steadfast, O God; my heart is steadfast;

I will sing and chant praise to You, my glory. Alleluia.

● *Prayer: Cleanse My Heart, page* 31.

Gospel. *John 4, 46-53.* At that time, there was a certain royal official whose son was lying sick at Capharnaum. When he heard that Jesus had come from Judea into Galilee, he went to Him and besought Him to come down and heal his son, for he was at the point of death. Jesus therefore said to him, "Unless you see signs and wonders, you do not believe." The royal official said to Him, "Sir, come down before my child dies." Jesus said to him, "Go your way, your son lives." The man believed the word that Jesus spoke to him, and departed. But even as he was now going down, his servants met him and brought word saying that his son lived. He asked of them therefore the hour in which he had got better. And they told him, "Yesterday, at the seventh hour, the fever left him." The father knew then that it was at that very hour in which Jesus had said to him, "Your son lives." And he himself believed, and his whole household. *S.* Praise be to You, O Christ.

● *Creed, page* 33.

Offertory. *Ps. 136, 1.* By the streams of Babylon we sat and wept when we remembered you, O Sion.

● *Offertory Prayers, page 35.*

Secret. May these mysteries, we beseech You, O Lord, afford us a heavenly remedy, and cleanse away the vices of our hearts. Through our Lord, etc.

● *Preface, page 43.*

Communion. *Ps. 118, 49. 50.* Remember Your word to Your servant, O Lord, since You have given me hope. This is my comfort in my affliction.

P. The Lord be with you. *S.* And with your spirit. ↰

Postcommunion. That we may be rendered worthy of these sacred gifts, grant us, we beseech You, O Lord, always to observe Your commandments. Through our Lord, etc. *S.* Amen.

● *Final Prayers, page 73.*

"You say it; I am a King."

FEAST OF CHRIST THE KING

LAST SUNDAY IN OCTOBER

WHITE VESTMENTS

THOUGHT FOR TODAY: Jesus said: "My kingdom is not of this world," but it is in this world. He came to establish a kingdom of truth for our intellect; a kingdom of justice and holiness for our will; a kingdom of love and peace for our heart. If we follow Him, He will lead us into His eternal kingdom.

● *Beginning of Mass, page 19.*

Introit. *Apoc. 5, 12; 1, 6.* Worthy is the Lamb Who was slain to receive power, and divinity, and wisdom, and strength, and honor. To Him belong glory and dominion forever and ever. *Ps. 71, 1.* O God, with Your judgment endow the King, and with Your justice, the King's son. ℣. Glory be.

● *Kyrie and Gloria, page 27.*

Prayer. Almighty and everlasting God, You willed to restore all things in Your beloved Son, the King of all creation; mercifully grant that all the families of nations that have been disunited by the wound of sin may become subject to His most sweet dominion. Who with You, etc. S. Amen. ⮧

Epistle. *Col. 1, 12-20.* Brethren: We give thanks to God the Father Who has made us worthy to share the lot of the saints in light. He has rescued us from the power of darkness, and transferred us into the kingdom of His beloved Son, in Whom we have our redemption through His blood, the remission of our sins. He is the image of the invisible God, the firstborn of every creature. For in Him were created all things in the heavens and on the earth, things visible and things invisible, whether Thrones, or Dominations, or Principalities, or Powers. All things have been created through and unto Him, and He is before all creatures, and in Him all things hold together. Again, He is the head of the body, the Church; He, Who is the beginning, the firstborn from the dead, that in all things He may have the first place. For it has pleased God the Father that in Him all His fullness should dwell, and that through Him He should reconcile to Himself all things, whether on the earth or in the heavens, making peace through the blood of His Cross, in Christ Jesus our Lord. *S.* Thanks be to God. ↴

Gradual. *Ps. 71, 8. 11.* He shall rule from sea to sea, and from the River to the ends of the earth. ℣. All kings shall pay Him homage, all nations shall serve Him.

Alleluia, alleluia. ℣. *Dan. 7, 4.* His power shall be an everlasting power which shall not be taken away: and His kingdom shall not be destroyed. Alleluia.

● Prayer: Cleanse My Heart, page **31**.

Gospel. *John 18, 33-37.* At that time, Pilate said to Jesus: "Are You the King of the Jews?" Jesus answered, "Do You say this of yourself, or have others told you of Me?" Pilate answered, "Am I a Jew? Your own people and the chief priests have delivered You to me. What have You done?" Jesus answered, "My kingdom is not of this world. If My kingdom were of this world, My followers would certainly have fought that I might not be delivered to the Jews. But, as it is, My kingdom is not from here." Pilate therefore said to Him, "You are then a King?" Jesus answered, "You say it; I am a King. This is why I was born, and

why I have come into the world, to bear
witness to the truth. Everyone who is of
the truth hears My voice." *S.* Praise be to
You, O Christ.

● *Creed, page 33.*

Offertory. *Ps. 2, 8.* Ask of Me and I will
give You the nations for an inheritance
and the ends of the earth for Your possession.

● *Offertory Prayers, page 35.*

Secret. O Lord, we offer You the Victim
of man's reconciliation; grant, we beseech
You, that He Whom we immolate by these
present sacrifices, may bestow on all nations, the gifts of unity and peace, Jesus
Christ, Your Son, our Lord. Who with You,
etc. ⟩

Preface of Christ the King

P. World without end. *S.* Amen. *P.* The Lord
be with you. *S.* And with your spirit. *P.* Lift up
your hearts. *S.* We have lifted them up to the
Lord. *P.* Let us give thanks to the Lord, our
God. *S.* It is fitting and just.

It is fitting indeed and just, right and
helpful to salvation, for us always and everywhere to give thanks to You, O Holy Lord,
Father Almighty, Everlasting God. Who
with the oil of gladness have anointed Your

Only-begotten Son, our Lord Jesus Christ, as eternal High Priest and universal King; that offering Himself on the altar of the Cross as an immaculate and peaceful oblation, He might complete the pledges of human redemption; and all creation being made subject to His dominion, He might deliver into the hands of Your infinite Majesty an eternal and universal kingdom: a kingdom of truth and life, a kingdom of holiness and grace, a kingdom of justice, love and peace. And therefore with Angels and Archangels, with Thrones and Dominations, and with the whole host of the heavenly army, we sing a hymn to Your glory, saying again and again: Holy, Holy, Holy, Lord God of Hosts. Heaven and earth are filled with Your glory. Hosanna in the highest. Blessed is He Who comes in the Name of the Lord. Hosanna in the highest.

● *Canon, page 47.*

Communion. *Ps. 28, 10. 11.* The Lord is enthroned as King forever; may the Lord bless His people with peace.

P. The Lord be with you. *S.* And with your spirit. ↰

Postcommunion. Having received the food of immortality, we beseech You, O

Lord, that we who glory in our warfare under the banners of Christ our King, may reign with Him forever in His heavenly dwelling place. Who with You, etc. S. Amen.

● *Final Prayers, page 73.*

"The master handed him over to the torturers."

TWENTY-FIRST SUNDAY AFTER PENTECOST

GREEN VESTMENTS

THOUGHT FOR TODAY: We say in the Our Father: "Forgive us our trespasses as we forgive those who trespass against us." But those who do not forgive think only of revenge, and never forget an offense. They act like the "wicked servant." "Blessed are the merciful: for they shall obtain mercy."

● *Beginning of Mass, page* **19.**

Introit. *Esther 13, 9. 10. 11.* In Your will are all things, O Lord; and there is none that can resist Your will: for You have made all things, heaven and earth, and all things that are under the cope of heaven. You are Lord of all. *Ps. 118, 1.* Happy are they whose way is blameless, who walk in the law of the Lord. ℣. Glory be.

● *Kyrie and Gloria, page* 27.

Prayer. Guard Your household, we beseech You, O Lord, with continued goodness; that, through Your protection, it may be free from all adversities, and by good works be devoted to Your Name. Through our Lord, etc. S. Amen. ↝

Epistle. *Eph. 6, 10-17.* Brethren: Be strengthened in the Lord and in the might of His power. Put on the armor of God, that you may be able to stand against the wiles of the devil. For our wrestling is not against flesh and blood, but against the Principalities and the Powers, against the world rulers of this darkness, against the spiritual forces of wickedness on high. Therefore, take up the armor of God, that you may be able to resist the evil day, and stand in all things perfect. Stand, therefore, having girded your loins with truth, and having your feet shod with the readiness of the gospel of peace, in all things taking up the shield of faith, with which you may be able to quench all the fiery darts of the most wicked one. And take unto you the helmet of salvation and the sword of the spirit, that is, the word of God. S. Thanks be to God. ↝

Gradual. *Ps. 89, 1-2.* O Lord, You have been our refuge through all generations. ℣.

Before the mountains were begotten and the earth and the world were brought forth, from everlasting to everlasting You are God.

Alleluia, alleluia. ℣. *Ps. 113, 1*. When Israel came forth from Egypt, the house of Jacob from a people of alien tongue. Alleluia.

● *Prayer: Cleanse My Heart, page* 31.

Gospel. *Matt. 18, 23-35*. At that time, Jesus spoke to His disciples this parable: "The kingdom of heaven is likened to a king who desired to settle accounts with his servants. And when he had begun the settlement, one was brought to him who owed him ten thousand talents. And as he had no means of paying, his master ordered him to be sold, with his wife and children and all that he had, and payment to be made. But the servant fell down and besought him, saying, 'Have patience with me and I will pay you all!' And moved with compassion, the master of that servant released him, and forgave him the debt. But as the servant went out, he met one of his fellow-servants who owed him a hundred denarii, and he laid hold of him and throttled him, saying, 'Pay what you owe.' His fellow-servant therefore fell down and began to entreat him, saying, 'Have patience with me and I will pay you all.' But he would not; but went away and cast him into prison until he should pay what was due. His fellow-servants, therefore, seeing what had happened, were very much saddened, and they went and informed their master of what had taken place. Then his master called him, and said to him, "Wicked servant! I forgave you all the debt, because you entreated me. Should not you also have had pity on your fellow-servant, even as I had pity on you?' And his master, being angry, handed him over to the torturers until he should pay all that was due to him. So also My heavenly Father will do to you, if you do not each forgive your brothers from your hearts." S. Praise be to You, O Christ.

● Creed, page 33.

Offertory. *Job 1.* There was a man in the land of Us, whose name was Job, simple, and upright, and fearing God, whom Satan besought that he might tempt: and power was given him from the Lord over his possessions and his flesh; and he destroyed all his substance and his children, and wounded his flesh also with a grievous ulcer.

● Offertory Prayers, page 35.

Secret. Mercifully receive, O Lord, this sacrifice, by which You have been pleased to be pacified and to restore salvation to us by Your powerful mercy. Through our Lord, etc.

● *Preface, page* 43.

Communion. *Ps. 118, 81. 84. 86.* My soul pines for Your salvation; I hope in Your word. When will You do judgment on my persecutors? The wicked have persecuted me wrongfully; help me, O Lord my God!

P. The Lord be with you. *S.* And with your spirit. ↴

Postcommunion. Having received the food of immortality, we beseech You, O Lord, that what has passed our lips, we may cherish in purity of heart. Through our Lord, etc. *S.* Amen.

● *Final Prayers, page* 73.

*"Render, therefore, to Cæsar the things that are Cæsar's,
and to God the things that are God's."*

TWENTY-SECOND SUNDAY
AFTER PENTECOST

GREEN VESTMENTS

THOUGHT FOR TODAY: Man was made by God
and continually needs His sustaining hand.
Hence he does not possess absolute dominion
over his life. It is our obligation to take reasonable care of our body and to use it in the service
of God and our fellowmen, and to cultivate our
spiritual life, so that we may be "without offense
unto the day of Christ."

● *Beginning of Mass, page* 19.

Introit. *Ps. 129, 3. 4.* If You, O Lord,
mark iniquities, Lord, who can stand? But
with You is forgiveness, O God of Israel.
Ps. 129, 1. 2. Out of the depths I cry to
You, O Lord; Lord, hear my voice. ℣. Glory
be.

● *Kyrie and Gloria, page* 27.

Prayer. O God, our refuge and strength, the author of all piety, give ear to the devout prayers of Your Church; and grant that what we ask with faith, we may obtain effectually. Through our Lord, etc. S. Amen. ↴

Epistle. *Phil. 1, 6-11.* Brethren: I am convinced that the Lord Jesus Who has begun a good work in you will bring it to perfection until the day of Christ Jesus. And I have the right to feel so about you all, because I have you in my heart, all of you, alike in my chains and in the defense and confirmation of the gospel, as sharers in my joy. For God is my witness how I long for you all in the heart of Christ Jesus. And this I pray, that your charity may more and more abound in knowledge and all discernment, so that you may approve the better things, that you may be upright and without offense unto the day of Christ, filled with the fruit of justice, through Jesus Christ, to the glory and praise of God. S. Thanks be to God. ↴

Gradual. *Ps. 132, 1-2.* Behold how good it is, and how pleasant, where brethren dwell as one! ℣. It is as when the precious ointment upon the head runs down over the beard, the beard of Aaron.

Alleluia, alleluia. ℣. *Ps. 113, 11.* Those who fear the Lord trust in the Lord; He is their help and their shield. Alleluia.

● Prayer: Cleanse My Heart, page 31.

Gospel. *Matt. 22, 15-21.* At that time, the Pharisees went and took counsel how they might trap Jesus in His talk. And they sent to Him their disciples with the Herodians, saying, "Master, we know that You are truthful, and that You teach the way of God in truth, and that You care naught for any man; for You do not regard the person of men. Tell us, therefore, what do You think: Is it lawful to give tribute to Cæsar, or not?" But Jesus, knowing their wickedness, said, "Why do you test Me, you hypocrites? Show Me the coin of the tribute." So they offered Him a denarius. Then Jesus said to them, "Whose are this image and the inscription?" They said to Him, "Cæsar's." Then He said to them, "Render, therefore, to Cæsar the things that are Cæsar's, and to God the things that are God's." S. Praise be to You, O Christ.

● Creed, page 33.

Offertory. *Esther 14, 12. 13.* Remember me, O Lord, You Who rule above all power: and give a well-ordered speech in my mouth, that my words may be pleasing in the sight of the prince.

● *Offertory Prayers, page 35.*

Secret. Grant, O merciful God, that this salutary oblation may forever free us from our faults, and shield us from all adversities. Through our Lord, etc.

● *Preface, page 43.*

Communion. *Ps. 16, 6.* I call upon You, for You will answer me, O God; incline Your ear to me; hear my word.

P. The Lord be with you. *S.* And with your spirit. ➔

Postcommunion. We have partaken, O Lord, of the gifts of this sacred mystery, and humbly beseech You, that what You have commanded us to do in remembrance of You may profit us as an aid to our weakness. Who live, etc. *S.* Amen.

● *Final Prayers, page 73.*

"He went in and took her by the hand . . ."

TWENTY-THIRD SUNDAY AFTER PENTECOST

GREEN VESTMENTS

THOUGHT FOR TODAY: The same Jesus Who raised the maid to life again, will make our body "like to the body of His glory." Therefore, let us not yield to blind passions, but rather let us consider all that we do in the light of eternity.

If there are only twenty-three Sundays after Pentecost, the Mass of the "Last Sunday after Pentecost," page 372, is said today.

● *Beginning of Mass, page 19.*

Introit. *Jer. 29, 11. 12. 14.* The Lord says: "I think thoughts of peace, and not of affliction: you shall call upon Me, and I will hear you; and I will bring back your captivity from all places." *Ps. 84, 2.* You have favored, O Lord, Your land; You have restored the well-being of Jacob. ℣. Glory be.

● *Kyrie and Gloria, page 27.*

Prayer. Absolve Your people from their offenses, we beseech You, O Lord; that through Your bountiful goodness we may be delivered from the bonds of sin, which through our frailty we have contracted. Through our Lord, etc. S. Amen. ⤴

Epistle. *Phil. 3, 17-21; 4, 1-3.* Brethren: Be imitators of me, and mark those who walk after the pattern you have in us. For many walk, of whom I have told you often and now tell you even weeping, that they are enemies of the cross of Christ. Their end is ruin, their god is the belly, their glory is in their shame, they mind the things of earth. But our citizenship is in heaven from which also we eagerly await a Savior, our Lord Jesus Christ, Who will refashion the body of our lowliness, conforming it to the body of His glory by exerting the power by which He is able also to subject all things to Himself. So then, my brethren, beloved and longed for, my joy and my crown, stand fast thus in the Lord, beloved. I entreat Evodia and I exhort Syntyche to be of one mind in the Lord. And I beseech you also, my loyal comrade, help them, for they have toiled with me in the gospel, as have Clement and the rest of my fellow-workers whose names are in the book of life. S. Thanks be to God. ⤵

Gradual. *Ps. 43, 8-9.* You saved us, O Lord, from our foes, and those who hated us You put to shame. ℣. In God we gloried day by day; Your Name we praised always.

Alleluia, alleluia. ℣. *Ps. 129, 1. 2.* Out of the depths I cry to You, O Lord; Lord, hear my prayer. Alleluia.

● *Prayer: Cleanse My Heart, page* 31.

Gospel. *Matt. 9, 18-26.* At that time, as Jesus was speaking to the crowds, behold, a ruler came up and worshipped Him, saying, "Lord, my daughter has just now died; but come and lay Your hand upon her, and she will return to life." And Jesus arose and followed him, and so did His disciples. Now a woman who for twelve years had been suffering from hemorrhage, came up behind Him and touched the tassel of His cloak, saying to herself, "If I touch but His cloak I shall be saved." But Jesus, turning and seeing her, said, "Take courage, daughter; your faith has saved you." And the woman was restored to health from that moment.

And when Jesus came to the ruler's house, and saw the flute players and the crowd making a din, He said, "Begone, the girl is asleep, not dead." And they laughed Him to scorn. But when the crowd had been put out, He went in and took her by the hand; and the girl arose. And the report of this spread throughout all that district. *S.* Praise be to You, O Christ.

● Creed, page 33.

Offertory. *Ps. 129, 1. 2.* Out of the depths I cry to You, O Lord; Lord, hear my prayer; out of the depths I cry to You, O Lord.

● Offertory Prayers, page 35.

Secret. We offer You, O Lord, this sacrifice of praise as an additional act of homage; that what You have granted to us without any merit of ours, You would mercifully accomplish. Through our Lord, etc.

● Preface, page 43.

Communion. *Mark 11, 24.* Amen I say to you, all things whatever you ask for in prayer, believe that you shall receive, and it shall be done to you.

P. The Lord be with you. *S.* And with your spirit. ➤

Postcommunion. We beseech You, almighty God, not to allow those to be subject to human dangers, whom You grant to rejoice in the participation of divine mysteries. Through our Lord, etc. S. Amen.

● *Final Prayers, page 73.*

ADDITIONAL MASS NO. I

GREEN VESTMENTS

When there are more than 24 Sundays after Pentecost, one or more of the following Masses are said. See the Liturgical Calendar.

● *Beginning of Mass, page 19.*

Introit. *Jer. 29.* The Lord says: "I think thoughts of peace, and not of affliction: you shall call upon Me, and I will hear you; and I will bring back your captivity from all places." *Ps. 84.* You have favored, O Lord, Your land; You have restored the well-being of Jacob. ℣. Glory be.

● *Kyrie and Gloria, page 27.*

● *Prayer, page 144.*   ● *Epistle, page 145.*

Gradual. *Ps. 43.* You saved us, O Lord, from our foes, and those who hated us You put to shame. ℣. In God we gloried day by day; Your Name we praised always. Alleluia, alleluia. ℣. *Ps. 129.* Out of the depths I cry to You, O Lord; Lord, hear my prayer. Alleluia.

● *Prayer: Cleanse My Heart, page 31.*

● *Gospel, page 146.*   ● *Creed, page 33.*

Offertory. *Ps. 129.* Out of the depths I cry to You, O Lord; Lord, hear my prayer; out of the depths I cry to You, O Lord.

● *Offertory Prayers, page 35.*

● *Secret, page 147.*   ● *Preface, page 43.*

Communion. *Mark 11.* Amen I say to you, all things whatever you ask for in prayer, believe that you shall receive, and it shall be done to you.

● *Postcommunion, p. 147.*   ● *Final Prayers, p. 73.*

820-13

ADDITIONAL MASS NO. 2

GREEN VESTMENTS

● *Beginning of Mass, page* 19.

Introit. *Jer. 29.* The Lord says: "I think thoughts of peace, and not of affliction: you shall call upon Me, and I will hear you; and I will bring back your captivity from all places." *Ps. 84.* You have favored, O Lord, Your land; You have restored the well-being of Jacob. ℣. Glory be.

● *Kyrie and Gloria, page* 27.

● *Prayer, page* 140.　　● *Epistle, page* 141.

Gradual. *Ps. 43.* You saved us, O Lord, from our foes, and those who hated us You put to shame. ℣. In God we gloried day by day; Your Name we praised always. Alleluia, alleluia. ℣. *Ps. 129.* Out of the depths I cry to You, O Lord; Lord, hear my prayer. Alleluia.

● *Prayer: Cleanse My Heart, page* 31.

● *Gospel, page* 142.　　● *Creed, page* 33.

Offertory. *Ps. 129.* Out of the depths I cry to You, O Lord; Lord, hear my prayer; out of the depths I cry to You, O Lord.

● *Offertory Prayers, page* 35.

● *Secret, page* 143.　　● *Preface, page* 43.

Communion. *Mark 11.* Amen I say to you, all things whatever you ask for in prayer, believe that you shall receive, and it shall be done to you.

● *Postcommunion, p.* 143.　　● *Final Prayers, p.* 73.

ADDITIONAL MASS NO. 3

GREEN VESTMENTS

● *Beginning of Mass, page* 19.

Introit. *Jer. 29.* The Lord says: "I think thoughts of peace, and not of affliction: you shall call upon Me, and I will hear you; and I will bring back your captivity from all places." *Ps. 84.* You have favored, O Lord, Your land; You have restored the well-being of Jacob. ℣. Glory be.

● *Kyrie and Gloria, page* 27.

● *Prayer, page* 137.   ● *Epistle, page* 138.

Gradual. *Ps. 43.* You saved us, O Lord, from our foes, and those who hated us You put to shame. ℣. In God we gloried day by day; Your Name we praised always. Alleluia, alleluia. ℣. *Ps. 129.* Out of the depths I cry to You, O Lord; Lord, hear my prayer. Alleluia.

● *Prayer: Cleanse My Heart, page* 31.

● *Gospel, page* 138.   ● *Creed, page* 33.

Offertory. *Ps. 129.* Out of the depths I cry to You, O Lord; Lord, hear my prayer; out of the depths I cry to You, O Lord.

● *Offertory Prayers, page* 35.

● *Secret, page* 139.   ● *Preface, page* 43.

Communion. *Mark 11.* Amen I say to you, all things whatever you ask for in prayer, believe that you shall receive, and it shall be done to you.

● *Postcommunion, p.* 139.   ● *Final Prayers, p.* 73.

"And He will send forth His angels with a trumpet..."

TWENTY-FOURTH AND LAST SUNDAY AFTER PENTECOST

GREEN VESTMENTS

THOUGHT FOR TODAY: At the end of the ecclesiastical year the Church earnestly reminds us of the judgment that we must pass before the all-knowing God. It is wise to anticipate that judgment in frequent and contrite confession, and always to live in friendly union with Jesus in the Blessed Sacrament Who will be our Judge.

This Mass is always said on the Last Sunday after Pentecost.

● *Beginning of Mass, page 19.*

Introit. *Jer. 29, 11. 12. 14.* The Lord says: "I think thoughts of peace, and not of affliction: you shall call upon Me, and I will hear you; and I will bring back your captivity from all places." *Ps. 84, 2.* You have favored, O Lord, Your land; You have restored the well-being of Jacob. ℣. Glory be.

● *Kyrie and Gloria, page* 27.

Prayer. Stir up, we beseech You, O Lord, the wills of Your faithful people; that more earnestly seeking after the fruit of good works, they may receive more abundant helps from Your mercy. Through our Lord, etc. *S.* Amen. ↴

Epistle. *Col. 1, 9-14.* Brethren: We have been praying for you unceasingly, asking that you may be filled with knowledge of God's will, in all spiritual wisdom and understanding. May you walk worthily of God and please Him in all things, bearing fruit in every good work and growing in the knowledge of God. May you be completely strengthened through His glorious power unto perfect patience and long-suffering; joyfully rendering thanks to God the Father, Who has made us worthy to share the lot of the saints in light. He has rescued us from the power of darkness and transferred us into the kingdom of His beloved Son, in Whom we have our redemption, through His Blood, the remission of our sins. *S.* Thanks be to God. ↴

Gradual. *Ps. 43, 8-9.* You saved us, O Lord, from our foes, and those who hated

374 LAST SUNDAY AFTER PENTECOST

us You put to shame. ℣. In God we gloried
day by day; Your Name we praised always.

Alleluia, alleluia. ℣. *Ps. 129, 1. 2.* Out of
the depths I cry to You, O Lord; Lord, hear
my prayer. Alleluia.

● *Prayer: Cleanse My Heart, page* 31.

Gospel. *Matt. 24, 15-35.* At that time,
Jesus said to His disciples: "When you see
the abomination of desolation, which was
spoken of by Daniel the prophet, standing
in the holy place——let him who reads understand——then let those who are in Judea
flee to the mountains; and let him who is
on the housetop not go down to take anything from his house; and let him who is
in the field not turn back to take his cloak.
But woe to those who are with child, or
have infants at the breast in those days!
But pray that your flight may not be in the
winter, or on the Sabbath. For then there
will be great tribulation, such as has not
been from the beginning of the world until
now, nor will be. And unless those days had
been shortened, no living creature would be
saved. But for the sake of the elect those
days will be shortened. Then if anyone say
to you, 'Behold, here is the Christ,' or, 'There
He is,' do not believe it. For false christs
and false prophets will arise, and will show

great signs and wonders, so as to lead astray, if possible, even the elect. Behold, I have told it to you beforehand. If therefore they say to you, 'Behold, He is in the desert,' do not go forth; 'Behold, He is in the inner chambers,' do not believe it. For as the lightning comes forth from the east and shines even to the west, so also will the coming of the Son of Man be. Wherever the body is, there will the eagles be gathered together. But immediately after the tribulation of those days, the sun will be darkened, and the moon will not give her light, and the stars will fall from heaven, and the powers of heaven will be shaken. And then will appear the sign of the Son of Man in heaven; and then will all tribes of the earth mourn, and they will see the Son of Man coming upon the clouds of heaven with great power and majesty. And He will send forth His angels with a trumpet and a great sound, and they will gather His elect from the four winds, from one end of the heavens to the other. Now from the fig tree learn this parable. When its branch is now tender, and the leaves break forth, you know that summer is near. Even so, when you see all these things, know that it is near, even at the door. Amen I say to you, this generation will not pass away till all these things have been accomplished. Heaven and earth will pass away, but My words will not pass away." *S.* Praise be to You, O Christ.

● *Creed, page 33.*

Offertory. *Ps. 129, 1. 2.* Out of the depths I cry to You, O Lord; Lord, hear my prayer; out of the depths I cry to You, O Lord.

● *Offertory Prayers, page 35.*

Secret. Be propitious, O Lord, to our supplications, and accepting the offerings and prayers of Your people, convert the hearts of us all to Yourself, that being freed from earthly desires, we may pass on to the desires of heaven. Through our Lord, etc.

● *Preface, page 43.*

Communion. *Mark 11, 24.* Amen I say to you, all things whatever you ask for in prayer, believe that you shall receive, and it shall be done to you.

P. The Lord be with you. *S.* And with your spirit. ↴

Postcommunion. Grant, we beseech You, O Lord, that by this sacrament, which we have received, whatever is corrupted in our souls may be restored by the gift of its efficiency. Through our Lord, etc. *S.* Amen.

● *Final Prayers, page 73.*

"I am the Immaculate Conception."

Dec. 8 - IMMACULATE CONCEPTION

WHITE VESTMENTS

THOUGHT FOR TODAY: Because Mary was chosen to be the Mother of God, the singular privilege was bestowed upon her by which, in the first instant of her Conception, in view of the merits of Jesus Christ, she was preserved from all stain of original sin. Unable to imitate her in her original sinlessness, let us follow her example of loving fidelity to God.

● *Beginning of Mass, page 19.*

Introit. *Isa. 61, 10.* I will greatly rejoice in the Lord, and my soul shall be joyful in my God: for He has clothed me with the garments of salvation, and with the robe of justice He has covered me, as a bride adorned with her jewels. *Ps. 29, 2.* I will extol You, O Lord, for You drew me clear and did not let my enemies rejoice over me. ℣. Glory be.

– 377 –

● *Kyrie and Gloria, page* **27.**

Prayer. O God, by the Immaculate Conception of the Virgin You prepared a worthy habitation for Your Son; we beseech You, that, as by the foreseen death of this same Son You preserved her from all stain of sin, so You would grant us also, through her intercession, to come to You with pure hearts. Through the same, etc. S. Amen. ↰

Epistle. *Prov. 8. 22-35.* The Lord begot me, the firstborn of His ways, the forerunner of His prodigies of long ago; from of old I was poured forth, at the first, before the earth. When there were no depths I was brought forth, when there were no fountains or springs of water; before the mountains were settled into place, before the hills, I was brought forth; while as yet the earth and the fields were not made, nor the first clods of the world. When He established the heavens I was there, when He marked out the vault over the face of the deep; when He made firm the skies above, and poised the fountains of waters; when He set for the sea its limit, so that the waters should not transgress His command; when He fixed fast the foundations of the earth; then was I beside Him as His craftsman, and I was His delight day by day, playing before Him all the while, playing on the surface of His earth and I found delight in the sons of men. So now, O children, listen to me; happy those who keep my ways. Hear instruction, and be wise, and refuse it not. Happy the man who obeys me, watching daily at my gates, waiting at my doorposts; for he who finds me finds life, and wins favor from the Lord. *S.* Thanks be to God. ↰

Gradual. *Judith 13, 23.* Blessed are you, O Virgin Mary, by the Lord the most high God, above all women upon the earth. ℣. *Jud. 15, 10.* You are the glory of Jerusalem, you are the joy of Israel, you are the honor of our people.

Alleluia, alleluia. ℣. *Cant. 4, 7.* You are all-beautiful, O Mary, and there is in you no stain of original sin. Alleluia.

During Paschaltime, the Gradual is omitted and the following Alleluia is said:

Alleluia, alleluia. ℣. *Judith 15, 10.* You are the glory of Jerusalem, you are the joy of Israel, you are the honor of our people. Alleluia. ℣. *Cant. 4, 7.* You are all-beautiful O Mary, and there is in you no stain of original sin. Alleluia.

● *Prayer: Cleanse My Heart, page* 31.

Gospel. *Luke 1, 26-28.* At that time, the angel Gabriel was sent from God to a town of Galilee called Nazareth, to a virgin betrothed to a man named Joseph, of the house of David, and the virgin's name was Mary. And when the angel had come to her, he said, "Hail, full of grace, the Lord is with you. Blessed are you among women." *S.* Praise be to You, O Christ.

● *Creed, page 33.*

Offertory. *Luke 1, 28.* Hail, Mary, full of grace; the Lord is with you; blessed are you among women. Alleluia.

● *Offertory Prayers, page 35.*

Secret. Receive the saving oblation which we offer to You, O Lord, on the solemn feast of the Immaculate Conception of the Blessed Virgin Mary, and grant that, as we confess that, by Your preventing grace, she was kept free from every stain of sin, so, by her intercession, we may be freed from all sin. Through our Lord, etc. ↰

Preface of the Blessed Virgin

P. World without end. *S.* Amen. *P.* The Lord be with you. *S.* And with your spirit. *P.* Lift up your hearts. *S.* We have lifted them up to the Lord. *P.* Let us give thanks to the Lord, our God. *S.* It is fitting and just.

It is fitting indeed and just, right and helpful to salvation, for us always and everywhere to give thanks to You, O Holy Lord, Father Almighty, Everlasting God, and that we should praise, bless, and proclaim You in the Immaculate Conception (*on the Feast of the Assumption substitute*: Assumption) of the Blessed Mary, ever Virgin; for she conceived Your Only-begotten Son by the overshadowing of the Holy Spirit, and while the glory of her virginity remained, brought forth to the world the Eternal Light, Jesus Christ our Lord. Through Whom the angels praise Your Majesty, the Dominations worship it, the Powers are in awe. The heavens and the heavenly hosts, and the blessed Seraphim join together in celebrating their joy. With these we pray You, join our own voices also, while we say with lowly praise: Holy, Holy, Holy, Lord God of hosts. Heaven and earth are filled with Your glory. Hosanna in the highest. Blessed is He who comes in the Name of the Lord. Hosanna in the highest.

● *Canon, page 47.*

Communion. Glorious things are said of you, O Mary, for He Who is mighty has done great things for you.

P. The Lord be with you. *S.* And with your spirit. ↝

Postcommunion. May the sacrament which we have received, O Lord, our God, heal in us the wounds of that sin, from which You, by a singular privilege, preserved immaculate the Conception of Blessed Mary. Through our Lord, etc. *S.* Amen.

● *Final Prayers, page 73.*

"The Lord clothed . . . him with a robe of glory."

Mar. 19 - FEAST OF SAINT JOSEPH

SPOUSE OF THE BLESSED VIRGIN MARY,
CONFESSOR AND PATRON OF THE
UNIVERSAL CHURCH

WHITE VESTMENTS

THOUGHT FOR TODAY: The greatness of Saint Joseph lies in his inner life and in his relation to Jesus and Mary. We pray to him for help in temporal needs, for progress in the spiritual life, and for a happy death.

If the Feast of St. Joseph falls in Holy Week, it is celebrated on the Tuesday after Low Sunday.

● *Beginning of Mass, page 19.*

Introit. *Ps. 91, 13-14.* The just man shall flourish like the palm tree, like a cedar of Lebanon shall he grow; planted in the house of the Lord, in the courts of our God. (*P.T.* Alleluia, alleluia.) *Ps. 91, 2.* It is good to give thanks to the Lord, to sing to Your Name, Most High. ℣. Glory be.

● *Kyrie and Gloria, page 27.*

Prayer. We beseech You, O Lord, that we may be assisted by the merits of the Spouse of Your most holy Mother, so that what we cannot obtain by our own power may be given to us through his intercession. Who live, etc. S. Amen. ↰

Epistle. *Ecclus. 45, 1-6.* Beloved of God and men, whose memory is held in benediction. He made him like the Saints in glory, and magnified him in the fear of his enemies, and with his words He made prodigies to cease. He glorified him in the sight of kings, and gave him Commandments in the sight of his people, and revealed to him His glory. He sanctified him in his faith and meekness, and chose him out of all flesh. For He heard him and his voice, and brought him into a cloud. And, face to face, He gave him the Commandments, the law of life and understanding. S. Thanks be to God. ↰

Gradual. *Ps. 20, 4-5.* O Lord, You welcomed him with goodly blessings, You placed on his head a crown of pure gold. ℣. He asked life of You: You gave him length of days forever and ever.

Tract. *Ps. 111, 1-3.* Happy the man who fears the Lord, who greatly delights in His commands. ℣. His posterity shall be mighty upon the earth; the upright generation shall be blessed. ℣. Wealth and riches shall be in his house; his generosity shall endure forever.

During Paschaltime, the Gradual and the Tract are omitted and the following Alleluia is said:

Alleluia, alleluia. ℣. *Ecclus. 45, 9.* The Lord loved him, and adorned him; He clothed him with a robe of glory. Alleluia. ℣. *Osee 14, 6.* The just man shall spring as the lily; and shall flourish forever before the Lord. Alleluia.

● *Prayer: Cleanse My Heart, page* 31.

Gospel. *Matt. 1, 18-21.* When Mary the Mother of Jesus had been betrothed to Joseph, before they came together, she was found to be with child by the Holy Spirit. But Joseph her husband, being a just man, and not wishing to expose her to reproach, was minded to put her away privately. But while he thought on these things, behold, an angel of the Lord appeared to him in a dream, saying, "Do not be afraid, Joseph, son of David, to take to yourself Mary your wife, for that which is begotten in her is of the Holy Spirit. And she shall bring forth a Son, and you shall call His Name Jesus;

for He shall save His people from their sins." *S.* Praise be to You, O Christ.

- Creed, page 33.

Offertory. *Ps. 88, 25.* My faithfulness and My kindness shall be with him; and through My Name shall his horn be exalted. (*P.T.* Alleluia.)

- Offertory Prayers, page 35.

Secret. We render to You, O Lord, the debt of our service, humbly entreating You to preserve Your own gifts within us by the prayers of Blessed Joseph, Spouse of the Mother of Your Son, Jesus Christ, our Lord, on whose holy feast we offer You this sacrifice of praise. Through the same, etc. ↱

Preface of St. Joseph

P. World without end. *S.* Amen. *P.* The Lord be with you. *S.* And with your spirit. *P.* Lift up your hearts. *S.* We have lifted them up to the Lord. *P.* Let us give thanks to the Lord, our God. *S.* It is fitting and just.

It is fitting indeed and just, right and helpful to salvation, for us always and everywhere to give thanks to You, O Holy Lord, Father Almighty, Everlasting God; and magnify You with due praise, bless and proclaim You on the feast of Blessed Joseph; who, as a just man, was given by You to be the spouse of the Virgin Mother of God, and as a faithful and prudent servant, was set over Your family, that with fatherly care he might guard Your Only-begotten Son, Jesus Christ our Lord, conceived by the overshadowing of the Holy Spirit. Through Whom the Angels praise Your Majesty, the Dominations worship it, the Powers are in awe. The heavens and the heavenly hosts, and the blessed Seraphim join together in celebrating their joy. With these we pray You, join our own voices also, while we say with lowly praise: Holy, Holy, Holy, Lord God of hosts. Heaven and earth are filled with Your glory. Hosanna in the highest. Blessed is He Who comes in the Name of the Lord. Hosanna in the highest.

● *Canon, page 47.*

Communion. *Matt. 1, 20.* Do not be afraid, Joseph, son of David, to take to yourself Mary your wife, for that which is begotten in her is of the Holy Spirit. (*P.T.* Alleluia.)

P. The Lord be with you. *S.* And with your spirit. ↱

Postcommunion. Be present with us, we beseech You, O merciful God, and by the intercession of Blessed Joseph, Your Confessor, mercifully guard Your gifts bestowed upon us. Through our Lord, etc. *S.* Amen.

● *Final Prayers, page 73.*

"Alleluia! Alleluia! Mary is taken up into heaven."

Aug. 15 - THE ASSUMPTION OF THE BLESSED VIRGIN MARY

WHITE VESTMENTS

THOUGHT FOR TODAY: This feast celebrates the privilege of Mary, solemnly defined by the Church, proclaiming that the body of the Blessed Virgin Mary was gloriously assumed into heaven. He Who is mighty has done great things for her in the first instant of her Conception. He also preserved her body from corruption in imitation of the body of her Son which was formed in her womb.

● *Beginning of Mass, page 19.*

Introit. *Apoc. 12, 1.* A great sign appeared in heaven: a woman clothed with the sun, and the moon was under her feet, and upon her head a crown of twelve stars. *Ps. 97, 1.* Sing to the Lord a new song, for He has done wondrous deeds. ℣. Glory be.

● *Kyrie and Gloria, page 27.*

Prayer. O almighty and eternal God, Who assumed into celestial glory, in body and soul, the Immaculate Virgin Mary, the mother of Your Son, grant we beseech You, that ever intent on heavenly things, we may be worthy to share in her glory. Through the same, etc. S. Amen. ⌐

Epistle. *Judith 13, 22-25; 15, 10.* The Lord has blessed you by His power, because by you He has brought our enemies to naught. Blessed are you, O daughter, by the Lord the most high God, above all women upon the earth. Blessed be the Lord Who made heaven and earth, Who has directed you to the cutting off the head of the prince of our enemies, because He has so magnified your name this day, that your praise shall not depart out of the mouth of men who shall be mindful of the power of the Lord forever: for you have not spared your life, by reason of the distress and tribulation of your people, but have prevented our ruin in the presence of our God. You are the glory of Jerusalem, you are the joy of Israel, you are the honor of our people. S. Thanks be to God. ⌐

Gradual. *Ps. 44, 11-12. 14.* Hear, O daughter, and see; turn your ear; for the king shall desire your beauty. ℣. All glorious is the King's daughter as she enters; her raiment is threaded with spun gold.

Alleluia, alleluia. ℣. Mary is taken up into heaven: the host of angels rejoice. Alleluia.

● *Prayer: Cleanse My Heart, page* 31.

Gospel. *Luke 1, 41-50.* At that time, Elizabeth was filled with the Holy Spirit, and cried out with a loud voice, saying, "Blessed are you among women and blessed is the fruit of your womb! And how have I deserved that the mother of my Lord should come to me? For behold, the moment that the sound of your greeting came to my ears, the babe in my womb leapt for joy. And blessed is she who has believed, because the things promised her by the Lord shall be accomplished." And Mary said, "My soul magnifies the Lord, and my spirit rejoices in God my Savior; because He has regarded the lowliness of His handmaid; for, behold, henceforth all generations shall call me blessed. Because He Who is mighty has done great things for me, and holy is His Name; and His mercy is from generation to generation on those who fear Him." S. Praise be to You, O Christ.

● *Creed, page* 33.

Offertory. *Gen. 3, 15.* I will put enmity between you and the Woman, between your seed and her seed.

● *Offertory Prayers, page 35.*

Secret. May the offering of our devotion ascend to You, O Lord, and through the intercession of the Most Blessed Virgin Mary, assumed into heaven, may our hearts, fired by the flame of charity, incessantly long for You. Through our Lord, etc.

● *Preface of the Blessed Virgin, page 380.*

Communion. *Luke 1, 48-49.* All generations shall call me blessed, because He Who is mighty has done great things for me.

P. The Lord be with you. *S.* And with your spirit. ↱

Postcommunion. Having received Your salutary sacraments, grant, we beseech You, O Lord, that through the merits and intercession of the Blessed Virgin Mary, assumed into heaven, we may be brought to the glory of the resurrection. Through our Lord, etc. *S.* Amen.

● *Final Prayers, page 73.*

———◆———

"Blessed are the clean of heart for they shall see God."

Nov. 1 - FEAST OF ALL SAINTS

WHITE VESTMENTS

THOUGHT FOR TODAY: We celebrate today the feast of all servants of God who reached their eternal goal. They lived once in the "valley of tears" as we do. With their help and God's grace we hope to fight the good fight on earth and to share their happiness in the life hereafter.

● *Beginning of Mass, page 19.*

Introit. Let us all rejoice in the Lord, celebrating a feast day in honor of all the saints: at whose solemnity the angels rejoice, and give praise to the Son of God. *Ps. 32, 1.* Exult, you just, in the Lord; praise from the upright is fitting. ℣. Glory be.

● *Kyrie and Gloria, page 27.*

Prayer. Almighty and everlasting God, You have granted us to venerate in one solemn feast the merits of all Your saints; we beseech You, that, since so many are praying for us, You would pour forth upon us the desired abundance of Your mercy. Through our Lord, etc. S. Amen. ⌐

Epistle. *Apoc. 7, 2-12.* In those days, behold, I, John, saw another angel ascending from the rising of the sun, having the seal of the living God; and he cried with a loud voice to the four angels, who had it in their power to harm the earth and the sea, saying, "Do not harm the earth or the sea or the trees, till we have sealed the servants of our God on their foreheads." And I heard the number of those who were sealed, a hundred and forty-four thousand sealed, out of every tribe of the children of Israel; of the tribe of Juda, twelve thousand sealed; of the tribe of Ruben, twelve thousand; of the tribe of Gad, twelve thousand; of the tribe of Aser, twelve thousand; of the tribe of Nephthali, twelve thousand; of the tribe of Manasses, twelve thousand; of the tribe of Simeon, twelve thousand; of the tribe of Levi, twelve thousand; of the tribe of Issachar, twelve thousand; of the tribe of Zabulon, twelve thousand; of the tribe of Joseph, twelve thousand; of the tribe of Benjamin, twelve thousand sealed. After this I saw a great multitude which no man could number, out of all nations and tribes and peoples and tongues, standing before the throne and before the Lamb, clothed in white robes, and with palms in their hands. And they cried with a loud voice, saying, "Salvation belongs to our God Who sits upon the throne, and to the Lamb." And all the angels were standing round about the throne, and the elders and the four living creatures; and they fell on their faces before the throne and worshipped God, saying, "Amen. Blessing and glory and wisdom and thanksgiving and honor and power and strength to our God forever and ever. Amen." S. Thanks be to God. ⸽

Gradual. *Ps. 33, 10. 11.* Fear the Lord, you His holy ones, for naught is lacking to those who fear Him. ℣. But those who seek the Lord want for no good thing.

Alleluia, alleluia. ℣. *Matt. 11, 28.* Come to Me all you who labor and are burdened, and I will give you rest. Alleluia.

● Prayer: Cleanse My Heart, page 31.

Gospel. *Matt. 5, 1-12.* At that time, Jesus, seeing the crowds, went up the mountain. And when He was seated, His disciples came to Him. And opening His mouth He taught them, saying, "Blessed are the poor in spirit, for theirs is the kingdom of heaven. Blessed are the meek, for they shall possess the earth. Blessed are they who mourn, for they shall be comforted. Blessed are they who hunger and thirst for justice, for they shall be satisfied. Blessed are the merciful, for they shall obtain mercy. Blessed are the clean of heart, for they shall see God. Blessed are the peacemakers, for they shall be called children of God. Blessed are they who suffer persecution for justice' sake, for theirs is the kingdom of heaven. Blessed are you when men reproach you, and persecute you, and, speaking falsely, say all manner of evil against you, for My sake. Rejoice and exult, because your reward is great in heaven." *S.* Praise be to You, O Christ.

● Creed, *page* 33.

Offertory. *Wis. 3, 1-2. 3.* The souls of the just are in the hand of God, and no torment shall touch them. They seemed, in the view of the foolish, to be dead. But they are in peace. Alleluia.

● Offertory Prayers, *page* 35.

Secret. We offer to You, O Lord, the gifts of our devotion; may they please You for the honor of all the just, and, by Your

mercy, profit us to salvation. Through our
Lord, etc.

● *Preface, page 261.*

Communion. *Matt. 5, 8-10.* Blessed are
the clean of heart, for they shall see God;
blessed are the peacemakers, for they shall
be called children of God; blessed are they
who suffer persecution for justice' sake, for
theirs is the kingdom of heaven.

P. The Lord be with you. *S.* And with
your spirit. ↱

Postcommunion. Grant, we beseech You,
O Lord, that Your faithful people may always rejoice in honoring all Your saints, and
may be defended by their unceasing prayers.
Through our Lord, etc. *S.* Amen.

● *Final Prayers, page 73.*

*"What therefore God has joined together,
let no man put asunder."*

THE NUPTIAL MASS

THOUGHT FOR TODAY: For Christians, marriage is not only a very important contract, a source of life, but is the most intimate and sublime union between husband and wife. This union of love and confidence has been raised by our Lord to the dignity of a great sacrament and, if consummated, can only be dissolved by death.

MARRIAGE SERVICE

The Priest asks the bridegroom, who stands or kneels at the right side of the bride:

N . . . , will you take N . . . , here present, for your lawful wife, according to the rite of our holy Mother, the Church? *Response:* I will.

Then the Priest asks the bride:

N . . . , will you take N . . . , here present, for your lawful husband, according to the rite of our holy Mother, the Church? *Response:* I will.

The bridegroom now holds the bride's right hand in his own right hand, and prompted by the Priest, promises her his troth in these words:

I, N . . . take you, N . . . , for my lawful wife, to have and to hold, from this day forward, for better, for worse, for richer, for poorer, in sickness and in health, until death do us part.

Now loosening their hands and joining them again, the bride, prompted by the Priest, says:

I, N . . . take you, N . . . , for my lawful husband, to have and to hold, from this day forward, for better, for worse, for richer, for poorer, in sickness and in health, until death do us part.

The bridegroom and bride may kneel or stand and the Priest says:

I join you together in marriage, in the name of the Father, and of the Son, ✠ and of the Holy Spirit. *S.* Amen.

He then sprinkles them with holy water. This done, the Priest blesses the ring, saying:

Priest. Our help ✠ is in the name of the Lord.

Server. Who made heaven and earth.

P. O Lord, hear my prayer. *S.* And let my cry come to You. *P.* The Lord be with you. *S.* And with your spirit.

Let us pray. Bless ✠, O Lord, this ring, which we bless ✠ in Your name, that she who is to wear it, keeping true faith to her husband, may abide in Your peace and obedience to Your will, and ever live in mutual love. Through Christ our Lord. *S.* Amen.

The Priest sprinkles the ring with holy water in the form of a Cross; and the bridegroom, having received the ring from the hand of the Priest, puts it on the ring finger of the left hand of the bride, saying:

With this ring I wed you, and I pledge you my fidelity.

The Priest then says:

In the name of the Father, and of the Son, ✠ and of the Holy Spirit. *S.* Amen.

P. Confirm, O God, that which You have wrought in us. *S.* From Your holy temple, which is in Jerusalem.

Lord, have mercy, Christ, have mercy. Lord, have mercy. Our Father, etc. (*silently.*)

P. And lead us not into temptation. *S.* But deliver us from evil. *P.* Save Your servants. *S.* Who hope in You, O my God. *P.* Send them help, O Lord, from the Sanctuary. *S.* And defend them out of Sion. *P.* Be to them, O Lord, a tower of strength. *S.* From the face of the enemy. *P.* O Lord, hear my prayer. *S.* And let my cry come to You. *P.* The Lord be with you. *S.* And with your spirit.

Let us pray. Look, O Lord, we beseech You, upon these Your servants, and graciously protect Your own institution, whereby You have provided for the propagation of mankind, that they who are joined together by Your authority may be preserved by Your help. Through Christ our Lord. S. Amen.

THE NUPTIAL MASS

● *Beginning of Mass, page 19.*

Introit. *Tob. 7, 15; 8, 19.* May the God of Israel join you together: and may He be with you, Who was merciful to two only children: and now, O Lord, make them bless You more fully. (*P.T.* Alleluia, alleluia.) *Ps. 127, 1.* Happy are you who fear the Lord, who walk in His ways! ℣. Glory be.

● *Kyrie, page 27. Omit Gloria.*

Prayer. Graciously hear us, almighty and merciful God, that, what is performed by our ministry may be fulfilled by Your blessing. Through our Lord, etc. S. Amen. ➥

Epistle. *Eph. 5, 22-33.* Brethren: Let wives be subject to their husbands as to the Lord: because a husband is head of the wife, just as Christ is head of the Church, being Himself Savior of the body. But just as the Church is subject to Christ, so also let wives be to their husbands in all things. Husbands, love your wives, just as Christ also loved the Church, and delivered Himself up for her, that He might sanctify her, cleansing her in the bath of water by means of the word; in order that He might present to Himself the Church in all her glory, not

having spot or wrinkle or any such thing,
but that she might be holy and without
blemish. Even thus ought husbands also to
love their wives as their own bodies. He
who loves his own wife, loves himself. For
no one ever hated his own flesh; on the
contrary he nourishes and cherishes it, as
Christ also does the Church (because we
are members of His body, made from His
flesh and from His bones). "For this cause
a man shall leave his father and mother,
and cleave to his wife; and the two shall
become one flesh." This is a great mystery
—I mean in reference to Christ and to the
Church. However, let each one of you also
love his wife just as he loves himself; and
let the wife respect her husband. S. Thanks
be to God. ⇗

Gradual. *Ps. 127, 3.* Your wife shall be
like a fruitful vine in the recesses of your
home. ℣. Your children like olive plants
around your table.

Alleluia, alleluia. ℣. *Ps. 19, 3.* May the
Lord send you help from the sanctuary, from
Sion may He sustain you. Alleluia.

*After Septuagesima, omit Alleluia and versicle,
and say:*

Tract. *Ps. 127, 4-6.* Behold, thus is the
man blessed who fears the Lord. ℣. The

Lord bless you from Sion: may you see the prosperity of Jerusalem all the days of your life. ℣. May you see your children's children. Peace be upon Israel!

During Paschaltime, omit Gradual and say:

Alleluia, alleluia. ℣. *Ps. 19, 3.* May the Lord send you help from the sanctuary, from Sion may He sustain you. Alleluia. ℣. *Ps. 133, 3.* May the Lord bless you from Sion, the Maker of heaven and earth. Alleluia.

● *Prayer: Cleanse My Heart, page 31.*

Gospel. *Matt. 19, 3-6.* At that time, there came to Jesus some Pharisees, testing Him, and saying, "Is it lawful for a man to put away his wife for any cause?" But He answered and said to them, "Have you not read that the Creator, from the beginning, made them male and female, and said, 'For this cause a man shall leave his father and mother, and cleave to his wife, and the two shall become one flesh'? Therefore now they are no longer two, but one flesh. What therefore God has joined together, let no man put asunder." S. Praise be to You, O Christ.

P. The Lord be with you. *S.* And with your spirit. ↘

Offertory. *Ps. 30, 15. 16.* My trust is in You, O Lord; I say, "You are my God." In Your hands is my destiny. (*P.T.* Alleluia.)

● *Offertory Prayers, page 35.*

Secret. Accept, we beseech You, O Lord, the gifts offered for the sacred bond of marriage; and dispose according to Your will, that which is instituted by Your bounty. Through our Lord, etc.

● *Preface, page 261.*

After the "Our Father" the Priest turns to the bridal couple and says:

Prayer. Be appeased, O Lord, by our humble prayers, and in Your kindness assist this institution of marriage which You have ordained for the propagation of the human race; so that this union made here, joined by Your authority, may be preserved by Your help. Through our Lord, etc. S. Amen. ↰

Prayer. O God, by Your mighty power You have made all things out of nothing. First, You set the beginnings of the universe in order. Then, You made man in Your image, and appointed woman to be his inseparable helpmate. Thus You made woman's body from the flesh of man, thereby teaching that what You have been pleased to institute from one principle might never lawfully be put asunder. O God, You have sanctified marriage by a mystery so excellent that in the marriage union You foreshadowed the union of Christ and the Church. O God, You join woman to man, and You endow that fellowship with a blessing which was not taken away in punishment for original sin, nor by the sentence of the flood. Look, in Your mercy, upon this Your handmaid, about to be joined in wedlock, who entreats You to protect and strengthen her. Let the yoke of marriage to her be one of love and peace. Faithful and chaste, let her marry in Christ. Let her ever follow the model of holy women: let her be dear to her husband like Rachel; wise like Rebecca; long-lived and faithful like Sara. Let the author of sin work none of his evil deeds within her; let her ever keep the Faith and the Commandments. Let her be true to one wedlock and shun all sinful embraces. Let her strengthen weakness by stern discipline. Let her be grave in demeanor, honorable for her modesty, learned in heavenly doctrine, fruitful in children. Let her life be good and innocent. Let her come finally to the rest of the blessed in the kingdom of heaven. May they both see their children's children to the third and fourth generation, thus attaining the old age which they desire. Through the same, etc. S. Amen.

The Priest then continues as usual with the Prayer: "Deliver us, we beseech You," page 61.

Communion. *Ps. 127, 4. 6.* Behold, thus is the man blessed who fears the Lord; may you see your children's children. Peace be upon Israel! (*P.T.* Alleluia.)

P. The Lord be with you. *S.* And with your spirit. ↘

Postcommunion. We beseech You, almighty God, to accompany the institutions of Your providence with gracious favor; that You may preserve with lasting peace those whom You have joined in lawful union. Through our Lord, etc. S. Amen.

● *Final Prayers, page 73.*

The Priest, before giving the blessing, turns toward the Bridegroom and Bride, saying:

May the God of Abraham, the God of Isaac, and the God of Jacob be with you, and may He fulfill His blessing in you; that you may see your children's children even to the third and fourth generation, and thereafter may have life everlasting by the grace of our Lord Jesus Christ, Who with the Father and the Holy Spirit lives and reigns, God, world without end. S. Amen.

———◇———

"Eternal rest give to them, O Lord; and let perpetual light shine upon them."

DAILY MASS FOR THE DEAD
BLACK VESTMENTS

The following Mass for all the Faithful Departed may be used whenever a Requiem Mass is said. As of Jan. 1, 1961, the only Prayer, Secret and Postcommunion required to be said are those "For All the Faithful Departed" given in the third place below. However, the Priest has the option of adding another Prayer, Secret and Postcommunion—such as one of those printed in the first and second places below.

Ps. 42, "Do me justice, etc." is omitted.

● *Beginning of Mass, page 19.*

Introit. *4 Esd. 2, 34. 35.* Eternal rest give to them, O Lord; and let perpetual light shine upon them. *Ps. 64, 2. 3.* To You we owe our hymn of praise, O God, in Sion; to You must vows be fulfilled in Jerusalem. Hear my prayer; to You all flesh must come. ℣. Eternal rest, etc. (*Repeat as far as Ps.*)

Kyrie. Lord, have mercy. (*3 times.*)
Christ, have mercy. (*3 times.*)
Lord, have mercy. (*3 times.*)

P. The Lord be with you.

S. And with your spirit. ➘

1. *For Deceased Bishops and Priests:*

Prayer. O God, in the apostolic priesthood, You raised Your servants (N. Your servant) to the dignity of the episcopate (priesthood); grant, we beseech You, that they (he) may be numbered with Your bishops and priests forever. Through our Lord, etc. *S.* Amen.

2. *For Deceased Brethren, Relations and Benefactors:*

Prayer. O God, the Giver of pardon and the lover of man's salvation, we beseech Your mercy, through the intercession of Blessed Mary ever Virgin and of all Your saints, to grant to the souls of the brethren, relations and benefactors of our congregation who have passed out of this life, the companionship of everlasting bliss.

3. *For All the Faithful Departed:*

Prayer. O God, the Creator and Redeemer of all the faithful, grant to the souls of Your servants and handmaids, the remission of all their sins, that, through devout prayers, they may obtain the pardon which they always desired. Who live, etc. S. Amen. ➶

Epistle. *Apoc. 14, 13.* In those days, I heard a voice from heaven saying, "Write: Blessed are the dead who die in the Lord henceforth. Yes, says the Spirit, let them rest from their labors, for their works follow them." S. Thanks be to God. ➶

Gradual. *4 Esd. 2, 34. 35.* Eternal rest give to them, O Lord; and let perpetual light shine upon them. ℣. *Ps. 111, 7.* The just man shall be in everlasting remembrance; an evil report he shall not fear.

Tract. Absolve, O Lord, the souls of all the faithful departed from every bond of sin. ℣. And by the help of Your grace may they be enabled to escape the judgment of punishment. ℣. And enjoy the bliss of everlasting light.

● *Prayer: Cleanse My Heart, page 31.*

Gospel. *John 6, 51-55.* At that time, Jesus said to the multitudes of the Jews, "I am the living bread that has come down from heaven. If anyone eat of this bread he shall live forever; and the bread that I will give is My Flesh for the life of the world." The Jews on that account argued with one another, saying, "How can this man give us His Flesh to eat?" Jesus therefore said to them, "Amen, amen, I say to you, unless you eat the Flesh of the Son of Man, and drink His Blood, you shall not have life in you. He who eats My Flesh and drinks My Blood has life everlasting and I will raise him up on the last day." *S.* Praise be to You, O Christ.

P. The Lord be with you. *S.* And with your spirit. ↴

Offertory. O Lord Jesus Christ, King of glory, deliver the souls of all the faithful departed from the pains of hell and from the bottomless pit; deliver them from the lion's mouth, that hell swallow them not up, that they fall not into darkness, but let the holy standard-bearer Michael bring them into that holy light which You promised of old to Abraham and to his seed. ℣. We offer You, O Lord, sacrifices and prayers of praise: receive them in behalf of those souls we commemorate this day. Grant them, O Lord, to pass from death to life: that life which You promised of old to Abraham and to his seed.

● *Offertory Prayers, page 35.*

1. *For Deceased Bishops and Priests:*

Secret. Accept, we beseech You, O Lord, for the souls of Your servants, bishops (priests), the sacrifice which we offer, and let those whom in this world You raised to episcopal (sacerdotal) rank, be admitted into the company of Your saints. Through our Lord, etc. *S.* Amen.

2. *For Deceased Brethren, Relations and Benefactors:*

Secret. O God, Whose mercies are numberless, graciously receive our humble prayers, and through these sacraments of our salvation, grant to the souls of our brethren, relations and benefactors, who by Your grace did confess Your Name, the remission of all their sins.

3. *For All the Faithful Departed:*

Secret. Mercifully regard, we beseech You, O Lord, the sacrifice which we offer You for the souls of Your servants and handmaids, that, to those on whom You conferred the favor of the Christian Faith You would also grant its reward. Through our Lord, etc. ➘

Preface for the Dead

P. World without end. *S.* Amen. *P.* The Lord be with you. *S.* And with your spirit. *P.* Lift up your hearts. *S.* We have lifted them up to the Lord. *P.* Let us give thanks to the Lord, our God. *S.* It is fitting and just.

It is fitting indeed and just, right and helpful to salvation, for us always and everywhere to give thanks to You, O Holy Lord, Father Almighty, Everlasting God, through Christ our Lord. In Whom the hope of a blessed resurrection has shone upon us, that those whom the certainty of dying afflicts, may be consoled by the promise of future immortality. For to Your faithful, O Lord, life is changed, not taken away; and the abode of this earthly sojourn being dissolved, an eternal dwelling is prepared in heaven. And therefore with Angels and Archangels, with Thrones and Dominations, and with the whole host of the heavenly army, we sing a hymn to Your glory, saying again and again: Holy, Holy, Holy, Lord God of hosts. Heaven and earth are filled with Your glory. Hosanna in the highest. Blessed is He Who comes in the Name of the Lord. Hosanna in the highest.

● *Canon, page* 47.

Communion. *4 Esd. 2, 34. 35.* May light eternal shine upon them, O Lord, with Your saints forevermore, for You are gracious. ℣. Eternal rest give to them, O Lord; and let perpetual light shine upon them: with Your saints forever, for You are gracious.

1. *For Deceased Bishops and Priests*:

Postcommunion. O Lord, may the mercies which we implore, benefit the souls of Your servants, bishops (priests), that, in Your mercy, they may be united to You forevermore, who hoped and believed in You. Through our Lord, etc. S. Amen.

2. *For Deceased Brethren, Relations and Benefactors*:

Postcommunion. Grant, we beseech You, almighty and merciful God, that the souls of our brethren, relations and benefactors, for whom we have offered this sacrifice in praise of Your Majesty, by virtue of this sacrament, may be freed from all their sins, and by Your mercy, receive the bliss of eternal light.

3. *For All the Faithful Departed*:

Postcommunion. May the prayer of Your suppliant people, we beseech You, O Lord, benefit the souls of Your servants and handmaids, that You may deliver them from all their sins, and make them sharers in Your Redemption. Who live, etc. S. Amen.

● *Final Prayers, page 73.*

"*I am the Way, the Truth, and the Life.*"

TREASURY OF PRAYERS

The Sign of the Cross

An indulgence of 3 years; with holy water, an indulgence of 7 years. (No. 678.)

IN THE name of the Father, and of the Son, ✠ and of the Holy Spirit. Amen.

The Lord's Prayer

OUR Father Who art in heaven, hallowed be Thy Name; Thy kingdom come; Thy will be done on earth as it is in heaven. Give us this day our daily bread; and forgive us our trespasses as we forgive those who trespass against us; and lead us not into temptation, but deliver us from evil. Amen.

The Hail Mary

HAIL Mary, full of grace! the Lord is with thee; blessed art thou among women, and blessed is the fruit of thy womb, Jesus. Holy Mary, Mother of God, pray for us sinners now and at the hour of our death. Amen.

The indulgences quoted in this Missal are taken from the 1950 Vatican edition of the "Enchiridion Indulgentiarum."

Glory be to the Father

When devoutly recited in the early morning, at noon and in the evening with the intention of giving thanks to the Most Blessed Trinity for the excellent gifts and privileges granted to the B.V.M., an indulgence of 500 days is granted on each of the aforesaid parts of the day this prayer is recited. A plenary indulgence under the usual conditions if devoutly recited three times daily for a month. (No. 47.)

GLORY be to the Father, and to the Son, and to the Holy Spirit. As it was in the beginning, is now, and ever shall be, world without end. Amen.

The Apostles' Creed

An indulgence of 5 years. A plenary indulgence under the usual conditions if devoutly recited daily for a month. (No. 43.)

I BELIEVE in God, the Father Almighty, Creator of heaven and earth; and in Jesus Christ, His only Son, our Lord; Who was conceived by the Holy Ghost, born of the Virgin Mary, suffered under Pontius Pilate, was crucified, died and was buried. He descended into hell; the third day He arose again from the dead; He ascended into heaven, sitteth at the right hand of God, the Father Almighty; from thence He shall come to judge the living and the dead. I believe in the Holy Ghost, the Holy Catholic Church, the communion of Saints, the forgiveness of sins, the resurrection of the body, and life everlasting. Amen.

The Confiteor, page 23.

An Act of Faith

An indulgence of 3 years for each of the following four prayers. A plenary indulgence under the usual conditions if any of the following four prayers are recited daily for a month. (No. 36.)

O MY God, I firmly believe that Thou art one God in three Divine Persons, Father, Son and Holy Ghost; I believe that Thy Divine Son became man and died for our sins, and that He will come to judge the living and the dead. I believe these and all the truths which the Holy Catholic Church teaches because Thou hast revealed them, Who canst neither deceive nor be deceived.

An Act of Hope

O MY God, relying on Thy almighty power and infinite mercy and promises, I hope to obtain pardon of my sins, the help of Thy grace, and life everlasting, through the merits of Jesus Christ, my Lord and Redeemer.

An Act of Love

O MY God, I love Thee above all things, with my whole heart and soul, because Thou art all-good and worthy of all love. I love my neighbor as myself for the love of Thee. I forgive all who have injured me, and ask pardon of all whom I have injured.

Act of Contrition

O MY God, I am heartily sorry for having offended Thee, and I detest all my sins because of Thy just punishments, but most of all because they offend Thee, my God, Who art all-good and deserving of all my love. I firmly resolve with the help of Thy grace, to sin no more and to avoid the near occasions of sin. Amen.

The Angelus

The faithful who recite the Angelus or the Regina Coeli at dawn, at noon and at eventide, or as soon as possible thereafter, or who merely recite the Hail Mary five times, may gain an indulgence of 10 years each time. A plenary indulgence under the usual conditions if recited daily for a month. (No. 331.)

℣. The angel of the Lord declared to Mary.

℟. And she conceived of the Holy Spirit. Hail Mary, etc.

℣. Behold the handmaid of the Lord.

℞. Be it done to me according to your world. Hail Mary, etc.

℣. And the Word was made flesh.

℞. And dwelt among us. Hail Mary, etc.

℣. Pray for us, O holy Mother of God.

℞. That we may be made worthy of the promises of Christ.

Let us pray

POUR forth, we beseech You, O Lord, Your grace into our hearts, that we to whom the Incarnation of Christ, Your Son, was made known by the message of an angel, may by His Passion and Cross be brought to the glory of His Resurrection. Through the same Christ our Lord. Amen.

Regina Coeli

(*Said during Paschaltime instead of the Angelus*)

Queen of heaven, rejoice. Alleluia.

For He whom you deserved to bear. Alleluia.

Has risen as He said. Alleluia.

Pray for us to God. Alleluia.

℣. Rejoice and be glad, O Virgin Mary. Alleluia.

℟. For the Lord is truly risen. Alleluia.

Let us pray

O GOD, Who by the Resurrection of Your Son, our Lord Jesus Christ, vouchsafed to give joy to the whole world; grant, we beseech You, that, through the intercession of the Virgin Mary, His Mother, we may attain the joys of eternal life. Through the same Christ our Lord. Amen.

Grace before Meals

BLESS us, O Lord, and these Your gifts, which we are about to receive from Your bounty. Through Christ our Lord. Amen.

Grace after Meals

WE GIVE You thanks, Almighty God, for all Your benefits; Who live and reign, world without end. Amen.

MORNING PRAYERS

Say the Angelus, page 416.

Morning Offering

When recited in the morning, an indulgence of 5 years. A plenary indulgence under the usual conditions when recited daily for a month. (No. 60.)

LORD God Almighty, Who have brought us to the beginning of this day, defend us during this day by Your power, that we may not fall into sin but that all our words, thoughts and deeds may always proceed and be directed toward that which is just in Your sight.

Prayer to the Holy Spirit

An indulgence of 5 years. A plenary indulgence under the usual conditions, if recited daily for a month. (No. 287.)

COME, Holy Spirit, fill the hearts of Your faithful and kindle in them the fire of Your love.

℣. Send forth Your Spirit, and they shall be created.

℟. And You shall renew the face of the earth.

Let us pray

O God, Who taught the hearts of the faithful by the light of the Holy Spirit; grant that, by the gift of the same Spirit, we may be always truly wise, and ever rejoice in His consolation. Through Christ our Lord. ℟. Amen.

Into Your Hands, O Lord

An indulgence of 3 years. A plenary indulgence under the usual conditions, if recited daily for a month. (No. 55.)

INTO Your hands, O Lord, and the hands of Your Angels, I place and entrust this day my own soul, my relations, my benefactors, my friends and enemies, and all Catholic people; keep us during this day, by the merits and intercession of the Blessed Virgin Mary and all the Saints, from the vices, evil desires, sins, and temptations of the devil, from sudden and unprovided death, and from the pains of hell. May the light of the Holy Spirit and Your grace shine in my heart. Let me ever obey Your commandments, and let me never be separated from You, Who live and reign with God the Father and the same Holy Spirit, God, world without end. Amen. —St. Edmund

Spiritual Communion

An indulgence of 3 years. A plenary indulgence under the usual conditions, if recited daily for a month. (No. 164.)

MY JESUS, I believe that You are in the Blessed Sacrament. I love You above all things, and I long for You in my soul. Since I cannot now receive You sacramentally, come at least spiritually into my heart. As though You were already come, I embrace You and unite myself entirely to You; never permit me to be separated from You.

The Litany of the Holy Name of Jesus

An indulgence of 7 years. A plenary indulgence once a month under the usual conditions when this Litany is recited daily for a month. (No. 114.)

LORD, have mercy.
Christ, have mercy.
Lord, have mercy.
Jesus, hear us.
Jesus, graciously hear us.
God, the Father of Heaven,*
God the Son, Redeemer of the world,
God the Holy Spirit,
Holy Trinity, one God,
Jesus, Son of the living God,
Jesus, Splendor of the Father,
Jesus, Brightness of eternal Light,
Jesus, King of Glory,
Jesus, Sun of Justice,
Jesus, Son of the Virgin Mary,
Jesus, most amiable,

Jesus, most admirable,
Jesus, the mighty God,
Jesus, Father of the world to come,
Jesus, Angel of great counsel,
Jesus, most powerful,
Jesus, most patient,
Jesus, most obedient,
Jesus, meek and humble of heart,
Jesus, Lover of Chastity,
Jesus, our Lover,
Jesus, God of Peace,
Jesus, Author of Life,
Jesus, Model of Virtues,
Jesus, zealous for souls,
Jesus, our God,
Jesus, our Refuge,
Jesus, Father of the Poor,

Have mercy on us.

Jesus, Treasure of the Faithful,*

Jesus, good Shepherd,

Jesus, true Light,

Jesus, eternal Wisdom,

Jesus, infinite Goodness,

Jesus, our Way and our Life,

Jesus, joy of Angels,

Jesus, King of the Patriarchs,

Jesus, Master of the Apostles,

Jesus, Teacher of the Evangelists,

Jesus, Strength of Martyrs,

Jesus, Light of Confessors,

Jesus, Purity of Virgins,

Jesus, Crown of all Saints,

Be merciful, *spare us, O Jesus!*

Be merciful, *graciously hear us, O Jesus!*

From all evil,†

From all sin,

From Your wrath,

From the snares of the devil,

From the spirit of fornication,

From everlasting death,

From the neglect of Your inspirations,

Through the mystery of Your holy incarnation,

Through Your nativity,

Through Your infancy,

Through Your most divine life,

Through Your labors,

Through Your agony and passion,

Through Your Cross and dereliction,

Through Your sufferings,

Through Your death and burial,

Through Your resurrection,

Through Your ascension,

Through Your institution of the Most Holy Eucharist,

Through Your joys,

Through Your glory,

Lamb of God, You Who take away the sins of the world, *spare us, O Jesus!*

Lamb of God, You Who take away the sins of the world, *hear us, O Jesus!*

Lamb of God, You Who take away the sins of the world, *have mercy on us, O Jesus!*

Jesus, hear us.

Jesus, graciously hear us.

*Have mercy on us.

†Deliver us, O Jesus.

Let us pray

O Lord Jesus Christ, Who have said, "Ask, and you shall receive; seek, and you shall find; knock, and it shall be opened to you"; mercifully attend to our supplications, and grant us the grace of Your most divine love, that we may love You with all our hearts, and in all our words and actions, and never cease to praise You.

Make us, O Lord, to have a perpetual fear and love for Your holy Name, for You never fail to govern those whom You do solidly establish in Your love. Who live and reign, world without end. Amen.

———◆———

EVENING PRAYERS

Say the Angelus, page 416.

A Prayer for Protection

An indulgence of 500 days when said in the evening. (No. 63.)

O MY God, I adore You and I love You with all my heart. I thank You for having created me, for having made me a Christian and for having watched over me this day. Pardon me for the evil I have done this day; and if I have done any good, deign to accept it. Watch over me while I take my rest and deliver me from danger. May Your grace be always with me. Amen.

Prayer for the Faithful Departed

An indulgence of 3 years. A plenary indulgence under the usual conditions, if recited daily for a month. (No. 597.)

O LORD Jesus Christ, King of glory, deliver the souls of all the faithful departed from the pains of hell and from the bottomless pit; deliver them from the lion's mouth, that hell swallow them not up, that they fall not into darkness, but let the holy standard-bearer Michael bring them into that holy light which You promised to Abraham and his seed.

Prayer of St. Alphonsus

When recited before going to sleep, an indulgence of 3 years, once a day. A plenary indulgence under the usual conditions, if recited daily for a month. (No. 99.)

JESUS CHRIST, my God, I adore You and I thank You for the many favors You have bestowed on me this day. I offer You my sleep and all the moments of this night, and I pray You to preserve me from sin. Therefore, I place myself in Your most sacred side, and under the mantle of our Blessed Lady, my Mother. May the holy angels assist me and keep me in peace, and may Your blessing be upon me.

Prayer for the Home

When said in the evening, an indulgence of 5 years. A plenary indulgence under the usual conditions, if recited daily for a month. (No. 62.)

WE BESEECH You, O Lord, visit this home, and drive far from it all the snares of the enemy: let Your holy angels dwell therein so as to preserve us in peace; and let Your blessing be always upon us. Through Christ our Lord. Amen.

Prayer to the Guardian Angel

An indulgence of 300 days. A plenary indulgence under the usual conditions, if recited daily for a month. (No. 452.)

Angel of God, my guardian dear,
  To whom His love commits me here,
Ever this night be at my side,
  To light and guard, to rule and guide.
    Amen.

The Litany of the Blessed Virgin Mary

An indulgence of 7 years. A plenary indulgence once a month under the usual conditions, if this Litany with its versicle and prayer is recited daily for a month. (No. 319.)

LORD, have mercy.
  Christ, have mercy.
Lord, have mercy.
Christ, hear us.
Christ, graciously hear us.

God, the Father of Heaven, *have mercy on us.*
God the Son, Redeemer of the world, *have mercy on us.*

God the Holy Spirit, *have mercy on us.*

Holy Trinity, One God, *have mercy on us.*

Holy Mary,*

Holy Mother of God,

Holy Virgin of virgins,

Mother of Christ,

Mother of divine grace,

Mother most pure,

Mother most chaste,

Mother inviolate,

Mother undefiled,

Mother most amiable,

Mother most admirable,

Mother of good counsel,

Mother of our Creator,

Mother of our Savior,

Virgin most prudent,

Virgin most venerable,

Virgin most renowned,

Virgin most powerful,

Virgin most merciful,

Virgin most faithful,

Mirror of justice,

Seat of wisdom,

Cause of our joy,

Spiritual vessel,

Vessel of honor,

Singular vessel of devotion,

Mystical rose,

Tower of David,

Tower of ivory,

House of gold,

Ark of the covenant,

Gate of heaven,

Morning star,

Health of the sick,

Refuge of sinners,

Comforter of the afflicted,

Help of Christians,

Queen of Angels,

Queen of Patriarchs,

Queen of Prophets,

Queen of Apostles,

Queen of Martyrs,

Queen of Confessors,

Queen of Virgins,

Queen of all Saints,

Queen conceived without original sin,

Queen assumed into heaven,

Queen of the most holy Rosary,

Queen of Peace,

Lamb of God, You Who take away the sins of the world, *spare us, O Lord!*

Lamb of God, You Who take away the sins of the world, *graciously hear us, O Lord!*

Lamb of God, You Who take away the sins of the world, *have mercy on us.*

℣. Pray for us, O holy Mother of God.

℟. That we may be made worthy of the promises of Christ.

Pray for us.

Let us pray

Grant, we beseech You, O Lord God, that we Your servants, may enjoy lasting health of mind and body, and by the glorious intercession of the Blessed Mary, ever Virgin, be delivered from present sorrow and enter into the joy of eternal happiness. Through Christ our Lord. Amen.

———◇———

BENEDICTION OF THE BLESSED SACRAMENT

O Salutaris

O SALUTARIS Hóstia	O SAVING Victim, opening wide
Quæ cæli pandis óstium:	The gate of heav'n to man below:
Bella premunt hostília,	Our foes press on from every side;
Da robur, fer auxílium.	Your aid supply, Your strength bestow.
Uni trinóque Dómino,	To Your great Name be endless praise,
Sit sempitérna glória,	Immortal Godhead, One in Three!
Qui vitam sine término	O grant us endless length of days,
Nobis donet in pátria. Amen.	With You in our true country. Amen.

Tantum Ergo

TANTUM ergo Sacraméntum,
Venerémur cérnui:

Et antíquum documéntum
Novo cedat rítui;

Præstet fides suppleméntum
Sénsuum deféctui.

Genitóri, Genitóque
Laus et jubilátio,

Salus, honor, virtus quoque,
Sit et benedíctio:
Procedénti ab utróque

Compar sit laudátio
Amen.

℣. Panem de cælo præstitísti eis. (Alleluia.)

℞. Omne delectaméntum in se habéntem. (Alleluia.)

DOWN in adoration falling,
Lo! the Sacred Host we hail;

Lo! o'er ancient forms departing
Newer rites of grace prevail;

Faith for all defects supplying
Where the feeble senses fail.

To the everlasting Father,
And the Son who reigns on high,

With the Holy Spirit proceeding
Forth from each eternally,
Be salvation, honor, blessing,

Might and endless majesty! Amen.

℣. You gave them bread from heaven. (Alleluia.)

℞. Containing in itself all sweetness. (Alleluia.)

Let us pray

O God, under a wonderful Sacrament, You have left us a memorial of Your Passion; grant us, we beseech You, so to venerate the sacred mysteries of Your Body and Blood that we may ever feel within us the fruit of Your redemption. Who live, etc.

The Divine Praises

An indulgence of 3 years. An indulgence of 5 years if said publicly. A plenary indulgence under the usual conditions if said daily for a month. (No. 696.)

BLESSED be God. Blessed be His Holy Name. Blessed be Jesus Christ, true God and true Man. Blessed be the Name of Jesus. Blessed be His Most Sacred Heart. Blessed be His Most Precious Blood. Blessed be Jesus in the Most Holy Sacrament of the Altar. Blessed be the great Mother of God, Mary most Holy. Blessed be her Holy and Immaculate Conception. Blessed be her Glorious Assumption. Blessed be the Name of Mary, Virgin and Mother. Blessed be St. Joseph, her most chaste spouse. Blessed be God in His Angels and in His Saints.

Hymn — "Holy God"

Holy God, we praise Thy name!
Lord of all, we bow before Thee!
All on earth Thy sceptre claim,
All in heaven above adore Thee.
Infinite Thy vast domain,
Everlasting is Thy reign.

Hark! the loud celestial hymn,
Angel choirs above are raising;
Cherubim and seraphim,
In unceasing chorus praising,
Fill the heavens with sweet accord;
Holy, holy, holy Lord!

THE FORTY HOURS' DEVOTION

This devotion, during which the Blessed Sacrament is publicly exposed for the veneration of the faithful for forty hours, in memory of the forty hours during which the Body of our Savior remained in the sepulchre, was begun at Milan in 1534.

During the Forty Hours' Exposition of the Blessed Sacrament, if a visit is made, during which the faithful recite five times the Our Father, Hail Mary, *and* Glory be *and add one* Our Father, Hail Mary, *and* Glory be *for the intentions of our Holy Father, an indulgence of 15 years. Those who go to confession and receive Holy Communion, may gain a plenary indulgence on each of the days of the exposition.* (No. 169.)

THE SACRAMENT OF PENANCE

PRAYERS BEFORE CONFESSION

Prayer for a Good Confession

An indulgence of 3 years. (No. 207.)

BEHOLD me at Your feet, O Jesus of Nazareth; behold the most miserable of creatures, who presents himself before You, humbled and penitent. Have mercy on me, O Lord, according to Your great mercy. I sinned, and my sins were committed against You. And yet my soul belongs to You because You have created and redeemed it with Your Precious Blood. May Your work not be in vain! Have pity on me; give me tears of repentance; pardon me, for I am Your child; pardon me as You pardoned the penitent thief; watch over me from the height of heaven and bless me.

I believe in God, etc.

Examination of Conscience

Begin by examining yourself on your last Confession and Communion: whether a grievous sin was forgotten through want of proper examination, concealed or disguised through shame; whether you confessed without a true sorrow, a firm purpose of amendment, and of repairing the evil done to your neighbor. Then examine yourself on the Ten Commandments, the Commandments of the Church, and the duties of your state in life. Do not neglect to consider the various ways in which we may become accessories to the sins of others.

The Ten Commandments:

1st. Did I wilfully doubt my Catholic Faith? make use of superstitious practices? deliberately omit daily prayers? wilfully despair of God's mercy or presume upon it to commit sin?

2nd. Did I use the name of God irreverently? call God to witness without good reason? or a falsehood?

3rd. Did I intentionally miss Mass on Sunday or a holy day of obligation? perform servile work?

4th. Did I disobey, criticize, show disrespect to parents or superiors?

5th. Did I harm anyone? become angry or speak unkindly to another? refuse to apologize or forgive? give bad example, tempt to sin, or ridicule another's good intentions? curse another? Did I injure my health by excessive amusements, eating or drinking? Did I give in to sadness?

6th and 9th. Did I take wilful pleasure in impure thoughts or desires? speak impurely or listen to impure conversation? allow unlawful intimacies? engage in passionate dancing? read immoral books and magazines? attend immoral plays, floor shows or motion pictures? commit an impure act with myself or others?

7th and 10th. Did I steal or help others to steal? desire to steal? Did I wilfully or negligently keep goods loaned to me as my own? Did I waste money? destroy or damage another's property?

8th. Did I lie to save myself or others? Did I injure the good name of another either by publicizing his wrong-doing without necessity (detraction) or telling others of misdeeds he never committed (slander)? Did I deliberately misinterpret the motives of another?

The Commandments of the Church:

Did I hear Mass on days of obligation? Did I abstain from meat on appointed days? fast (if 21 years old)? Did I go to confession and communion at Easter time? Did I contribute to the support of our pastor? Did I make plans for marriage outside the laws of the Church?

Say an Act of Contrition, page 416.

The Form of Confession

1. When the Priest opens the slide, make the Sign of the Cross and say: "Bless me, father, for I have sinned. It is (*state the time*) since my last confession."

2. Tell how long it is since your last confession, without waiting to be asked.

3. Give, as nearly as possible, the number of mortal sins. As to venial sins, telling the number is optional.

4. Distinguish between temptation and sin: between mortal and venial sins, particularly in regard to impure thoughts, imaginations and feelings. They become sins only when deliberately admitted, and mortal sins when wilfully entertained, although your conscience has warned you of their danger and of the obligation to reject them. You may include temptations by saying simply, "I had some impure thoughts, but did my best to banish them."

5. At the conclusion, if only venial sins have been confessed, include some sin of your past life, previously confessed, for which you are heartily sorry.

6. Listen carefully to the advice the Priest may give you. Answer his questions clearly, without any irrelevant details. Accept the penance he imposes.

7. While he is saying the words of absolution make an act of loving contrition, trusting in God's mercy and resolving to do all that you can to please Him.

PRAYERS AFTER CONFESSION

Act of Reparation

An indulgence of 500 days, once a day. A plenary indulgence under the usual conditions, if recited daily for a month. (No. 100.)

O JESUS, Son of the living God, my Savior and Redeemer, behold us prostrate at Your feet. We beg pardon, and make this act of reparation for all the blasphemies uttered against Your Holy Name, for all the outrages committed against You in the most holy Sacrament of the altar, for all irreverence shown to Your most Blessed and Immaculate Mother, and for all the calumnies spoken against Your spouse, our holy Mother, the Catholic Church. O Jesus, Who said: *Whatever you shall ask the Father in My Name, that I will do,* we pray and beseech You for our brethren who are living in danger of sin, that You preserve them from the seductions of apostasy. Save them who stand over the abyss; give them light and knowledge of the truth, power and strength in the conflict against evil, and perseverance in faith and active charity. And therefore, most merciful Jesus, do we pray to the Father in Your Name, with Whom You live and reign, in the unity of the Holy Spirit, world without end. Amen.

Act of Firm Purpose

An indulgence of 500 days. A plenary indulgence under the usual conditions, if devoutly recited daily for a month. (No. 112.)

GIVE me a change of heart, O Jesus, You Who have sacrificed Yourself for love of me! Make known to my spirit the excellence of Your sacred humiliations. Let me begin today, illumined by Your light, to destroy this part of the natural man which lives in me in its entirety. This is the main source of my misery, the obstacle that constantly keeps me from Your love.

(R. Card. Merry del Val)

DEVOTIONS FOR HOLY COMMUNION

PRAYERS BEFORE HOLY COMMUNION

Prayer of St. Thomas Aquinas

An indulgence of 3 years. A plenary indulgence once a month, for daily recitation under the usual conditions. (No. 158.)

ALMIGHTY and eternal God, I approach the sacrament of Your Only-begotten Son, our Lord Jesus Christ. As a sick man I approach the physician of life; as a man unclean, I come to the fountain of mercy; blind, to the light of eternal brightness; poor and needy, to the Lord of heaven and earth. I beseech You, therefore, in Your boundless mercy, to heal my sickness, to wash away my defilements, to enlighten my blindness, to enrich my poverty, and to clothe my nakedness; that I may receive the Bread of angels, the King of kings, the Lord of lords, with such reverence and humility, such contrition and faith, such purpose and intention, as may help the salvation of my soul. Grant, I beseech You, that I may receive not only the Sacrament of the Body and Blood of our Lord, but also the whole grace and virtue of the Sacrament. O most indulgent God, grant me so to receive the Body of Your Only-begotten Son, our Lord Jesus Christ, which He took of the Virgin Mary, that I may be found worthy to be incorporated with His Mystical Body and numbered among His members. O most loving Father, grant that I may one day forever contemplate Him unveiled and face to face, Whom, on my pilgrimage, I receive under a veil, Your beloved Son, Who lives and reigns with You in the unity of the Holy Spirit, God, world without end. Amen.

Prayer for a Worthy Communion

An indulgence of 5 years. A plenary indulgence if devoutly recited daily for a month with the addition of sacramental confession, a visit to a church or public oratory, and prayer for the intentions of the Pope. (No. 155.)

LET not the partaking of Your Body, O Lord Jesus Christ, which I, though unworthy, presume to receive, turn to my judgment and condemnation; but through Your goodness, may it become a safeguard and an effective remedy, both of soul and body. Who live and reign, world without end. Amen.

Prayer to the Blessed Virgin

An indulgence of 3 years. (No. 747.)

O MOST Blessed Virgin Mary, most loving and most merciful Mother, I a wretched and unworthy sinner, come before you, with the heartfelt prayer, that in your goodness you would deign graciously to be near me and all who throughout the whole Church are to receive the Body and Blood of your Son this day, even as you stood by your most dear Son as He hung on the Cross, that, aided by your gracious help, we may worthily offer up a pure and acceptable sacrifice in the sight of the most high and undivided Trinity. Amen.

Prayer to St. Joseph

An indulgence of 3 years. (No. 747.)

O BLESSED Joseph, happy man, to whom it was given not only to see and to hear that God Whom many kings longed to see, and saw not, to hear, and heard not; but also to carry Him in your arms, to embrace Him, to clothe Him, and to guard and defend Him.

℣. Pray for us, O Blessed Joseph.

℟. That we may be made worthy of the promises of Christ.

Let us pray

O God Who have given us a royal priesthood, we beseech You, that as Blessed Joseph was found worthy to touch with his hands, and to bear in his arms, Your Only-begotten Son, born of the Virgin Mary, so may we be made fit, by cleanness of heart and blamelessness of life, to minister at Your holy altar; may we, this day, with reverent devotion partake of the Sacred Body and Blood of Your Only-begotten Son, and may we in the world to come be accounted worthy of receiving an everlasting reward. Through the same Christ our Lord. Amen.

Spiritual Communion, page 420.

THANKSGIVING AFTER COMMUNION

Prayer to Christ the King

A plenary indulgence once a day. (No. 272.)

O CHRIST Jesus, I acknowledge You King of the Universe. All that has been created has been made for You. Exercise upon me all Your rights. I renew my baptismal promises, renouncing Satan and all his works and pomps. I promise to live a

good Christian life and to do all in my
power to procure the triumph of the rights
of God and Your Church. Divine Heart of
Jesus, I offer You my poor actions in order
to obtain that all hearts may acknowledge
Your sacred Royalty, and that thus the
reign of Your peace may be established
throughout the universe. Amen.

Prayer of St. Thomas Aquinas

An indulgence of 3 years. (No. 160.)

I THANK You, O holy Lord, almighty
Father, eternal God, Who have deigned,
not through any merits of mine, but out of
the condescension of Your goodness, to satisfy me a sinner, Your unworthy servant,
with the precious Body and Blood of Your
Son, our Lord Jesus Christ. I pray that this
holy Communion be not a condemnation
to punishment for me, but a saving plea
to forgiveness. May it be to me the armor
of faith and the shield of a good will.
May it be the emptying out of my vices
and the extinction of all lustful desires; an
increase of charity and patience, of humility
and obedience, and of all virtues; a strong
defense against the snares of all my enemies,
visible and invisible; the perfect quieting of
all my evil impulses of flesh and spirit,

binding me firmly to You, the one true God; and a happy ending of my life. I pray too that You will deign to bring me a sinner to that ineffable banquet, where You with Your Son and the Holy Spirit, are to Your Saints true light, fulfillment of desires, eternal joy, unalloyed gladness, and perfect bliss. Through the same Christ our Lord. Amen.

Prayer of St. Bonaventure

PIERCE, O most sweet Lord Jesus Christ, my inmost soul with the most joyous and healthful pang of Your love, with true, serene, and most holy apostolic charity, so that my soul may always languish and melt with love and longing for You, that it may yearn for You and Your dwelling-place, and long to be dissolved and to be with You. Grant that my soul may hunger after You, the bread of angels, the refreshment of holy souls, our daily and supersubstantial bread, having all sweetness and savor and every delight to the taste. Let my heart always hunger and feed upon You, Whom the angels yearn to look upon, and may my inmost soul be filled with the sweetness of Your savor. May it always thirst after You, the source of life, the source of wisdom and knowledge, the source of eternal light, the torrent of pleasure, the richness of the house of God. May it always compass You, seek You, find You, run to You, attain to You, meditate upon You, speak of You, and do all things for the honor and glory of Your holy Name, with humility and discretion, with love and delight, with readiness and affection, and with perseverance to the end. Be alone always my hope and my whole confidence, my riches, my delight, my pleasure and my joy; my rest and tranquillity; my peace, my sweetness and my fragrance; my sweet savor, my food and refreshment; my refuge and my help; my wisdom and portion, my possession and my treasure, in Whom may my mind and my heart be always fixed and firm and rooted immovably. Amen.

Adoro Te

An indulgence of 5 years. An indulgence of 7 years if this hymn or only the last two verses are recited before the Blessed Sacrament. A plenary indulgence under the usual conditions, if this hymn is recited daily for a month. (No. 166.)

O HIDDEN Godhead, humbly I adore You,
Who truly are beneath the forms in my view.

To You I bow my heart and bend the knee,
Since, contemplating You, all fails for me.
Sight, touch and taste in You are each
     deceived:
The ear alone most safely is believed.

I firmly hold whate'er God's Son has spoken,
Than Truth's own word there is no truer
     token.

God only on the Cross was hid from view,
But here hides Deity and Manhood too;
And I in both professing firm belief,
Make mine the prayer of the repentant thief.

Your wounds, as Thomas saw, I do not see,
Yet You confess my Lord and God to be.
My faith confirm and childlike trust impart,
And may I love You, Lord, with all my
     heart.

O Blest Memorial of our Lord's own dying:
O Living Bread, to mortals life supplying:
Become indeed the life of my own mind,
So that in You I may all sweetness find.

O Pelican, self-wounding on the Rood,
Me unclean man yet cleanse with Your
     own Blood,
Of which a single drop, for sinners spilt,
Can purge this wicked world of all its guilt.

O Jesus Whom at present veiled I see,
What I so thirst for, do You grant to me:

That I may see Your Blessed Self unfolding,
And may find rest Your glory in beholding.
  Amen.

Offering and Prayer of St. Ignatius Loyola

An indulgence of 3 years. A plenary indulgence under the usual conditions, if devoutly recited daily for a month. (No. 52.)

TAKE O Lord, and receive my entire liberty, my memory, my understanding and my whole will. All that I am and all that I possess You have given me: I surrender it all to You to be disposed of according to Your will. Give me only Your love and Your grace; with these I will be rich enough, and will desire nothing more.

Anima Christi

An indulgence of 300 days every time. 7 years after Communion. A plenary indulgence under the usual conditions once a month for those who recite it every day. (No. 131.)

SOUL of Christ, sanctify me.
  Body of Christ, save me.
Blood of Christ, inebriate me.
Water from the side of Christ, wash me.
Passion of Christ, strengthen me.
O good Jesus, hear me.
Within Your wounds hide me.
Separated from You let me never be.

From the malignant enemy, defend me.
At the hour of death, call me.
And close to You bid me.
That with Your saints I may be
Praising You, forever and ever. Amen.

Indulgenced Prayer Before a Crucifix

An indulgence of 10 years. A plenary indulgence may be gained by all, who having confessed and received Holy Communion, recite this prayer before an image of Christ crucified and also pray for the intentions of the Holy Father. (No. 201.)

BEHOLD, O kind and most sweet Jesus, I cast myself upon my knees in Your sight, and with the most fervent desire of my soul I pray and beseech You that You would impress upon my heart lively sentiments of Faith, Hope and Charity, with true repentance for my sins, and a firm desire of amendment, while with deep affection and grief of soul I ponder within myself and mentally contemplate Your five most precious wounds; having before my eyes that which David spoke in prophecy of You, O good Jesus: They have pierced my hands and feet; they have numbered all my bones.

THE WAY OF THE CROSS

The Way of the Cross is a devotion in which we accompany, in spirit, our Blessed Lord in His sorrowful journey to Calvary, and devoutly meditate on His sufferings and death.

INDULGENCES

Those who devoutly make the Stations of the Cross, may gain a plenary indulgence. An added plenary indulgence with the reception of Holy Communion on the same day, or within a month after having made the Stations of the Cross 10 times.

Those who are lawfully hindered from making the Stations of the Cross, may gain the same indulgences if they hold a Crucifix, blessed for this purpose in their hand, and piously recite twenty times Our Father, Hail Mary, and Glory be, one for each Station, five for the five Sacred Wounds of our Lord, and one for the intention of the Holy Father. If prevented from doing this, an indulgence of 10 years for each recitation of Our Father, Hail Mary and Glory be.

I. Jesus Is Condemned to Death

O Jesus, You desired to die for me that I may receive the supernatural life, sanctifying grace, and become a child of God. How precious must be that life. Teach me to appreciate it more and more.

II. Jesus Bears His Cross

O Jesus, You have chosen to die the disgraceful death on the Cross. You have paid a high price for my redemption and the life of grace that was bestowed upon me. May I love You always.

III. Jesus Falls the First Time

O Jesus, Your painful fall under the Cross and Your quick rise teach me to repent and rise instantly should I ever be forgetful of Your love and commit a mortal sin. Make me strong to conquer my wicked passions.

IV. Jesus Meets His Mother

O Jesus, Your afflicted Mother was resigned to Your Passion because she is my Mother also, and wants to see me live and die as a child of God. Grant me a tender love of Your holy Mother.

V. Jesus Is Helped by Simon

O Jesus, Simon first reluctantly helped You to carry the Cross. Make me better understand the value of my sufferings which should lead me closer to You, as Simon was united with You through the Cross.

VI. Jesus and Veronica

O Jesus, how graciously did You reward that courageous woman. When I side with You against sin and temptation, You surely will increase the beauty of my soul and fill me with joy and peace. Jesus, give me courage.

VII. Jesus Falls a Second Time

O Jesus, despite my good resolutions I have sinned repeatedly. But Your sufferings assure me of forgiveness if only I return to You with a contrite heart. I repent for having offended You.

VIII. Jesus Speaks to the Women

O Jesus, You told the women of Jerusalem to weep rather over themselves. Make me weep over my sins which caused Your sufferings and the loss of my friendship with You.

IX. Jesus Falls a Third Time

O Jesus, I see You bowed to the earth enduring the pains of extreme exhaustion. Grant that I never yield to despair but come to You for help in hardship and spiritual distress.

X. Jesus Stripped of His Garments

O Jesus, You permitted Yourself to be stripped of Your garments. Grant, that I may sacrifice all my attachments rather than imperil the divine life of my soul.

XI. Jesus Is Nailed to the Cross

O Jesus, how could I complain of being nailed to God's commandments which are given for my salvation when I see You nailed to the Cross. Strengthen my faith and increase my love for You.

XII. Jesus Dies on the Cross

O Jesus, dying on the Cross, You preached love and forgiveness. May I be thankful that You have made me a child of God. Help me to forgive all those who have injured me.

XIII. Jesus Is Taken from the Cross

O Jesus, a sword of grief pierced Your Mother's heart when You were lying lifeless in her arms. Grant me through her intercession to lead the life of a loyal child of Mary.

XIV. Jesus Is Laid in the Tomb

O Jesus, Your enemies triumphed when they sealed Your tomb. But Your eternal triumph began on Easter morning. Strengthen my good will to live for You until the divine life of my soul will be manifested in the bliss of heaven.

PRAYERS AND DEVOTIONS TO THE SACRED HEART OF JESUS

June — Month of the Sacred Heart

During the month of June or any month designated by the Bishop of the Diocese, the faithful who devoutly take part in public services in honor of the Sacred Heart of Jesus may gain an indulgence of 10 years on any day of the month. A plenary indulgence, if they are present at these services on at least 10 days with the addition of Confession, Communion and pray for the intentions of the Supreme Pontiff.

Those who perform their devotions privately during such a month, may gain an indulgence of 7 years on any day of the month. A plenary indulgence under the usual conditions, if they perform these devotions daily during the month and are lawfully prevented from taking part in the public exercises. (No. 253.)

First Friday Devotions

Those who assist at the public exercises in honor of the Sacred Heart, may gain a plenary indulgence with the addition of Confession, Communion and prayers for the intentions of the Holy Father.

Those who on the First Friday recite privately some prayers in reparation for the injuries against the Sacred Heart, may gain a plenary indulgence under the usual conditions. If, moreover, a public service is held, this latter indulgence can be gained only by those who are lawfully prevented from assisting at such a service.

Those who recite devout prayers of reparation on other Fridays of the year, may gain an indulgence of 7 years once on each Friday. (No. 252.)

Those who receive Holy Communion on any of the five Fridays immediately preceding the Feast of the Sacred Heart, may gain a plenary indulgence, if they go to confession, visit some church or public oratory and pray for the intentions of the Holy Father. (No. 254.)

Promises of the Sacred Heart

1. I will give to My Faithful all the graces necessary in their state of life.

2. I will establish peace in their homes.

3. I will comfort them in all their afflictions.

4. I will be their secure refuge during life, and above all in death.

5. I will bestow abundant blessings upon all their undertakings.

6. Sinners shall find in My Heart the source and the infinite ocean of mercy.

7. Tepid souls shall become fervent.

8. Fervent souls shall quickly mount to high perfection.

9. I will bless every place in which an image of My Heart shall be exposed and honored.

10. I will give to priests the gift of touching the most hardened hearts.

11. Those who shall promote this devotion shall have their names written in My Heart, never to be effaced.

12. I promise you in the excessive mercy of My Heart that My all-powerful love will grant to all those who communicate on the First Friday in nine consecutive months the grace of final penitence; they shall not die in My disgrace nor without receiving their Sacraments. My Divine Heart shall be their safe refuge in this last moment.

Act of Reparation to the Sacred Heart of Jesus

An indulgence of 5 years. A plenary indulgence once a month for daily devout recitation under the conditions of Confession, Communion and a visit to a church or public oratory.

When said with the Litany of the Sacred Heart, page 455, on the Feast itself, in the presence of the Blessed Sacrament, an indulgence of 7 years. A plenary indulgence under the conditions of Confession and Communion. (No. 224.)

O MOST sweet Jesus, Whose overflowing charity for men is requited by so much forgetfulness, negligence and contempt, behold us prostrate before Your altar, (if said elsewhere, *in Your presence*) eager to repair by a special act of homage the cruel indifference and injuries, to which Your loving Heart is everywhere subject.

Mindful, alas, that we ourselves have had a share in such great indignities, which we now deplore from the depths of our hearts, we humbly ask Your pardon and declare our readiness to atone by voluntary expiation not only for our own personal offenses, but also for the sins of those, who, straying far from the path of salvation, refuse in their obstinate infidelity to follow You, their Shepherd and Leader, or, renouncing the vows of their baptism, have cast off the sweet yoke of Your Law.

We are now resolved to expiate each and every deplorable outrage committed against You; we are determined to make amends for the manifold offenses against Christian modesty in unbecoming dress and behavior, for all the foul seductions laid to ensnare the feet of the innocent, for the frequent violation of Sundays and holy days, and the shocking blasphemies uttered against You and Your Saints. We wish also to make amends for the insults to which Your Vicar on earth and Your priests are subjected, for the profanation, by conscious neglect or terrible acts of sacrilege, of the very Sacrament of Your divine love; and lastly for the public crimes of nations who resist the rights and the teaching authority of the Church which You have founded.

Would, O divine Jesus, that we were able to wash away such abominations with our blood. We now offer, in reparation for these violations of Your divine honor, the satisfaction You did once make to Your eternal Father on the Cross and which You continue to renew daily on our altars; we offer it in union with the acts of atonement of Your Virgin Mother and all the Saints and of the pious faithful on earth; and we sincerely promise to make recompense, as far as we can with the help of Your grace, for all neglect of Your great love and for the sins we and others have committed in the past. Henceforth we will live a life of unwavering faith, of purity, of conduct, of perfect observance of the precepts of the Gospel and especially that of charity. We promise to the best of our power to prevent others from offending You and to bring as many as possible to follow You.

O loving Jesus, through the intercession of the Blessed Virgin Mary, our model in reparation, deign to receive the voluntary offering we make of this act of expiation; and by the crowning of perseverance keep us faithful to death in our duty and the allegiance we owe to You, so that we may all one day come to that happy home, where You with the Father and the Holy Spirit live and reign, world without end. Amen.

Consecration of the Human Race to the Sacred Heart of Jesus

MOST sweet Jesus, Redeemer of the human race, look down upon us humbly prostrate before Your altar (or *in Your presence*). We are Yours, and Yours we wish to be; but, to be more surely united with You, behold each one of us freely consecrates himself today to Your Most Sacred Heart.

Many indeed have never known You; many too, despising Your precepts, have rejected You. Have mercy on them all, most merciful Jesus, and draw them to Your Sacred Heart.

Be King, O Lord, not only of the faithful who have never forsaken You, but also of the prodigal children who have abandoned You; grant that they may quickly return to their Father's house lest they die of wretchedness and hunger.

Be King of those who are deceived by erroneous opinions, or whom discord keeps aloof; call them back to the harbor of truth and unity of faith, so that soon there may but one flock and one Shepherd.

Grant, O Lord, to Your Church assurance of freedom and immunity from harm; give peace and order to all nations, and make the earth resound from pole to pole with one cry: Praise to the Divine Heart that wrought our salvation; to It be glory and honor forever. Amen.

The Litany of the Most Sacred Heart of Jesus

An indulgence of 7 years. A plenary indulgence once a month under the usual conditions, if the entire Litany with its versicles and prayer is recited daily for a month. (No. 245.)

LORD, have mercy.
Christ, have mercy.
Lord, have mercy.
Christ, have mercy.
Christ, hear us.
Christ, graciously hear us.
God, the Father of Heaven,*
God the Son, Redeemer of the world,
God, the Holy Spirit,
Holy Trinity, One God,
Heart of Jesus, Son of the Eternal Father,
Heart of Jesus, formed by the Holy Spirit in the womb of the Virgin Mother,
Heart of Jesus, substantially united to the Word of God,
Heart of Jesus, of Infinite Majesty,
Heart of Jesus, Sacred Temple of God,
Heart of Jesus, Tabernacle of the Most High,
Heart of Jesus, House of God and Gate of Heaven,

Heart of Jesus, burning furnace of charity,
Heart of Jesus, abode of justice and love,
Heart of Jesus, full of goodness and love,
Heart of Jesus, abyss of all virtues,
Heart of Jesus, most worthy of all praise,
Heart of Jesus, King and center of all hearts,
Heart of Jesus, in Whom are all the treasures of wisdom and knowledge,
Heart of Jesus, in Whom dwells the fullness of divinity,
Heart of Jesus, in Whom the Father was well pleased,
Heart of Jesus, of Whose fullness we have all received,
Heart of Jesus, desire of the everlasting hills,
Heart of Jesus, patient and most merciful,
Heart of Jesus, enriching all who invoke You,

Have mercy on us.

Heart of Jesus, fountain of life and holiness,*

Heart of Jesus, propitiation for our sins,

Heart of Jesus, loaded down with opprobrium,

Heart of Jesus, bruised for our offenses,

Heart of Jesus, obedient to death,

Heart of Jesus, pierced with a lance,

Heart of Jesus, source of all consolation,

Heart of Jesus, our life and resurrection,

Heart of Jesus, our peace and reconciliation,

Heart of Jesus, Victim for our sins,

Heart of Jesus, salvation of those who trust in You,

Heart of Jesus, hope of those who die in You,

Heart of Jesus, delight of all the Saints,

Lamb of God, You Who take away the sins of the world, *spare us, O Lord.*

Lamb of God, You Who take away the sins of the world, *graciously hear us, O Lord.*

Lamb of God, You Who take away the sins of the world, *have mercy on us.*

℣. Jesus, meek and humble of heart.

℟. Make our hearts like Yours.

Have mercy on us.

Let us pray

Almighty and eternal God, look upon the Heart of Your most beloved Son and upon the praises and satisfaction which He offers You in the name of sinners; and to those who implore Your mercy do You of Your great goodness grant forgiveness in the Name of the same Jesus Christ, Your Son, Who with You lives and reigns world without end. Amen.

PRAYERS AND DEVOTIONS TO THE BLESSED VIRGIN MARY

The Memorare

An indulgence of 3 years. A plenary indulgence under the usual conditions, if said daily for a month. (No. 339.)

REMEMBER, O most gracious Virgin Mary, that never was it known that anyone who fled to your protection, implored your help or sought your intercession, was left unaided. Relying on this confidence, I fly to you, O Virgin of virgins, my mother. To you I come, before you I stand, sinful and sorrowful. O Mother of the Word Incarnate, despise not my petitions, but in your mercy hear and answer me. Amen.

Prayer to the Immaculate Conception

O HOLY Mary, Mother of our Lord Jesus Christ, Queen of Heaven and Mistress of the World, you never forsake or despise anyone; look upon us with an eye of pity, and beg of your beloved Son the pardon of all our sins; that we who now devoutly celebrate your Immaculate Conception may receive the reward of eternal joy through the mercy of Jesus Christ, our

Lord, Whom you, pure Virgin, did bring into the world, and Who, with the Father and the Holy Spirit in perfect Trinity, lives and reigns, one God, world without end. Amen.

THE ROSARY OF THE BLESSED VIRGIN MARY

TRADITION affirms that St. Dominic, the founder of the Order of Preachers, was inspired to preach the Rosary devotion to the people, as a powerful weapon in the spiritual war against the Albigensian heresy. This blessed formula of prayer unites to the repetition of the Angelic Salutation and the Lord's Prayer, a devout consideration of the principal events in the Life of Our Lord and His Blessed Mother.

Innumerable benefits have been conferred on mankind through the Rosary. The hope of the Christian world in its war against communism finds its confirmation in the rapid development of the Rosary Crusade the beginnings of which can be seen in Mary's apparition to Bernadette at Lourdes in 1858. In 1883 the great Pope Leo XIII issued the first of twelve encyclicals which were devoted exclusively to explaining and recommending the Rosary. According to him, the Rosary is "one of the most beautiful manifestations of the spirit of prayer," "the cue to the order of faith and the perfect beauty of the devotion due to Mary," "a résumé of the Gospel," "the surest way to interest Mary in the unity of the Church," in brief "a most excellent manner of praying." He desired to see the Rosary in the hands of every Catholic.

HOW TO SAY THE ROSARY

The Apostles' Creed *is said on the Crucifix; the* Our Father *is said on each of the Large Beads;*

the Hail Mary *on each of the Small Beads; the* Glory Be to the Father *after the three Hail Marys at the beginning of the Rosary, and after each group of Small Beads.*

When the hands are occupied (driving a car, etc.) the indulgences for saying the Rosary may be gained as long as the beads are on one's person.

The Joyful Mysteries

Mondays, Thursdays, the Sundays of Advent, and Sundays from Epiphany until Lent.

1. Annunciation (*Humility*)
2. Visitation (*Charity*)
3. Birth of our Lord (*Poverty*)
4. Presentation (*Obedience*)
5. Finding in the Temple (*Piety*)

The Sorrowful Mysteries

Tuesdays, Fridays throughout the year; and daily from Ash Wednesday until Easter Sunday.

1. Agony in the Garden (*Contrition*)
2. Scourging at the Pillar (*Purity*)
3. Crowning with Thorns (*Courage*)
4. Carrying of the Cross (*Patience*)
5. The Crucifixion (*Self-denial*)

The Glorious Mysteries

Wednesdays, Saturdays, and the Sundays from Easter until Advent.

1. Resurrection of Christ (*Faith*)
2. Ascension of Christ (*Hope*)
3. Descent of the Holy Spirit (*Love*)
4. Assumption (*Eternal happiness*)
5. Crowning of B.V.M. (*Devotion to Mary*)

The Five First Saturdays

Mary's Great Promise at Fatima

The observance of the First Saturday in honor of the Immaculate Heart of Mary is intended to console her Immaculate Heart, and to make reparation to it for all the blasphemies and ingratitude of men.

This devotion and the wonderful promises connected with it were revealed by the Blessed Virgin with these words recorded by Lucy, one of the three children to whom the Blessed Virgin appeared at Fatima, Portugal, in 1917:

I promise to help at the hour of death, with the graces needed for salvation, whoever on the First Saturday of five consecutive months shall:

1. *Confess and receive Holy Communion.*

2. *Recite five decades of the Rosary.*

3. *And keep me company for fifteen minutes while meditating on the fifteen mysteries of the Rosary, with the intention of making reparation to me.*

NOTE: Confession during the week, preceding the first Friday, will suffice for the first Saturday, or conversely when Saturday is the first day of the month. The Rosary may be recited at any convenient time of the day, and the fifteen-minute meditation may be made at any time during the day on the fifteen mysteries of the Rosary. A sermon for the occasion may be substituted for the meditation.

NOVENA IN HONOR OF OUR LADY OF THE MIRACULOUS MEDAL

Reprinted with the permission of the Central Association of the Miraculous Medal, Germantown, Philadelphia, Pa.

In 1830, our Blessed Lady appeared to Catherine Labouré, a French Sister of Charity, and directed her to have a medal struck, now universally venerated as the "Miraculous Medal." By means of this medal, God has seen fit to work many wonders for His own glory and for the salvation of souls.

The faithful are urged to make the Miraculous Medal Perpetual Novena in their respective parishes. This is one of the ways they have of showing devotion to Our Lady of the Miraculous Medal, and a means of obtaining many blessings.

PRAYERS OF THE NOVENA

All Stand and Sing:

MOTHER DEAREST, MOTHER FAIREST

Mother dearest, Mother fairest,
    Help of all who call on thee,
Virgin purest, brightest, rarest,
    Help us, help, we cry to thee.

Chorus:

Mary, help us, help we pray,
Mary, help us, help we pray,
Help us in all care and sorrow;
Mary, help us, help we pray.

READING OF ANNOUNCEMENTS AND FAVORS

Priest: In the Name of the Father, and of the Son, and of the Holy Ghost.

People: Amen.

Priest: O Holy Ghost, fill the hearts of Thy faithful, and kindle in them the fire of Thy love.

Send forth Thy Spirit, and they shall be created.

People: And Thou shalt renew the face of the earth.

Priest: Let us pray. O God, Who didst instruct the hearts of the faithful by the light of the Holy Spirit, grant us in the same Spirit to be truly wise and ever to rejoice in His consolation, through Jesus Christ our Lord.

People: Amen.

Priest: O Mary, conceived without sin.

People: Pray for us who have recourse to thee. (3 times.)

PRAYER

Priest and People: O Lord Jesus Christ, Who hast vouchsafed to glorify by numberless miracles, the Blessed Virgin Mary, Immaculate from the first moment of her Conception, grant that all who devoutly implore her protection on earth, may eternally enjoy Thy presence in heaven, Who, with the

Father and Holy Ghost, livest and reignest, God, forever and ever. Amen.

O Lord Jesus Christ, Who for the accomplishment of Thy greatest works, hast chosen the weak things of the world, that no flesh may glory in Thy sight, and Who for a better and more widely diffused belief, in the Immaculate Conception of Thy Mother, hast wished that the Miraculous Medal be manifested to Saint Catherine Labouré; grant, we beseech Thee, that filled with like humility, we may glorify this mystery by word and work. Amen.

MEMORARE

Priest and People: Remember, O most compassionate Virgin Mary, that never was it known, that anyone who fled to thy protection, implored thy assistance or sought thy intercession, was left unaided. Inspired with this confidence, we fly unto thee, O Virgin of virgins, our Mother; to thee we come, before thee we kneel, sinful and sorrowful. O Mother of the Word Incarnate, despise not our petitions, but in thy clemency hear and answer them. Amen.

NOVENA PRAYER

Priest and People: O Immaculate Virgin Mary, Mother of our Lord Jesus and our Mother, penetrated with the most lively confidence, in thy all powerful and never failing intercession, manifested so often through the Miraculous Medal, we thy loving and trustful children, implore thee to obtain for us the graces and favors we ask during this Novena, if they be beneficial to our immortal souls, and the souls for whom we pray. (*Here privately mention your petitions.*) Thou knowest, O Mary, how often our souls have been the sanctuaries of thy Son, Who hates iniquity. Obtain for us then, a deep hatred of sin, and that purity of heart which will attach us to God alone, so that our every thought, word and deed, may tend to His greater glory. Obtain for us also a spirit of prayer and self-denial, that we may recover by penance what we have lost by sin, and at length attain to that blessed abode, where thou art the Queen of angels and of men. Amen.

AN ACT OF CONSECRATION TO OUR LADY OF THE MIRACULOUS MEDAL

Priest and People: O Virgin Mother of God, Mary Immaculate, we dedicate and consecrate ourselves to thee, under the title of Our Lady of the Miraculous Medal. May this Medal be for each one of us, a sure sign of thy affection for us, and a constant reminder of our duties toward thee. Ever while wearing it, may we be blessed by thy

THE CHILD JESUS AND SAINT JOSEPH

MADONNA OF THE STREETS

loving protection, and preserved in the grace of thy Son. O most powerful Virgin, Mother of our Savior, keep us close to thee every moment of our lives. Obtain for us, thy children, the grace of a happy death; so that, in union with thee, we may enjoy the bliss of heaven forever. Amen.

Priest: O Mary, conceived without sin.

People: Pray for us who have recourse to thee. (3 times.)

All Seated: SHORT SERMON

    Mother dear, O pray for me,
      Whilst far from heav'n and thee
    I wander in a fragile bark
      O'er life's tempestuous sea.
    O Virgin Mother, from thy throne,
      So bright in bliss above,
    Protect thy child, and cheer my path
      With thy sweet smile of love.
    Chorus: Mother dear, remember me,
      And never cease thy care,
    Till in heaven eternally
      Thy love and bliss I share.
    Mother dear, O pray for me,
      Should pleasure's siren lay
    E'er tempt thy child to wander far
      From virtue's path away;
    When thorns beset life's devious way,
      And darkling waters flow,
    Then, Mary, aid thy weeping child,
      Thyself a Mother show.   *Chorus.*

After Benediction, page 427, the congregation sings:

"O Mary, conceived without sin, pray for us, pray for us. O Mary, conceived without sin, pray for us who have recourse to thee."

PRAYERS AND DEVOTIONS TO ST. JOSEPH

Patron of the Universal Church

INDULGENCES FOR THE MONTH OF MARCH

The faithful who take part in public devotions in honor of St. Joseph during the month of March or any other month of the year, may gain an indulgence of 7 years on any day of the month. A plenary indulgence if they take part in ten such devotions with the addition of Confession, Holy Communion and prayers for the intention of the Holy Father.

The faithful who perform private devotions to St. Joseph, may gain an indulgence of 5 years once, on any day of the month. A plenary indulgence under the usual conditions if these devotions are performed daily for a month provided that the faithful are lawfully hindered from making the same devotions publicly. (No. 466.)

Prayer to St. Joseph

An indulgence of 500 days. (No. 474.)

O GLORIOUS St. Joseph, you were chosen by God to be the reputed Father of Jesus, the most pure Spouse of Mary, ever Virgin and the Head of the Holy Family. You have been chosen by Christ's Vicar as the heavenly Patron and Protector of the Church founded by Christ. Therefore, with the greatest confidence I implore your powerful assistance for the whole Church militant. Protect, in a special manner, with true fatherly love, the sovereign Pontiff and all the bishops and priests in communion with the See of Peter. Be the protector of all who labor for souls amid the trials and tribulations of this life; and grant that all the nations of the earth may submit with docility to that Church out of which there is no salvation.

Dearest St Joseph, accept the offering I now make of myself to you. I dedicate myself to your service, and that you may ever be my Father, my Protector and my Guide in the way of salvation. Obtain for me great purity of heart and a fervent love for interior life. Grant that, after your example, all my actions may be directed to the greater glory of God, in union with the divine Heart of Jesus, the immaculate heart of Mary, and your own paternal heart. Finally, pray for me, that I may share in the peace and joy of your holy death. Amen.

Prayers To Be Recited During the Novena to St. Joseph

The faithful who take part in a public Novena to St. Joseph in preparation for his feast, may gain an indulgence of 7 years on any day. A plenary indulgence under the usual conditions of Confession, Holy Communion and prayers for the intention of the Holy Father.

*The faithful who make this Novena privately
with the intention of continuing for nine days, may
gain an indulgence of 5 years, once, on any day.
A plenary indulgence under the usual conditions at
the end of the Novena, provided that the faithful
are lawfully hindered from making this same Novena publicly.* (No. 467.)

MEMORARE TO ST. JOSEPH

REMEMBER, O most chaste spouse of
the Virgin Mary, that never was it
known that any who implored your help
and sought your intercession were left un-
assisted. Full of confidence in your power, I
fly unto you, and beg your protection. Despise not, O foster-father of the Redeemer,
my humble supplication but in your bounty,
hear and answer me. Amen.

Novena Prayer to Obtain a Special Favor

O BLESSED St. Joseph, tender-hearted
father, faithful guardian of Jesus, chaste
spouse of the Mother of God, I pray and
beseech you, to offer to God the Father,
His divine Son, bathed in blood on the
Cross for sinners, and through the thrice
holy Name of Jesus obtain for us of the
eternal Father the favor we implore.

Appease the Divine anger so justly inflamed by our crimes; beg of Jesus mercy
for your children. Amid the splendors of

eternity, forget not the sorrows of those who suffer, those who pray, those who weep; stay the almighty arm which smites us, that by your prayers and those of your most holy Spouse the Heart of Jesus may be moved to pity and to pardon. Amen.

The Litany of St. Joseph

An indulgence of 5 years. A plenary indulgence once a month under the usual conditions, if this Litany with its versicle and prayer is recited daily for a month. (No. 462.)

Lord, have mercy.
Christ, have mercy.
Lord, have mercy.
Christ, hear us.
Christ, graciously hear us.
God the Father of Heaven,*
God the Son, Redeemer of the world,
God the Holy Spirit,
Holy Trinity, One God,
Holy Mary,**
St. Joseph,
Renowned offspring of David,
Light of Patriarchs,
Spouse of the Mother of God,
Chaste guardian of the Virgin,
Foster father of the Son of God,
Diligent protector of Christ,
Head of the Holy Family,
Joseph most just,
Joseph most chaste,
Joseph most prudent,
Joseph most strong,
Joseph most obedient,
Joseph most faithful,
Mirror of patience,
Lover of poverty,
Model of artisans,
Glory of home life,
Guardian of virgins,
Pillar of families,
Solace of the wretched,
Hope of the sick,
Patron of the dying,
Terror of demons,
Protector of Holy Church,

Have mercy on us.
**Pray for us.*

Lamb of God, You Who take away the sins of the world, *spare us, O Lord!*

Lamb of God, You Who take away the sins of the world, *graciously hear us, O Lord!*

Lamb of God, You Who take away the sins of the world, *have mercy on us.*

℣. He made him the lord of His household.

℟. And prince over all His possessions.

Let us pray

O God, Who in Your ineffable providence did vouchsafe to choose Blessed Joseph to be the spouse of Your most holy Mother; grant, we beseech You, that we may be worthy to have him for our intercessor in heaven whom on earth we venerate as our Protector. Who live and reign, world without end. Amen.

A Workman's Prayer to St. Joseph

An indulgence of 500 days. (No. 478.)

GLORIOUS St. Joseph, model of all those who are devoted to labor, obtain for me the grace to work in a spirit of penance for the expiation of my many sins; to work conscientiously, putting the call of duty above my inclinations; to work with gratitude and joy, considering it an honor to employ and develop, by means of labor, the gifts received from God; to work with order, peace, moderation and patience, without ever recoiling before weariness or difficulties; to work, above all, with purity of intention, and with detachment from self, having always death before my eyes and the account which I must render of time lost, of talents wasted, of good omitted, of vain complacency in success, so fatal to the work of God. All for Jesus, all for Mary, all after your example, O Patriarch Joseph. Such shall be my watchword in life and in death. Amen.

Prayer

An indulgence of 3 years. A plenary indulgence under the usual conditions if devoutly recited daily for a month. (No. 479.)

SUPPORTED by the patronage of the Spouse of Your Most Holy Mother, we beseech Your clemency, O Lord, to make our hearts despise all earthly things and to love You, the true God, with perfect charity. Who live and reign, world without end. Amen.

FEASTS AND FASTS

I. Holy Days of Obligation

IN U.S.A.: All Sundays. — The Circumcision, *Jan. 1st*. — Ascension Day. — The Assumption, *Aug. 15th*. — All Saints, *Nov. 1st*. — Immaculate Conception, *Dec. 8th*. — Christmas, *Dec. 25th*.

IN CANADA: All Sundays. — The Circumcision, *Jan. 1st*. — The Epiphany, *Jan. 6th*. — The Ascension. — All Saints, *Nov. 1st*. — The Immaculate Conception, *Dec. 8th*. — Christmas Day, *Dec. 25th*.

IN AUSTRALIA: Same as U.S.A., except Immaculate Conception.

II. Fasting and Abstinence-Days

ABSTINENCE—Everyone over seven years of age is bound to observe the law of abstinence.

Complete abstinence is to be observed on Fridays, Ash Wednesday, Holy Saturday, the Vigil of the Immaculate Conception, and December 23. On days of complete abstinence meat, and soup or gravy made from meat, may not be used at all.

Partial abstinence is to be observed on Ember Wednesdays and Saturdays and on the Vigil of Pentecost. On days of partial abstinence meat, and soup or gravy made from meat, may be taken only at the principal meal.

FAST—Everyone over 21 and under 59 years of age is also bound to observe the law of fast on the weekdays of Lent, Ember Days, Holy Saturday, Vigils of Pentecost and the Immaculate Conception, and December 23.

On days of fast only one full meal is allowed. Two other meatless meals, sufficient to maintain strength, may be taken according to each one's needs; but together they should not equal another full meal.

Meat may be taken at the principal meal on a day of fast except on Fridays, Holy Saturday, Ash Wednesday, Vigil of the Immaculate Conception, and December 23.

Eating between meals is not permitted; but liquids, including milk and fruit juices, are allowed.

When health or ability to work would be seriously affected, the law does not oblige. In doubt concerning fast or abstinence, a parish priest or confessor should be consulted.

New Law of Eucharistic Fast

(From the Motu Proprio issued by His Holiness Pope Pius XII, March 19, 1957)

1. Priests and faithful, before Holy Mass or Holy Communion, respectively, must abstain for three hours from solid foods and alcoholic beverages, and for one hour from non-alcoholic beverages. Water does not break the fast.

2. From now on, the fast must be observed for the period of time indicated in Number One, even by those who celebrate or receive Holy Communion at midnight or in the first hours of the day.

3. The infirm, even if not bed-ridden, may take non-alcoholic beverages and that which is really and properly medicine, either in liquid or solid form, before Mass or Holy Communion without any time limit.

We strongly exhort priests and faithful who are able to do so to observe the old and venerable form of the Eucharistic fast before Mass and Holy Communion. All those who will make use of these concessions must compensate for the good received by becoming shining examples of a Christian life and principally with works of penance and charity.

The dispositions of this Motu Proprio will go into effect on March 25, 1957, the Feast of the Annunciation of the Blessed Virgin Mary. Every disposition whatsoever to the contrary is abrogated, even if it is worthy of special mention.

Given at Rome at St. Peter's, March 19, the Feast of St. Joseph, Patron of the Universal Church, 1957, the 19th year of Our pontificate.

Page of Today's Mass	SUNDAY OR FEASTDAY	YEAR				
		1961	1962	1963	1964	1965
110	Octave of Christmas.	1 Jan.	1 Jan.	1 Jan.	1 Jan.	1 Jan.
113	Holy Name.........	2 Jan.	2 Jan.	2 Jan.	5 Jan.	3 Jan.
117	Epiphany............	6 Jan.	6 Jan.	6 Jan.	6 Jan.	6 Jan.
123	Feast of Holy Family.	8 Jan.	7 Jan.	13 Jan.	12 Jan.	10 Jan.
128	2nd Sun. aft. Epiph...	15 Jan.	14 Jan.	20 Jan.	19 Jan.	17 Jan.
133	3rd Sun. aft. Epiph...	22 Jan.	21 Jan.	27 Jan.	....	24 Jan.
137	4th Sun. aft. Epiph...	....	28 Jan.	3 Feb.	....	31 Jan.
140	5th Sun. aft. Epiph...	....	4 Feb.	....	....	7 Feb.
144	6th Sun. aft. Epiph...	....	11 Feb.	.••.	....	
148	Septuagesima.......	29 Feb.	18 Feb.	10 Feb.	26 Jan.	14 Feb.
153	Sexagesima.........	5 Feb.	25 Feb.	17 Feb.	2 Feb.	21 Feb.
159	Quinquagesima......	12 Feb.	4 Mar.	24 Feb.	9 Feb.	28 Feb.
164	1st Sun. of Lent.....	19 Feb.	11 Mar.	3 Mar.	16 Feb.	7 Mar.
170	2nd Sun. of Lent....	26 Feb.	18 Mar.	10 Mar.	23 Feb.	14 Mar.
174	3rd Sun. of Lent.....	5 Mar.	25 Mar.	17 Mar.	1 Mar.	21 Mar.
179	4th Sun. of Lent.....	12 Mar.	1 Apr.	24 Mar.	8 Mar.	28 Mar.
184	Passion Sunday.....	19 Mar.	8 Apr.	31 Mar.	15 Mar.	4 Apr.
190	Palm Sunday........	26 Mar.	15 Apr.	7 Apr.	22 Mar.	11 Apr.
209	Easter Sunday......	2 Apr.	22 Apr.	14 Apr.	29 Apr.	18 Apr.
216	1st Sun. aft. Easter..	9 Apr.	29 Apr.	21 Apr.	5 Apr.	25 Apr.
221	2nd Sun. aft. Easter.	16 Apr.	6 May	28 Apr.	12 Apr.	2 May
224	3rd Sun. aft. Easter..	23 Apr	13 May	5 May	19 Apr.	9 May
228	4th Sun. aft. Easter..	30 Apr.	20 May	12 May	26 Apr.	16 May
232	5th Sun. aft. Easter..	7 May	27 May	19 May	3 May	23 May
236	Ascension Day......	11 May	31 May	23 May	7 May	27 May
241	Sun. aft. Ascension..	14 May	3 June	26 May	10 May	30 May
245	Pentecost...........	21 May	10 June	2 June	17 May	6 June
252	Trinity Sunday......	28 May	17 June	9 June	24 May	13 June
257	Corpus Christi.......	1 June	21 June	13 June	28 May	17 June
263	2nd Sun. aft. Pent...	4 June	24 June	16 June	31 May	20 June
267	Sacred Heart........	9 June	29 June	21 June	5 June	25 June
274	3rd Sun. aft. Pent....	11 June	1 July	23 June	7 June	27 June
278	4th Sun. aft. Pent....	18 June	8 July	30 June	14 June	4 July

Page of Today's Mass	SUNDAY OR FEASTDAY	YEAR				
		1961	1962	1963	1964	1965
282	5th Sun. aft. Pent.. .	25 June	15 July	7 July	21 June	11 July
286	6th Sun. aft. Pent....	2 July	22 July	14 July	28 June	18 July
291	7th Sun. aft. Pent....	9 July	29 July	21 July	5 July	25 July
295	8th Sun. aft. Pent....	16 July	5 Aug.	28 July	12 July	1 Aug.
299	9th Sun. aft. Pent....	23 July	12 Aug.	4 Aug.	19 July	8 Aug.
303	10th Sun. aft. Pent...	30 July	19 Aug.	11 Aug.	26 July	....
388	Assumption.........	15 Aug.	15 Aug.	15 Aug.	15 Aug.	15 Aug
307	11th Sun. aft. Pent ..	6 Aug.	26 Aug.	18 Aug.	2 Aug.	22 Aug.
311	12th Sun. aft Pent...	13 Aug.	2 Sept.	25 Aug.	9 Aug.	29 Aug.
316	13th Sun. aft. Pent...	20 Aug.	9 Sept.	1 Sept.	16 Aug.	5 Sept.
320	14th Sun. aft. Pent...	27 Aug.	16 Sept	8 Sept.	23 Aug.	12 Sept.
324	15th Sun. aft. Pent...	3 Sept.	23 Sept.	15 Sept.	30 Aug.	19 Sept.
328	16th Sun. aft. Pent...	10 Sept.	30 Sept.	22 Sept.	6 Sept.	26 Sept.
333	17th Sun. aft. Pent...	17 Sept.	7 Oct.	29 Sept.	13 Sept.	3 Oct.
337	18th Sun. aft. Pent...	24 Sept.	14 Oct.	6 Oct.	20 Sept.	10 Oct.
341	19th Sun. aft. Pent...	1 Oct.	21 Oct.	13 Oct.	27 Sept.	17 Oct.
345	20th Sun. aft. Pent...	8 Oct.	....	20 Oct.	4 Oct.	24 Oct.
355	21st Sun. aft. Pent...	15 Oct.	4 Nov.	....	11 Oct.	....
349	Christ the King......	29 Oct.	28 Oct.	27 Oct.	25 Oct.	31 Oct.
392	All Saints..........	1 Nov.	1 Nov.	1 Nov.	1 Nov.	1 Nov.
360	22nd Sun. aft. Pent..	22 Oct.	11 Nov.	3 Nov.	18 Oct.	7 Nov.
364	23rd Sun. aft. Pent...	....	18 Nov.	10 Nov.	....	14 Nov.
371	24th Sun. aft. Pent...	5 Nov.	....	*17 Nov.	....	....
370	25th Sun. aft. Pent...	12 Nov.	....	....	8 Nov.	....
369	26th Sun. aft. Pent...	19 Nov.	....	....	15 Nov.	....
372	Last Sun. aft. Pent...	26 Nov	25 Nov.	24 Nov.	22 Nov.	21 Nov.
84	1st Sun. of Advent...	3 Dec.	2 Dec.	1 Dec.	29 Nov.	28 Nov.
88	2nd Sun. of Advent..	10 Dec.	9 Dec.	....	6 Dec.	5 Dec.
377	Immaculate Concep..	8 Dec.	8 Dec.	8 Dec.	8 Dec.	8 Dec.
92	3rd Sun. of Advent..	17 Dec.	16 Dec	15 Dec.	13 Dec.	12 Dec.
96	4th Sun. of Advent..	24 Dec.	23 Dec.	22 Dec.	20 Dec.	19 Dec.
101	Christmas..........	25 Dec.	25 Dec	25 Dec.	25 Dec.	25 Dec.
106	Sun. btw. Chr. & N. Y.	31 Dec.	30 Dec.	29 Dec.	27 Dec.	26 Dec.

*Page 369

Page of Today's Mass	SUNDAY OR FEASTDAY	YEAR				
		1966	1967	1968	1969	1970
110	Octave of Christmas.	1 Jan.	1 Jan.	1 Jan.	1 Jan.	1 Jan.
113	Holy Name.........	2 Jan.	2 Jan.	2 Jan.	5 Jan.	4 Jan.
117	Epiphany...........	6 Jan.	6 Jan.	6 Jan.	6 Jan.	6 Jan.
123	Feast of Holy Family.	9 Jan.	8 Jan.	7 Jan.	12 Jan.	11 Jan.
128	2nd Sun. aft. Epiph...	16 Jan.	15 Jan.	14 Jan.	19 Jan.	18 Jan.
133	3rd Sun. aft. Epiph...	23 Jan.	....	21 Jan.	26 Jan.	....
137	4th Sun. aft. Epiph...	30 Jan.	....	28 Jan.	....	....
140	5th Sun. aft. Epiph...	....	....	4 Feb.	....	....
148	Septuagesima.......	6 Feb.	22 Jan.	11 Feb.	2 Feb.	25 Jan.
153	Sexagesima	13 Feb.	29 Jan.	18 Feb.	9 Feb.	1 Feb.
159	Quinquagesima......	20 Feb.	5 Feb.	25 Feb.	16 Feb.	8 Feb.
164	1st Sun. of Lent.....	27 Feb.	12 Feb.	3 Mar.	23 Feb.	15 Feb.
170	2nd Sun. of Lent....	6 Mar.	19 Feb.	10 Mar.	2 Mar.	22 Feb.
174	3rd Sun. of Lent.....	13 Mar.	26 Feb.	17 Mar.	9 Mar.	1 Mar.
179	4th Sun. of Lent.....	20 Mar.	5 Mar.	24 Mar.	16 Mar.	8 Mar.
184	Passion Sunday.....	27 Mar.	12 Mar.	31 Mar	23 Mar.	15 Mar.
190	Palm Sunday.......	3 Apr.	19 Mar.	7 Apr.	30 Mar.	22 Mar.
209	Easter Sunday......	10 Apr.	26 Mar.	14 Apr.	6 Apr.	29 Mar.
216	1st Sun. aft. Easter..	17 Apr.	2 Apr.	21 Apr.	13 Apr	5 Apr.
221	2nd Sun. aft. Easter..	24 Apr.	9 Apr.	28 Apr.	20 Apr.	12 Apr.
224	3rd Sun. aft. Easter..	1 May	16 Apr.	5 May	27 Apr.	19 Apr.
228	4th Sun. aft. Easter..	8 May	23 Apr.	12 May	4 May	26 Apr.
232	5th Sun. aft. Easter..	15 May	30 Apr.	19 May	11 May	3 May
236	Ascension Day......	19 May	4 May	23 May	15 May	7 May
241	Sun. aft. Ascension..	22 May	7 May	26 May	18 May	10 May
245	Pentecost...........	29 May	14 May	2 June	25 May	17 May
252	Trinity Sunday......	5 June	21 May	9 June	1 June	24 May
257	Corpus Christi......	9 June	25 May	13 June	5 June	28 May
263	2nd Sun. aft. Pent....	12 June	28 May	16 June	8 June	31 May
267	Sacred Heart.......	17 June	2 June	21 June	13 June	5 June
274	3rd Sun. aft. Pent....	19 June	4 June	23 June	15 June	7 June
278	4th Sun. aft. Pent....	26 June	11 June	30 June	22 June	14 June
282	5th Sun. aft. Pent...	3 July	18 June	7 July	29 June	21 June

Page of Today's Mass	SUNDAY OR FEASTDAY	YEAR				
		1966	1967	1968	1969	1970
286	6th Sun. aft. Pent....	10 July	25 June	14 July	6 July	28 June
291	7th Sun. aft. Pent....	17 July	2 July	21 July	13 July	5 July
295	8th Sun. aft. Pent...	24 July	9 July	28 July	20 July	12 July
299	9th Sun. aft. Pent...	31 July	16 July	4 Aug.	27 July	19 July
303	10th Sun. aft. Pent...	7 Aug.	23 July	11 Aug.	3 Aug.	26 July
388	Assumption.........	15 Aug.	15 Aug.	15 Aug.	15 Aug.	15 Aug.
307	11th Sun. aft. Pent...	14 Aug.	30 July	18 Aug.	10 Aug.	2 Aug.
311	12th Sun. aft. Pent...	21 Aug.	6 Aug.	25 Aug.	17 Aug.	9 Aug.
316	13th Sun. aft. Pent...	28 Aug.	13 Aug.	1 Sept.	24 Aug.	16 Aug.
320	14th Sun. aft. Pent...	4 Sept.	20 Aug.	8 Sept.	31 Aug.	23 Aug.
324	15th Sun. aft. Pent...	11 Sept.	27 Aug.	15 Sept.	7 Sept.	30 Aug.
328	16th Sun. aft. Pent...	18 Sept.	3 Sept	22 Sept.	14 Sept.	6 Sept.
333	17th Sun. aft. Pent...	25 Sept.	10 Sept.	29 Sept.	21 Sept.	13 Sept.
337	18th Sun. aft. Pent...	2 Oct.	17 Sept.	6 Oct.	28 Sept.	20 Sept.
341	19th Sun. aft. Pent...	9 Oct.	24 Sept.	13 Oct.	5 Oct.	27 Sept.
345	20th Sun. aft. Pent ..	16 Oct.	1 Oct.	20 Oct.	12 Oct.	4 Oct.
349	Christ the King......	30 Oct.	29 Oct.	27 Oct.	26 Oct.	25 Oct.
392	All Saints..........	1 Nov.	1 Nov.	1 Nov.	1 Nov.	1 Nov.
355	21st Sun. aft. Pent...	23 Oct.	8 Oct.	....	19 Oct.	11 Oct.
360	22nd Sun. aft. Pent...	....	15 Oct.	3 Nov.	....	18 Oct.
364	23rd Sun. aft. Pent...	6 Nov.	22 Oct.	10 Nov.	2 Nov.	....
369	24th Sun. aft. Pent...	13 Nov.	....	17 Nov.	**9 Nov.	....
371	25th Sun. aft. Pent...	....	5 Nov.	....	*16 Nov.	**8 Nov.
370	26th Sun. aft. Pent...	....	12 Nov	....	....	*15 Nov.
369	27th Sun. aft. Pent...	....	19 Nov.	....	....	....
372	Last Sun. aft Pent...	20 Nov.	26 Nov.	24 Nov.	23 Nov	22 Nov.
84	1st Sun. of Advent...	27 Nov.	3 Dec.	1 Dec.	30 Nov.	29 Nov.
88	2nd Sun. of Advent..	4 Dec.	10 Dec.	....	7 Dec.	6 Dec.
377	Immaculate Concep..	8 Dec.	8 Dec.	8 Dec.	8 Dec.	8 Dec.
92	3rd Sun. of Advent..	11 Dec.	17 Dec.	15 Dec.	14 Dec.	13 Dec.
96	4th Sun. of Advent..	18 Dec.	24 Dec.	22 Dec.	21 Dec.	20 Dec.
101	Christmas..........	25 Dec.	25 Dec.	25 Dec.	25 Dec.	25 Dec.
106	Sun. btw. Chr. & N.Y.	....	31 Dec.	29 Dec.	28 Dec.	27 Dec.

* Page 369   ** Page 370

Page of Today's Mass	SUNDAY OR FEASTDAY	YEAR				
		1971	1972	1973	1974	1975
110	Octave of Christmas.	1 Jan.	1 Jan.	1 Jan.	1 Jan	1 Jan.
113	Holy Name.........	3 Jan.	2 Jan.	2 Jan.	2 Jan.	5 Jan.
117	Epiphany............	6 Jan.	6 Jan.	6 Jan.	6 Jan.	6 Jan.
123	Feast of Holy Family.	10 Jan.	9 Jan.	7 Jan.	13 Jan.	12 Jan.
128	2nd Sun. aft. Epiph...	17 Jan.	16 Jan.	14 Jan.	20 Jan.	19 Jan.
133	3rd Sun. aft. Epiph...	24 Jan.	23 Jan.	21 Jan.	27 Jan.	....
137	4th Sun. aft. Epiph....	31 Jan.	....	28 Jan.	3 Feb.	....
140	5th Sun. aft. Epiph....	....	....	4 Feb.	....	....
144	6th Sun. aft. Epiph....	....	....	11 Feb.	....	....
148	Septuagesima.......	7 Feb.	30 Jan.	18 Feb.	10 Feb.	26 Jan.
153	Sexagesima.........	14 Feb.	6 Feb.	25 Feb.	17 Feb.	2 Feb.
159	Quinquagesima......	21 Feb.	13 Feb.	4 Mar.	24 Feb.	9 Feb.
164	1st Sun. of Lent.....	28 Feb.	20 Feb.	11 Mar.	3 Mar.	16 Feb.
170	2nd Sun. of Lent....	7 Mar.	27 Feb.	18 Mar.	10 Mar.	23 Feb.
174	3rd Sun. of Lent.....	14 Mar.	5 Mar.	25 Mar.	17 Mar.	2 Mar.
179	4th Sun. of Lent.....	21 Mar.	12 Mar.	1 Apr.	24 Mar.	9 Mar.
184	Passion Sunday.....	28 Mar.	19 Mar.	8 Apr.	31 Mar.	16 Mar.
190	Palm Sunday.......	4 Apr.	26 Mar.	15 Apr.	7 Apr.	23 Mar.
209	Easter Sunday......	11 Apr.	2 Apr.	22 Apr.	14 Apr.	30 Mar.
216	1st Sun. aft. Easter..	18 Apr.	9 Apr.	29 Apr.	21 Apr	6 Apr.
221	2nd Sun. aft. Easter..	25 Apr.	16 Apr.	6 May	28 Apr.	13 Apr.
224	3rd Sun. aft. Easter..	2 May	23 Apr.	13 May	5 May	20 Apr.
228	4th Sun. aft. Easter..	9 May	30 Apr.	20 May	12 May	27 Apr.
232	5th Sun. aft. Easter..	16 May	7 May	27 May	19 May	4 May
236	Ascension Day......	20 May	11 May	31 May	23 May	8 May
241	Sun. aft. Ascension...	23 May	14 May	3 June	26 May	11 May
245	Pentecost...........	30 May	21 May	10 June	2 June	18 May
252	Trinity Sunday......	6 June	28 May	17 June	9 June	25 May
257	Corpus Christi.......	10 June	1 June	21 June	13 June	29 May
263	2nd Sun. aft. Pent....	13 June	4 June	24 June	16 June	1 June
267	Sacred Heart.......	18 June	9 June	29 June	21 June	6 June
274	3rd Sun. aft. Pent....	20 June	11 June	1 July	23 June	8 June
278	4th Sun. aft. Pent.....	27 June	18 June	8 July	30 June	15 June

Page of Today's Mass	SUNDAY OR FEASTDAY	YEAR				
		1971	1972	1973	1974	1975
282	5th Sun. aft. Pent....	4 July	25 June	15 July	7 July	22 June
286	6th Sun. aft. Pent....	11 July	2 July	22 July	14 July	29 June
291	7th Sun. aft. Pent....	18 July	9 July	29 July	21 July	6 July
295	8th Sun. aft. Pent....	25 July	16 July	5 Aug.	28 July	13 July
299	9th Sun. aft. Pent....	1 Aug.	23 July	12 Aug	4 Aug.	20 July
303	10th Sun. aft. Pent...	8 Aug.	30 July	19 Aug.	11 Aug.	27 July
388	Assumption.........	15 Aug.	15 Aug.	15 Aug.	15 Aug.	15 Aug.
307	11th Sun. aft. Pent...	....	6 Aug.	26 Aug.	18 Aug.	3 Aug.
311	12th Sun. aft. Pent...	22 Aug.	13 Aug.	2 Sept.	25 Aug.	10 Aug.
316	13th Sun. aft. Pent...	29 Aug.	20 Aug.	9 Sept.	1 Sept.	17 Aug.
320	14th Sun. aft. Pent...	5 Sept.	27 Aug.	16 Sept.	8 Sept.	24 Aug.
324	15th Sun. aft. Pent...	12 Sept.	3 Sept.	23 Sept.	15 Sept.	31 Aug.
328	16th Sun. aft. Pent...	19 Sept.	10 Sept.	30 Sept.	22 Sept.	7 Sept.
333	17th Sun. aft. Pent...	26 Sept.	17 Sept.	7 Oct.	29 Sept.	14 Sept.
337	18th Sun. aft. Pent...	3 Oct.	24 Sept.	14 Oct.	6 Oct.	21 Sept.
341	19th Sun. aft. Pent...	10 Oct.	1 Oct.	21 Oct.	13 Oct.	28 Sept.
345	20th Sun. aft. Pent...	17 Oct.	8 Oct.	....	20 Oct.	5 Oct.
349	Christ the King......	31 Oct.	29 Oct.	28 Oct.	27 Oct.	26 Oct.
392	All Saints..........	1 Nov.	1 Nov.	1 Nov.	1 Nov.	1 Nov.
355	21st Sun. aft. Pent...	24 Oct.	15 Oct.	4 Nov.	....	12 Oct.
360	22nd Sun. aft. Pent...	....	22 Oct.	11 Nov.	3 Nov.	19 Oct.
364	23rd Sun. aft. Pent...	7 Nov.	....	18 Nov.	10 Nov	....
371	24th Sun. aft. Pent...	*14 Nov.	5 Nov	....	*17 Nov.	2 Nov.
370	25th Sun. aft. Pent...	....	12 Nov.	....	....	9 Nov.
369	26th Sun. aft. Pent...	....	19 Nov.	....	....	16 Nov.
372	Last Sun. aft. Pent...	21 Nov.	26 Nov.	25 Nov.	24 Nov.	23 Nov.
84	1st Sun. of Advent...	28 Nov.	3 Dec.	2 Dec.	1 Dec.	30 Nov.
88	2nd Sun. of Advent..	5 Dec.	10 Dec.	9 Dec.	....	7 Dec.
377	Immaculate Concep..	8 Dec.	8 Dec.	8 Dec.	8 Dec.	8 Dec.
92	3rd Sun. of Advent...	12 Dec.	17 Dec.	16 Dec.	15 Dec.	14 Dec.
96	4th Sun. of Advent...	19 Dec.	24 Dec.	23 Dec.	22 Dec.	21 Dec.
101	Christmas..........	25 Dec.	25 Dec.	25 Dec.	25 Dec.	25 Dec.
106	Sun. btw. Chr. & N. Y.	26 Dec.	31 Dec..	30 Dec.	29 Dec.	28 Dec.

* Page 369

OTHER OUTSTANDING CATHOLIC BOOKS

THE HOLY BIBLE — With all the latest official Confraternity translations, world-famous religious masterpieces in full color, extra large type throughout, paragraphed for easy reading. **Ask for No. 610.**

SAINT JOSEPH DAILY MISSAL—By Rev. H. Hoever. Truly the finest, most up-to-date Daily Missal. With extra large type, simplified arrangement, official Confraternity version, full color illus. **Ask for No. 810.**

2 VOLUME — SAINT JOSEPH DAILY MISSAL — Thin and compact. Easy-to-carry, easy-to-use with all the features of the 1 Volume Ed. **Ask for No. 840.**

SAINT JOSEPH "CONTINUOUS" SUNDAY MISSAL — By Rev. H. Hoever. New Missal with no cross references or page-turning. Full color illustrations, large type. Confraternity version. **Ask for No. 720.**

SAINT JOSEPH CHILDREN'S MISSAL — By Rev. H. Hoever. Easy-to-understand prayers. Full color illustrations of Sunday Gospels, Actions of the Priest, Stations and Rosary. Large type. **Ask for No. 806.**

SAINT JOSEPH CATHOLIC MANUAL — New handy Manual with Novenas, Mass Prayers, the Sacraments, Dictionary, Epistles and Gospels. Over 157 full color illustrations. 1,000 pages. **Ask for No. 812.**

SAINT JOSEPH PICTURE PRAYER BOOK — By Rev. L. Lovasik, S.V.D. Mass prayers and many little prayers children will easily understand. Beautiful full color pictures. Large type. **Ask for No. 802.**

LIVES OF THE SAINTS — By Rev. H. Hoever. Short life of a Saint and prayer for every day of the year. Large type, 70 colored illustrations. **Ask for No. 870.**

JESUS, MY LIFE—By Rev. L. Lovasik, S.V.D. All-new, beautifully illustrated prayer book devoted to Jesus. Large type. Colored illustrations. **Ask for No. 265.**

MARY, MY HOPE — By Rev. L. Lovasik, S.V.D. New prayer book for complete devotion to Mary. 23 full color illus., including the Rosary. **Ask for No. 365.**

CATHOLIC PICTURE BIBLE — By Rev. L. Lovasik, S.V.D. Inspiring for the whole family. Over 101 Bible stories illustrated in full color. **Ask for No. 435.**

WHEREVER CATHOLIC BOOKS ARE SOLD

(Over)

COMMEMORATION OF THE DEAD
(Express your intentions before Mass)

REMEMBER, O LORD, these Your servants and handmaids:

† . . . .

† . . . .

† . . . .

† . . . .

† . . . .

† . . . .

† . . . .

† . . . .

† . . . .

who have gone before us with the sign of faith. Grant them Your eternal light and peace. Through Christ our Lord. Amen.

— THE HOLY FAMILY —

Jesus, Mary and Joseph exemplify the proper relations that should exist between husband and wife, and parents and children. We should often ask them to sanctify our families by their example and intercession.

(Inside Back Cover)